Life Behind the Masks:
Surviving and Healing from
Mother-Daughter Sexual Abuse

Life Behind the Masks is one of the most powerful stories of overwhelming, tormented child abuse from a demonic mother, that I have ever read. Wilma was an amazing girl who was not going to allow her abuser to define who she was as a person. Her childhood of abuse and cruelty is one no child should ever have to experience, nor grow up thinking they are at fault.

Wilma's faith, determination, and resilience to not be defined by her abuse–and her courage to share her story–had a powerful impact on me. It has caused me to reflect over my educational career and search my memory for acts of kindness. Did I bring a light of sunshine into the lives of my students who were experiencing extreme pain outside of school? Did I protect students from the cruelty of being bullied and harassed by their peers?

Wilma's story is an invitation for all of us to be more sensitive and to seek out the wounded; to be the caring adult that can change a life path. Her story is a true miracle that gives all of us hope for innocent victims of abuse. *Life Behind the Masks* is a must read for anyone working with children.

~ Jim Sporleder, Trauma Informed Consultant
Retired Principal of Lincoln High School in Walla Walla, WA
Paper Tigers Documentary
National Trauma Responsive Trainer
National Trauma Responsive Conference Presenter
Author, *The Trauma Informed School*
Co-author with Heather T. Forbes, LCSW
Help for Billy, A Study Guide for Help for Billy

~

Stark and unfiltered. A survivor's account of her childhood marred by the trauma of maternal abuse. All the signs were there, but those who might have intervened either could not or would not see it. Frustratingly familiar. This book should be required reading for anyone who works with children or with survivors of abuse.

~ Susan Kostenko, M.D. (retired)
Adult Psychiatry and Substance Abuse

I met Wilma about 15 years ago before she discovered how good a writer she is. As a fellow survivor of sexual abuse, I know how difficult it can be to tell your story. Wilma has become a great inspiration to me. She shows us that victims can survive and even learn to tell their story. Wilma breaks the silence so many still endure, regarding this taboo subject. This is Wilma's tragic story, superbly written and I am so glad she is finally telling it.

~ Heather McDougal
Chief Operating Officer
CLI Select Agencies

~

I was so impressed with Wilma MacLiver's initial calling to write this book–she shared the idea that when she went to find books that spoke to mother-daughter incest there were none and she took this to mean she could make a difference for others who suffered similar situations. The book is clearly a testimony to that important endeavor, to her extraordinary spirit and to all the hope that lives for all children and adults to survive and forgive and live a life full of love and beauty after something so harrowing. Wilma MacLiver's book is a testimony to the human spirit. I hope everyone who needs to read this book finds it and then finds the grace Wilma did.

~ Heather Kirkpatrick, Ph.D.
President and Chief Executive Officer
Alder Graduate School of Education

~

Wow. Just wow. This book is a window into a societal wound; one that runs deep and dark, but it never gushes. It oozes, and therefore, too often, we can ignore it. Or pretend it's not there. Or look past it. This story moves us past those reflexes. What I love most about the book, is its stark and straightforward nature. Abuse often exists in the space between what we know and what we refuse to accept. MacLiver weaves a harrowing story of survival from a void into which we must all unflinchingly stare.

~ Ryan Stone, Ph.D.
Author, *Best Road Yet*

~

Wilma MacLiver's book opened a whole new world for me, that of childhood sexual abuse and the deep childhood trauma it carries. It helped me to grow in empathy and compassion. Sadly, there are many adults who can relate to what Wilma has experienced but who have not allowed themselves to face, reflect on, and heal from the abuse they experienced. Wilma's story is incredibly painful; but ultimately it is an uplifting book about great suffering and forgiveness.

~ James Encinas, Author
Wheeling to Healing...
sBroken Heart on a Bicycle,

Your Own Wheeling to Healing
A Guide to Healing Yourself and
Groups of People Who've Experienced
Adverse Childhood Experiences (ACEs)

FAMILY
does not mean:

Keeping secrets,

Walking on eggshells,

Lying to keep the peace,

Pretending others are healthy when they are not,

Tiptoeing around the truth,

Attending events that derail my healing,

Engaging in toxic behavior,

Defending my choices,

Remaining loyal to destructive patterns,

or sacrificing my needs in an

attempt to fix or save others.

~ Courtney J. Burg

LIFE
Behind the Masks
Surviving and Healing from Mother-Daughter Sexual Abuse

By
Wilma MacLiver

Writing Well, Ink
Phoenix, Arizona

LifeBehindtheMasks.com

Life Behind the Masks:
Surviving and Healing from
Mother-Daughter Sexual Abuse
by Wilma MacLiver

Life Behind the Masks:
Surviving and Healing from Mother-Daughter Sexual Abuse
Copyright © 2021 Wilma L. MacLiver

Editor: Mary L. Holden
Cover/Interior Design & Layout: Betsy McGrew
Cover/Interior Photos: Property of Wilma MacLiver
Back Cover Portrait: Adriane Ryann Thompson

Published by Writing Well, Ink
3310 W. Bell Road, Suite 182, Phoenix, AZ 85053
Printed in the United States of America
Library of Congress Cataloging-in-Publication Data
Paperback ISBN 978-1-7377631-9-2
ebook ISBN 978-1-7377631-8-5

All rights reserved. No part of this publication may be reproduced, distributed, digitally stored, or transmitted in any form or by any means, including photocopying, recording, or other electronic or mechanical methods, without the prior written permission of the publisher, except in the case of brief quotations embodied in critical reviews and certain other noncommercial uses permitted by copyright law.

Although the author and publisher have made every effort to ensure that the information in this book was correct at press time, the author and publisher do not assume and hereby disclaim any liability to any party for any loss, damage, or disruption caused by errors or omissions, whether such errors or omissions result from negligence, accident, or any other cause. The words are the author's alone, not those of Writing Well, Ink.

Adherence to all applicable laws and regulations, including international, federal, state and local governing professional licensing, business practices, advertising, and all other aspects of doing business in the US, Canada or any other jurisdiction is the sole responsibility of the reader and consumer.

Neither the author nor the publisher assumes any responsibility or liability whatsoever on behalf of the consumer or reader of this material. Any perceived slight of any individual or organization is purely unintentional.

The resources in this book are provided for informational purposes only and should not be used to replace the specialized training and professional judgment of a health care or mental health care professional.

Neither the author nor the publisher can be held responsible for the use of the information provided within this book. Please always consult a trained professional before making any decision regarding treatment of yourself or others.

For more information: Contact@WritingWellInk.com

For daughters everywhere.

An event has happened,
upon which it is difficult to speak,
and impossible to be silent.
~ Edmund Burke

It is not the critic who counts; not the man who points out how the strong man stumbles, or where the doer of deeds could have done them better. The credit belongs to the man who is actually in the arena, whose face is marred by dust and sweat and blood; who strives valiantly; who errs, who comes short again and again, because there is no effort without error and shortcoming; but who does actually strive to do the deeds; who knows great enthusiasms, the great devotions; who spends himself in a worthy cause; who at the best knows in the end the triumph of high achievement, and who at the worst, if he fails, at least fails while daring greatly, so that his place shall never be with those cold and timid souls who neither know victory nor defeat.

~ Theodore Roosevelt

Contents

Author's Note ~ xi
Forewords ~ xv
Introduction ~ xxiii
1964: Birth ~ 1
1965: 1 Year Old ~ 7
1966: 2 Years Old ~ 13
1967: 3 Years Old ~ 17
1968: 4 Years Old ~ 23
1969: 5 Years Old ~ 29
1970: 6 Years Old ~ 41
1971: 7 Years Old ~ 51
1972: 8 Years Old ~ 67
1973: 9 Years Old ~ 77
1974: 10 Years Old ~ 87
1975: 11 Years Old ~ 105
1976: 12 Years Old ~ 115
1977: 13 Years Old ~ 139
1978: 14 Years Old ~ 165
1979: 15 Years Old ~ 191
1980: Jan., Feb., Mar. ~ 217
1980: April, May, June ~ 243
1980: July, Aug., Sept. ~ 255
1980: Autumn Begins ~ 277
1980: Oct., Nov., Dec. ~ 285
1981 to 1985 ~ 299
1986 to 1995 ~ 309
1996 to 2015 ~ 341
Epilogue ~ 361
Statistics ~ 369
References & Resources ~ 373
Acknowledgments ~ 379
About the Author ~ 381

Author's Note

*Christ never intended to cover up the dark side of life,
but rather to illuminate a path through it.
If we want to create a different future,
we must have the courage to look at the past.*
~ Dan B. Allender, Ph.D.

Abused children live in environments that are beyond their comprehension. What actually happens to children in those circumstances is shocking and deplorable to read about.

The subject of child abuse is difficult, emotional, and disturbing, but it is real.

~

I learned to read in first grade.

I remember the awe and wonder I experienced when reading a book. It seemed amazing that reading could transform me to another place.

I didn't hear the playground bell when I was reading E.B. White's masterpiece because I was in the barn listening to Charlotte speak from high up in her web.

I was 10 years old when I first thought I would like to write a book. I started with a homemade diary.

I never imagined I would write about the nightmare of living in my mother's house, but as I sorted through a landfill of memories, I searched for a memoir similar to my own. I found books written by victims of abuse, but none that addressed Mother-Daughter Sexual Abuse (MDSA). My searches left me feeling isolated and different. I

Author's Note

decided then, that if I ever had the courage, I would write my memoir for other daughters who were searching.

This is the true account of my childhood–one that was terrorized by my mother.

During my early years, Hellen betrayed and abandoned her role as mother and became a predator from which I could not escape. The mother I depended on and trusted to love and protect me, instead exploited and destroyed my innocence.

Each chapter represents my life and memories as they progressed over time. To keep the memories authentic as they occurred, the first chapters are short, as I had to rely on family history. The chapters lengthen as I grew through childhood and into my teen years.

Each chapter contains headline stories of news events, providing a real-world timeline outside of my isolated situation.

The counselors, Pastor and Mrs. Sawyer, and later Dr. James Laine, often chose similar words during counseling. The end of each chapter contains their collective comments in the Counseling Notes.

I refer to Hellen as 'Mom' or 'my mother' in few places when necessary to clarify my thoughts at the time. Those exceptions aside, I refer to her by her birth name. Hellen's name has an unusual spelling and it befits the evil nature she possessed. Hellen used cusswords profusely; those have been excluded from this text. She also used slang in her speech. It is included in the dialogue to show her authentic style and low level of education.

I have conscientiously portrayed these events as they occurred, yet I've minimized parts of the text due to the personal nature of the abuse and to avoid details that might suggest voyeurism.

The names of most people in this book have been changed to respect their privacy. There are some exceptions, with permission. The descriptions of scenes, settings, events, characters, and conversations are authentic, though some conversations and details

Author's Note

cannot be remembered verbatim. In those cases, dialogue has been reassembled through meticulous research–at times requiring travel–via conversations with relatives and references to the journals I kept through the years. The dialogues are consistent with the research, and what I remember of how the events occurred, and how the people, including me, behaved and spoke. I cannot certify exact accuracy in every conversation, but I can certify its truth. Hellen's first name, height, weight, manner, speech, walk, nature, and everything else represented and stated about her as an individual, is authentic.

The following memoir is mine; written from my childlike perspective throughout the years I lived in Hellen's house.

New York – 1951
Hellen Bullard
20 years old

Forewords

At this writing, I have been a clinical pastoral counselor for 44 years. I have counseled many victims of molestation, rape, and abuse, but none like Wilma. Her abuse was beyond comprehension. Wilma's pain brought me to tears on many occasions. Her survival is a miracle.

Most molestation/rape/abuse victims will counsel for a while, take a break and return for counseling. Many don't stick it out long enough to find healing. For some, the pain is too great, and for others the binding shame–the belief that something is wrong with them that is not wrong with everyone else–stops them from opening up, even with a professional counselor.

Wilma was different. She came with a determination to heal from her traumatic childhood and a commitment to work through the painful memories. She never quit, but faithfully kept her weekly appointments. *Her healing is one of the most remarkable miracles I have witnessed in counseling.*

Wilma had a lot of support from God, Pastor Sawyer and his wife, and from her loving husband. Pastor Sawyer is one of the best pastors I have ever met.

As you read this book, you will only get a *watered-down view* of what she suffered. It may still be too hard to read. Her abuse was real, and the physical trauma she suffered has been medically confirmed by multiple medical doctors.

Wilma has been a real inspiration to me. I count it a blessing that God brought her into my life.

~ James A. Laine, Ph.D., Th.D., D.D., L.C.P.C

~

Forewords

I first met Wilma MacLiver at the Arizona Hemophilia and Thrombosis Center's (AzHTC) comprehensive multi-specialty clinic for persons with bleeding and clotting disorders. Wilma came to our clinic for evaluation of bleeding problems. Our clinic takes a holistic approach to medical care; all sub-specialty providers screen patients in this one clinic visit. I am one of about a dozen professionals and my specialty is in mental health assessment, diagnosis, and treatment. I am a licensed professional counselor.

During her clinic evaluation and screening, it was immediately apparent that Wilma had suffered severe, persistent, and pervasive early childhood trauma, neglect, and abuse. Her trauma included physical, sexual, psychological, and emotional abuse, as well as disrupted attachment with her primary caretaker–Hellen. Wilma met the diagnostic criteria for Post-Traumatic Stress Disorder (PTSD) and *she had clearly sustained,* among other physical harm, *several Traumatic Brain Injuries (TBI).* We started regular therapy appointments in mid-December.

Eye Movement Desensitization and Reprocessing (EMDR) is an evidence-based therapy known to be beneficial in reducing the symptoms in persons with PTSD and is one of the therapeutic modalities that I use in my practice.

Francine Shapiro, the founder of this therapy, explains in her book, *Getting Past Your Past,* that EMDR therapy targets what Shapiro calls, "unprocessed memories that contain…negative emotions, sensations and beliefs."

Wilma had experience with counseling when she came to me. I am sure that contributed to her success with therapy. However, her strongest attribute was her persistent desire to improve and reclaim her life. Somehow, despite all the damage and brainwashing that Hellen perpetrated on Wilma, she managed to come to me having an intact family life, social life, and spiritual life. Her work ethic is impeccable. Wilma never missed an appointment in the 25 sessions that we scheduled over a two-year period. She was always on time and prepared with notes, journal entries, questions, and insights. She relentlessly worked in and out of session. She persevered through mental blocks, intense emotions, tearful sessions, and the recovery of truly horrifying memories, always focused on the end goal of achieving emotional stability and mental well-being.

~ Maria Iannone, LPC
Arizona Hemophilia and Thrombosis Center
University of Arizona Medical Center

~

I was born into a typical American home…with my mom, pop, and one brother and sister. As a family, we attended school programs, scouts, celebrated birthdays and took family vacations. Growing up, I never once thought that I wasn't loved or important. I never once thought that my brother or sister was loved more than me…and they felt the same way. I never worried, or even considered that our home could break up, and it never did. I grew up loved and safe. I had *no idea* that other children were not loved and nurtured the same as me.

When Wilma and I met, we flipped over each other, dated, and married. Like most people, we had adjustments to married life, but something was different about our marriage from the relationship my parents had. Left to our own, at best we were going to be another troubled couple, but we were not left to our own. God was certainly involved and we had a great pastor. Before we met, we both made dedications to God, and we were committed to working things out. After all, we really did and still do, love each other.

At times, being born into a loving family was a disadvantage. I could not grasp the walls, the caves, the sudden changes in an evening, an outing, or a doctor visit. I had no idea that people could be triggered by a sound, a smell, or a word. As we received help, Wilma moved forward toward healing from her tragic childhood and I worked to understand a different perspective than mine. We had many long talks and at times, she'd reveal some of the evil Hellen had spouted, like, "What did I ever do to God to deserve a sorry excuse for a daughter like you?"

One evening Wilma was recalling the birth of our first son in the hospital and the love she had flooding over her as she held our baby whom she had only met moments before. I asked from a non-abused perspective, "Doesn't this show you that Hellen is a flake?"

Wilma responded from her abused perspective, "Oh no…if my mother could not have felt this love for me, then I must be *really* bad."

At that moment, I got it and my understanding was clear. Hellen was evil and Wilma was very affected by Hellen's cruelty and lies. It was a monumental moment for me.

I am very proud of Wilma. No matter how she felt about herself, it was always important to her that our children grew up in a loving home. Our children were very important to her and she stayed home to raise and nurture them. She was very involved in their education and their friends were over all the time. And, this was in the early phases of help being offered to her.

As more help became available, Wilma took small, cautious steps at the beginning, and then worked with a strong determination as time went on. Literally, she took each memory, lived it again, and put the blame where it belonged—*on the abuser.* She has not stopped healing; when the help made a difference in her life, she reached out to other hurting people. They know that she has been there. A connection is made.

Wilma had a tragic start to life. Her healing is a miracle. I got to be there to witness it.

~ Greg MacLiver

Forewords

It is a rare occasion that I would pen my thoughts to paper. Usually, they all fall out of my mouth at the most inappropriate time. However, after learning of the tragedies of my mother's youth, I have come to a conclusion. There is not an iron-clad knight in shining armor that has faced and conquered more demons of hell than my mother. The fact that she survived is incredible. But, it is courageous and commendable that she did not pass this evil to the next generation.

~ Ryan MacLiver

~

The announcer seemed confident until he said, "And now, please welcome Wilma...Mic...Liver, uh no Mac Leever...ur. MiCiver." The people who'd packed the theatre erupted in laughter as my mom entered from stage right. Smiling and waving as she crossed the stage, Wilma MacLiver was undaunted by the mispronunciation of her name.

My heart pounded. The cameras zeroed in on her. The huge screens radiated her warmth and confidence. The crowd was clapping and cheering.

I reflected. The announcer had misread my mom's name, and I was coming to the realization that I had been misreading her *life*.

Growing up, I had a mom who was there. I had a mom who cared. I had a mom who loved me unconditionally. And, I had a mom who I knew was different than other kids' moms. Something was wrong.

My brother and I grew up with Grandma MacLiver, and...my mom's mom. He and I never acknowledged Hellen as a grandma. Mom would yell at us for referring to her that way, but we never connected with Hellen. We visited her, but there was something in our little kid brains that could never make her out as a 'grandma.' She wasn't like Grandma MacLiver, and we didn't know why.

Our mom was fun. Our mom was sobering. Our mom was in the center of everything us boys were doing. Our mom was withdrawn.

Our mom would make us laugh. Our mom would cry.

She took us everywhere. We had the 'cool mom' on the street. All of the summer field trips…that was my mom's doing. Our mom drove us. Our mom went with us. Our mom was close. Our mom was far. Sometimes, she could feel so distant. Other times, she would get so close that no one would ever forget it. She marked our lives. She made a difference. She connected deep and personally with the people we knew–and even with strangers. She never let her friends get too close.

She could talk for hours. She could be extremely quiet and reflective. She could leave you feeling like you could never understand her. She could smile, and you knew she completely got you.

It was that smile I saw beaming from the stage and across the monitors that evening. The entire audience could feel that smile. That look. That 'I know you and I care' twinkle. The crowd was roaring.

She walked to the podium and delivered the first sentence of her GED graduating class speech: "Mark Twain said, 'There are two types of speakers; those who are nervous and those who are liars.'" Mom's voice echoed against the walls, but this was not supposed to be the opening line. I was laughing, but reeling in confusion because we had not written this line into the speech. Once again, her spontaneity and her wit arose and took us on a ride.

Life at home had always been that way. Moments of spontaneity. Moments of uncertainty.

This night would be no different. Several times throughout the speech, the crowd rose to their feet, cheering, only to be seated while wiping their tears moments later. She connected to their pains, to their hearts, and to their dreams. Their hearts were warmed by a conquering hero. She made them know they too could conquer. This was my mom. In 23 minutes, an entire audience in Phoenix's Orpheum Theatre experienced my mom. The highs. The lows. The laughter. The tears.

Forewords

Over the years, many people have experienced my mom. Kris was one of those individuals. He was a friend of mine in elementary school, and always in trouble. One day, Kris got into a fight. My mom, a duty aide at our school, was required to write a referral that could've meant expulsion. Kris fell to the ground with uncontrollable sobbing and told her, "My dad will beat me if I bring a referral home."

My mom connected. She knew the true meaning of the words. She knew the reaction. She hugged him instead. She talked to his heart. Kris would never forget that act of love. He would see her years later at a restaurant and excitedly walk over to hug her. Unfortunately, Kris never broke free from the pain of abuse. He was not able to rise above the shame.

Kris died. My mom cried.

I can never forget Kris. History repeats itself…unless a hero steps in to make a positive change. Too often, the cycle of abuse is passed from generation to generation.

Because of the strength and courage of my mom, the cycle of abuse was not passed on to my generation. I was born to a conqueror. I was born to someone who battled in the most personal way to change the course of history. Mine.

It is now time for you and I to turn the pages and read her life correctly for the first time.

~ Jeremy MacLiver

Introduction

Not to know is bad. Not to want to know is worse.
Not to hope is unthinkable. Not to care is unforgivable.
~ Nigerian saying

In the 1960s when I was a child, the United States did not have the laws to protect children like the ones today.

Since that time, states have created laws to identify, intervene, and protect children who live in situations of abuse. Also, public awareness of child abuse has increased since the time when such awareness would have been beneficial for me.

The laws focus on reportable agents, defined as teachers, medical professionals, coaches, counselors, clergy or those in frequent contact with children, and/or a child's family members. If the reportable agent has concerns–no actual proof is needed–then they are required to make a report to the local authorities for investigation.

I had the privilege of working with three experienced counselors. Pastor Sawyer and his wife were the first to recognize and address the trauma in my life. They provided the majority of the life-changing counseling I received. They continue to be an inspiration to me. In addition to counseling, they teach classes for those who have suffered trauma. They are a gift in my life, and I am grateful.

Pastor Sawyer's wife, Mrs. Sawyer, has been like a mother to me. Her wise counsel, steady encouragement, and Christian example has guided me since I was a young teen. I appreciate her gentle wisdom and love. I am where I am today because she willingly and graciously filled the role of a mother in my life.

Introduction

Pastor Sawyer introduced me to Dr. Laine. Together they offered clear, concise counseling.

The counselors worked diligently to explain the power of mind control. Abusers like Hellen begin when the child is preverbal, and methodically work to control the child forever. They create the child's reality. Pastor Sawyer told me, "Childhood is where our reality is formed."

I came to understand that through words, most abusers control their victims for life, not needing the aid of chains, locks, or ropes. Pastor Sawyer explained, "Their primary tools are manipulation, domination, and control."

Hellen had a brilliant mind, constantly seeking out new ways to cause torment and agony, while maintaining different levels of terror. She was methodical in her plan to increase the power and control she had over others, my siblings, and me.

We called her mom.

But...Hellen was incredible.

Incredibly evil.

Wilma MacLiver
April, 2021

1964: Birth

It's no wonder that truth is stranger than fiction.
Fiction has to make sense.
~ Mark Twain

The Times

In 1964, Ford Motor Company introduced the Mustang, the United States Postal Service added ZIP codes, Pop-Tarts marketed dessert for breakfast, and around the time of my birth, my parents realized the imminent death of their marriage.

My father, Angelo Proietti, was born in New York in 1914, just weeks after his parents emigrated through Ellis Island from Italy. He quit school in eighth grade to work and help provide for his family. Angelo was short in stature–less than five feet tall and weighed 200 pounds. Drafted into the military for World War II, he fought on Normandy Beach. When his tour of duty ended, he worked a factory job until he retired. He was naturally neat, clean, and well respected in the community. He enjoyed gardening and cooking.

My mother, Hellen Bullard, was born in Pennsylvania in 1931. Her father was from England and her mother was of Swedish descent. The fifth of six children, Hellen quit school in ninth grade because her obesity made it too difficult to fit in the desks. Hellen's severe obesity was an issue from the time she was a young girl until her death.

Relatives relayed their memories about the cruel and abusive nature of Hellen's mother.

Grandmother Bullard justified her brutal behavior under the banner of religion. Relatives commonly reported that grandmother was unreasonably strict with her children; beat them with switches and quoted scriptures while threatening them with hell fire. According to the reports, everyone including grandpa feared her.

~

*Grandma Bullard
Late 1940's
with unidentified man.*

*We have no pictures
of her smiling.*

*Hellen spoke of her mother
beating her and
forcing her to memorize
long passages of scripture.*

*Hellen never expressed any
fond memories of her mother
nor indicated any grief
about her death.*

~

Hellen's siblings escaped the family home through various methods. Two of her sisters carried shopping bags each day on the streetcar, slowly removing their belongings until none were left in their room. Others married at the first opportunity. Junior, her only brother, moved to another state in ninth grade, due to a stress-induced illness.

Relatives said that Hellen was her mother's slave, and they always felt sorry for her.

Grandmother died young at age 52 with a diagnosis of being 'full of cancer.' Hellen stayed in the family home and cared for her mother through her final days.

1964: Birth

Angelo and Hellen met as co-workers at the local factory. They married in 1956 when Angelo was 42 and Hellen was 25 years old. His wedding gift to Hellen was a new home, a new car, and a honeymoon to Florida, all paid for in cash.

~

1956 – Grandmother Proietti, Angelo and Hellen, Grandpa Bullard

~

My brother Hugh was born in 1958, then Danny in 1959, and my sister, Tracy, in 1960.

Hellen soon became the talk of their small town; known for her dirty house, not bathing her children, and leaving her babies in soiled diapers. My dad was called home from the factory countless times when Hellen threatened to commit suicide. She never did anything that endangered her life–just fits of crying, bouts of despondency, and expressions of rage. Word about her strange behavior quickly passed through the small-town grapevine.

~

My father purchased another new home close to the factory as the family grew. Still, Hellen cried and threatened suicide because she wanted to live near her father, approximately 30 miles away. My dad didn't want to drive the icy mountain roads in the winter to work at the factory.

Finally, after eight years living with Hellen's constant suicide threats and increasing depression, Angelo bought an empty lot near his father-in-law.

According to Hellen and Angelo, Hellen designed the custom home, and Angelo had it built according to her design. Construction went as planned and the home was completed two months before I was born.

~

Pennsylvania – 1963
The custom home
Angelo built for Hellen near Grandpa Bullard.

~

A scandal developed during the construction of the house and Hellen was once again the talk of the town and an embarrassment to our relatives. Hellen found out that she was pregnant with me and she was upset. She kept saying she did *"not* want this pregnancy."

There was talk among the community and extended family that Angelo was not my father. Just who the father was…well, this became the *family secret.* My siblings were too young to understand the talk.

1964: Birth

∼

Family history and photographs show that just before I was born, our family moved into the custom home that Hellen designed and my dad built for her. In the nine years they were married, it was their third new home.

I was born in the winter of 1964. Hellen had been upset that she was pregnant with me and throughout my life, she made it clear that she had "never wanted that pregnancy." Grandpa Bullard was a photographer and yet, there are no pictures of Hellen holding me as an infant. That has always puzzled me.

Near the time of my first birthday, Hellen prepared to leave my dad. For months, she stashed away the household expense money. She threw away the bills and late notices.

∼

New York – 1964
Angelo Proietti
51 years old

1964: Birth

~ Counseling Notes ~

Many years ago, I travelled to New York and Pennsylvania to interview relatives for this book. I asked about my mean grandmother and they had many memories to share.

The counselors said, "It's possible your grandmother was following a cycle of abuse in her own life. She used religion to abuse and torment her children to the point that five of them escaped her house, while Hellen remained trapped. Evidently, she was cruel enough that decades later when you interviewed relatives, they still had things to say about her."

~

I asked about why there would be no pictures of me as an infant when my grandfather was a photographer.

The counselors said, "The family secret may well be the answer to your question. It looks like Hellen was ducking, dodging, and covering as much as she could. Finally, she ran away from all of her family. Who and what she was running from, and trying to hide, the whole extent of it we will probably never know."

1965: 1 Year Old

Don't go around saying the world owes you a living.
The world owes you nothing. It was here first.
~ Mark Twain

The Times

In 1965, the first U.S. troops went into Vietnam, Winston Churchill died, Diet Pepsi and Applejacks were introduced into American diets, and after my first birthday, I didn't see my father again until I was 24 years old.

My first birthday was the only birthday I celebrated with my father.

Then, when I was 14 months old, Hellen flew my siblings and I across the country, separating us from our father by more than 2,500 miles.

~

There was snow on the ground when Hellen left my father and moved my siblings and me to Arizona. From that cold December day until my rescue 15 years later, life with Hellen only got worse.

After we left, my dad discovered the bills were three months behind, and his home was in foreclosure. He had lost everything.

The couple that purchased our foreclosed home said that Hellen left it a filthy mess, with mounds of unwashed clothes and dirty cloth diapers piled high in the basement.

1965: 1 Year Old

A neighbor loaned my father the money to buy an old travel trailer to live in. It was located just up the hill from the custom home he'd worked so hard to build.

~

Through the years, Hellen bragged about how crafty she had been and how gullible my dad was to think his bills were paid. I remember her saying, "Your father was just another stupid man. One among millions."

Hearing that as a child, I wondered, *if he is so stupid, why did you marry him?*

I didn't know much about my dad when I was growing up. Hellen told us he was mean and had often waved a gun as a threat. I had a few pictures of him in a box, but I had a hard time imagining Hellen's stories lining up to the man in the photos. It took almost 30 years to confirm my gut feelings: Hellen had lied about him.

~

So...the mystery left for me was, why did Hellen fight to live close to her father, then soon after the home was finished, move 2,500 miles away from everyone she knew? And...how hard was it for her to leave everything behind and go it alone with four little kids in Arizona? What was so pressing that she *had* to leave? What was she hiding? What or who was she running away from?

~

Before we left Pennsylvania, Hellen contacted a Baptist church in Phoenix and told its young minister that she was forced to leave her family, friends, and even her marriage to save her sickly daughters. The minister and his wife rented an apartment for us in preparation for our arrival.

When our plane landed at Sky Harbor airport, the minister and his wife met us at the airport. They drove us to a small, furnished apartment filled with food and necessities.

1965: 1 Year Old

Not long after we'd settled in, Hellen found another church she preferred to attend.

Hellen had a grudge against Baptists from her teen years, and she 'made even on it' by contacting a Baptist minister and his wife to use them before leaving my dad. Until she died, she laughed about how she "never wanted to be a dumb old Baptist anyway."

About two months later, my dad borrowed money and traveled to Phoenix. He arrived with hopes of reconciling his family, pleading with Hellen to return home. She refused. At the age of 51, he knew he had lost his family and flew back to Pennsylvania alone.

~

Years later, I asked my dad about his trip to Phoenix. In his thick Italian accent, he said, "Well, I did travel to Phoenix to try to get your mother to come back home. I tell ya, she cries and carries on until I build her the house she wants right by her father, and she ups and leaves a me! I didn't know what to do in that desert called Arizona."

"Did you look for work during your visit, dad?"

"Na. I was a too afraid if I started following your mother she'd just keep running away. I'd never have a-nothin'. She left me with nothin'. I lost ever'thing."

He paused for a moment. I waited as he gathered his thoughts. Then, swinging his hands before his chest, he confirmed what Hellen had bragged about for years. "You see, your mother, oh that woman… your mother threatened me with never seeing you kids again. I'd already lost everthin' I worked hard for, so I didn't trust her. I figured if I just went home, worked, and saved, like I'd always done, I could go before the judge and at least get visitation of you's kids. I knew the judge. Nice Italian guy. I thought he'd think kindly of me. I was tired of your mother's games."

After a pause, he continued, "All I ever wanted was to go to work and come home to a clean house, one that I was a willing to work

1965: 1 Year Old

hard to provide, and my wife and kids be there and be happy. I only wanted a simple, happy life. Is that a too much to ask?"

∼

There are conflicting reports of why Hellen left my dad and moved us across the country where she knew no one. Hellen said it was because Tracy and I had been ill with pneumonia. She said the doctors advised Arizona's sunny climate for our health. She claimed her husband and family didn't believe her, so they wouldn't help her.

In researching the pneumonia story, I interviewed my dad and several relatives in New York, Pennsylvania, Michigan, and Arizona. None of them heard the doctors advise a move across the country. Family members faintly remembered some type of bronchial illness (possibly pneumonia), but nothing serious enough to warrant a move to Arizona. My dad said, "I was never told by the doctors that moving to Arizona was necessary or even recommended. I would've done anything for you kids."

∼

As a kid, I used to wonder how the doctors on the East Coast handled pneumonia cases. Surely, they didn't send *everyone* "out West."

∼

Hellen's behavior, her choices, and her perversions however, told a different story.

Time would show that Hellen moved to hide a secret she was protecting about herself.

1965: 1 Year Old

~ Counseling Notes ~

I discussed my feelings about my father in the photos and how they did not fit Hellen's descriptions of him.

The counselors said, "Your gut feelings as a child regarding the photos of your father and the things Hellen said about him are interesting. It shows early on you were an independent thinker. You were not a follower. You couldn't align your gut feeling to what she told you about him being mean and waving a gun around in a threatening way. It's also interesting that you had the wisdom at a young age to keep your thoughts and feelings private.

Another area of your inquisitive thinking is how you put together Hellen's stories of how she wanted to live by her father, but a year later she moved 2,500 miles away. How old were you when you questioned that?"

"I think I was about 9 or 10 years old when I put that together."

"Did you ever ask her about that?"

"No. I wouldn't have dared."

"It was smart not to have questioned her."

"Did you have any idea at all that her move had anything to do with a family secret?"

"No. But the family secret that came out years later stunned me."

1965: 1 Year Old

~

I had so many questions about why Hellen would tear apart our family.

The counselors said, "Who knows what Hellen was running from? Whatever was going on tore apart your family and forever changed all of your lives. Child abuse and trauma is a multi-generational curse. The only way to put a stop to it is to get help. You *have* to work through it or you will just pass it to the next generation."

Phoenix, Arizona – 1965
Sky Harbor Airport

Hellen arriving with us four kids
for the first time.

1966: 2 Years Old

*It's not the size of the dog in the fight;
it's the size of the fight in the dog.*
~ Mark Twain

The Times

The year 1966 brought stereo cassette decks to store shelves, the first photos of the Earth were shot from the moon, Walt Disney died, and I ignored Hellen and prayed when I was scared.

My grandfather was helping us move and I was in the front seat of Hellen's car, watching as a U-Haul truck flipped onto its side and spun out of control on the interstate. Hellen pulled to the side of the road as I jumped up and down on the front seat while crying out, "Jesus, Jesus, Jesus."

"Shut up!" Hellen snapped.

I continued to pray as we watched the big truck spin on its side to the edge of the highway and finally stop at the brink of the pavement. I remember the sounds of screeching metal on the pavement slowly going silent. Hellen cried when the truck stopped at the edge. There was no guardrail and just over the edge was a deep canyon. My grandfather and my two brothers were inside the U-Haul, but they only had minor injuries. Our furniture was scattered across the lanes of the interstate.

I was 2½ years old.

1966: 2 Years Old

~

Through the years, Hellen told that story many times, giving God credit for helping us in that desperate moment. It is the only time I remember her giving God credit for anything good. It seems fitting that I kept that desperate prayer as my first memory because later I would find my own world spinning out of control and call on God for help.

Grandpa Bullard
65 years old
Around the time of the U-Haul Accident

1966: 2 Years Old

~ Counseling Notes ~

I asked why I would remember so vividly when our U-Haul truck flipped on its side when we were moving:

The counselors said, "Your courage shows through at just two years old. You watched the truck and kept praying despite Hellen's scolding. That is just a small inkling of the fight within you, which would sustain you in the years to come."

1967: 3 Years Old

The more you explain it, the more I don't understand it.
~ Mark Twain

The Times

In 1967, the Supreme Court ruled unconstitutional the state laws against interracial marriage, Mickey Mouse watches and jogging became popular, and by the time of my third birthday, I realized I had a secret.

One beautiful autumn day, Hellen hired a photographer to take our pictures. He was late, and I fell asleep on the couch while waiting. As I stirred from the short nap, I heard Hellen and my brother Hugh talking.

"Mom, what are those bruises on Wilma's legs?"

"Oh, she fell outside. If that little snot would just listen, she wouldn't be getting hurt like that."

Jerking on my shoulder, Hellen snapped, "Get up! You messed up your dress and your hair."

The photographer arrived and took group photos. I smiled as instructed until he took pictures of me alone. He told me to smile and I couldn't. I thought about Hugh and hoped he didn't believe what Hellen had said. I *hadn't* fallen outside and Hellen knew it. I instinctively knew I would be in trouble if I told anyone what Hellen did to me in her bed.

It was a secret.

1967: 3 Years Old

I felt very different from my sister and brothers.

When Hugh saw the bruises on my legs, I was naive to think he could make Hellen stop hitting me.

But...we both kept silent.

~

Picture day was the first realization that I couldn't tell anyone about the things Hellen did to me in her bed. I don't know when Hellen started sexually abusing me, *it just always was.*

I know for certain that the sexual abuse was well established by that day. I was too young to understand the troubled feelings I had when Hellen sexually abused me. Yet, even at three years of age I understood it was shameful. I don't remember if she told me not to tell anyone or not, I just remember it was a secret I felt 'yucky' about. Shaken by the realization I couldn't tell anyone, I began biting my nails, became afraid of the dark, and developed a speech impediment.

~

On the back of the picture, Hellen wrote: "Wilma – 3 yrs. old – Mom's little shadow."

The melancholy portrait taken that day later proved to be one of the truest reflections of those painful early years. It would be decades before I was able to speak about living in that nightmare. Although

1967: 3 Years Old

I was unable to cognitively recognize it then, Hellen's cruelty was methodically growing by the day.

~

Later in life, my brother Danny said, "From the time you were about 2½ years old, I used to wonder why you cried all the time. I was 8 years old and I clearly remember you being a sad little kid. Your crying really stood out in my mind. Even as we got older."

~

A few months later, Hellen was driving on a busy road when I opened the back door of the car and watched as the road flashed by. I just *had* to get away from Hellen. I still remember making the decision to jump. Then, I let go of the door handle and dropped out of the car. I hit the street, tumbling, rolling, everything blurry and noisy.

Suddenly, everything stopped. I lay in the road dazed and shocked. Hellen's back tire had run over my right foot, leaving it mangled and raw, the bone clearly exposed.

When my face slammed into the road, the impact knocked out my front teeth. I bled profusely from my mouth and nose. I had road burns and scrapes all over my body.

A man in an old, beat-up Volkswagen Beetle stopped. He gently picked me up and carried me to the sidewalk.

Some bystander put a sweater down, and he laid me on it. He spoke kind, comforting words. I felt unable to talk. I was in pain and began to cry when I saw that I was bleeding from head to toe.

The man looked around and asked, "What happened?"

"I was only driving 35 miles per hour, and she just opened the back door and fell out," Hellen explained while waving her arms.

"It looks like the back tire ran over her foot," Hellen muttered, as if to herself.

The man insisted on calling for an ambulance or at least helping us get to a hospital.

1967: 3 Years Old

Instead, Hellen lied to him and said she was a nurse, (she wasn't). "I'll take her to the hospital myself," she said to the man. "I can take care of everything from this point on."

The other bystander left. Hesitantly, the man got into his car and drove away.

Hellen drove straight home while scolding and cursing at me. "If you're stupid enough to jump out of the car, no one can help you. Why did you jump out of the car?"

"I was hot."

At home, I cried as Hellen poured rubbing alcohol on my foot and into the scrapes on my skin. The alcohol burned.

1967: 3 Years Old

~ Counseling Notes ~

For years, I berated myself repeatedly for being so dumb to have jumped out of a moving car. I hesitantly spoke about it in counseling.

The counselors said, "You were following a normal pattern of behavior for children under extreme stress. When a child is doing those things, it is a cry for help. A child doesn't look at the whole length of the decision. Desperate children do desperate things, unaware of the logical harm that can result."

1968: 4 Years Old

Nothing makes us so lonely as our secrets.
~ Paul Tournier

The Times

In 1968, Martin Luther King, Jr. and Robert Kennedy were assassinated. Following the assassinations, Sears & Roebuck removed toy guns from their catalog and ordered all 815 stores to quit advertising them. I turned four years old and asked for a bed for my birthday.

Having lost my front teeth when I jumped out of the car, my speech problems grew worse. I annoyed Hellen and she mocked me when I didn't pronounce the letter sounds of s, ch, and j the correct way.

"Wilma, you talk like a baby, and it's high time you snapped out of it."

I tried, but without front teeth, I couldn't make it happen. I noticed Hugh, Danny, and Tracy said things right. I felt different. The speech problem was confirmation that I was different.

~

My fourth birthday was approaching, and I asked for a bed like each of my siblings had. I felt like a baby because I was still sleeping in Hellen's bed.

"Mom, can I have a bed for my birthday?"

"No, not until you can learn how to be good."

I didn't know what she meant, but was too afraid to ask. My

1968: 4 Years Old

birthday passed, and I didn't get a bed. I couldn't have known it then, but Hellen would make getting a bed of my own a nightmare. The more I expressed the desire for a bed, the further the possibly of getting one became. I continued sleeping in Hellen's bed, and the sexual abuse continued.

~

That winter, Hellen met a family that lived a mile from our house. The husband smiled a lot, but he scared me, and I didn't know why. His wife was sweet, and I liked her. Their girls were 3 and 5 years old.

Hellen often left me at their house, each time reminding them that "Wilma is a brat, so feel free to spank her as often as necessary. She's a real troublemaker. Thanks for babysitting. I need the break."

I didn't know what the word "troublemaker" meant, or why she needed a break from me and not my siblings. Hellen's new friends seemed to understand.

I liked playing there because the girls let me choose which doll I wanted to play with and they had many to choose from. It was fun during the day. I also spent many nights there. I hated nighttime at their house and begged Hellen not to leave me there overnight. She often made me stay, and when I did, the father insisted on giving us baths before bed. Each time I told him, "I don't want a bath!" But he insisted that bath time was part of staying overnight.

He bathed his daughters first, and then directed them towards his wife for help with their pajamas. I was afraid when the mother and daughters left the bathroom. Alone in the bathroom, he did things to me like Hellen did, while helping me "get clean."

I was upset and confused by what he did to me in that bathtub. At home, Hellen did much of the same to me in her bed. Although sexual touch was part of my life, I felt uncomfortable and didn't know how to verbalize what I was thinking and feeling. So...the abuse continued.

1968: 4 Years Old

∼

Hellen's friendship with the family ended abruptly and without explanation.

One night around midnight, Hellen woke us up and told us, "get dressed and hurry." We left in a pickup truck that Hellen had borrowed.

Hellen drove through the dark streets to the family's house and told us to go inside. It felt creepy, and when we questioned her, she explained they had left town in an emergency and wouldn't be returning.

Inside the home, it looked as though they had taken a small amount of clothing and nothing else. The family photographs were still on the walls, dishes in the cabinets, food in the refrigerator, and the girls' dolls were still on their bed.

Hellen gave us boxes, newspapers for packing, and blankets. She ordered us to empty everything from the house. Throughout the night, we hauled truckloads of their belongings to our house. We left the house empty and, except for some cleaning that needed to be done, it was ready for another tenant.

I had an eerie feeling while driving away with the last of the family's belongings, just as the sun was rising over the mountains.

Later, Hellen said that somehow the dolls I loved had been 'lost' in the move.

∼

I never found out what Hellen did with the doll collection that the Weird Family left behind. I had been excited to hold them and care for them. Knowing Hellen, she had likely 'lost' them in the family's trash cans.

It seems odd that my memory has completely blocked the names of the family. I have thought of them as the 'Weird Family' through the years, so for this writing, I left them with no name, keeping the penning of this memoir authentic.

Several times after we were adults, my brother Danny and I asked Hellen about that family, how she knew they were going to leave town, and why they had left. We put some real pressure on her, yet we were unable to get any answers. Hellen had something to hide and she took the secrets about the Weird Family to her grave.

My hunch, and that is all it is, is that the man was on the run from the police for some reason.

1968: 4 Years Old

~ Counseling Notes ~

Danny and I both have a good memory and yet neither one of us can remember the name of the Weird Family. I was too young to have been keeping a journal at the time. I questioned this blank spot in both of our memories in counseling.

The counselors said, "It's interesting that you have no memory of the Weird Family's name and that Danny doesn't remember it either. Your memory has blacked that out and even the children's names. That's significant. Often when a parent is abusing a child, they will deliberately leave the child with a known abuser, so that if the child ever complains about inappropriate touching to a nurse or teacher, the parent can refer back to when the child 'stayed overnight at our friend's house.'

Again, it appears that throughout your life Hellen set up a pattern of making sure she had an alibi should you ever talk to someone in authority. It is sad for you that she used people and deliberately put you in harm's way to protect herself. She was sick."

~

"Also, Hellen continued to keep you waiting for a bed, when beds were clearly available from this family's house. Yet, she denied you a bed, and the little girls' dolls. That is cruel to dispose of exactly what you needed (the bed) and exactly what you

1968: 4 Years Old

desired (the dolls) with no explanation. In truth, there is no explanation for withholding a bed when she so willingly provided a bed for herself and your siblings. She was openly expressing cruelty.

Her message to you and your siblings was that you clearly didn't deserve the normal comforts of life. You were not worthy. You were not good enough. That was the message she wanted to instill in your mind, and to a point she was successful. She also worked to instill it in your siblings' minds that they were all different from you. That is a difficult division to heal when it goes on for as long as Hellen carried it on."

1969: 5 Years Old

Denial ain't just a river in Egypt.
~ Mark Twain

The Times

In 1969, Dwight D. Eisenhower died, Neil Armstrong walked on the moon, and I thought I was going to start kindergarten.

When I turned five, Hellen was a cashier at a convenience store and the manager rented her a television so we could watch Neil Armstrong's historic first steps on the moon. It was a small, black-and-white television, and there was snow on the screen.

~

That summer I looked forward to attending kindergarten. Finally, I would be going to school with my siblings.

One September morning, I smiled bravely while asking Hellen, "When am I going to school?"

"I have no intention of enrolling you in kindergarten."

"Why?"

"The school won't put up with stupid crybabies like you. You are not going there because you'll embarrass me. If you can learn to shut your mouth and do what you're told here, then I'll think about letting you go to school. You should be ashamed of yourself."

I was crushed.

1969: 5 Years Old

"Besides," she added, "kindergarten is just a stupid idea men came up with."

I believed her. I couldn't have a bed and now I couldn't go to school because I was bad. I decided I would try harder to be good, and maybe then, I could have a bed and go to school.

~

It appears kindergarten was just something else Hellen could and did withhold from me, while blaming me for not being 'allowed to attend.'

Skipping kindergarten was a disappointment, and it left me in Hellen's care, day and night. As a result, abuse and incest continued to be my reality. In essence, my kindergarten.

~

Hugh never seemed to get into much trouble. Hellen depended on him to babysit us and called him "the only man in the house." She needed him to be responsible, and he seemed to be. Throughout her life when Hellen got upset, Hugh could usually calm her down. He was smart; he won a scholarship and graduated from college. He had a big ego. He still does.

Danny was different. He was also smart, but he applied his mind to getting out of schoolwork. Danny was funny and often made the family laugh. He would say, "I didn't make honor roll this time, but I did make the principal's list," referring to the principal's discipline list. Danny was in trouble often because he hated school, sports, Boy Scouts, and church, anything that had rules. Over the years, his hatred for Hellen's rules flared, and he rebelled often.

Hellen told Danny, "You're just like Angelo. You walk like him and talk like him."

"And, just what would you like me to do about that?" he replied.

The remark usually got him into more trouble, yet sometimes Hellen would surprise us and laugh. Though Danny was funny, he had a lot of underlying anger, and when he was angry, I was scared of him.

1969: 5 Years Old

My sister, Tracy, was my first friend. She is smart and friendly. She also did well in school and participated in clubs. Teachers loved her outgoing, chatty personality. She won awards, earned good grades, and was awarded scholarships. Over the years, I desired to be like Tracy because Hellen seemed to like her. As far as I could tell, Tracy was everything Hellen said I failed to be.

Overall, it seemed as though Hellen loved Hugh and Tracy. Danny and I were often in trouble. I tried to please her, but I couldn't seem to.

~

One cold November evening, Hellen's sexual fondling took a new, perverted turn. I think it began because of her new job.

Hellen began working for Figurettes, a custom-fit undergarment company. Women could host a Figurettes party in their home, similar to a Tupperware party. Guests were offered a custom undergarment fitting in one of the bedrooms by the Figurettes sales consultant.

Tracy and I had to go with Hellen to her parties. I hated having to go with Hellen into the bedrooms and watch her as she custom-fitted women into the various undergarments the company offered. I was uncomfortable watching as the women undressed and Hellen touched them.

I wanted to stay in the living room, but Hellen insisted I stay with her.

After a few months, Hellen became one of the Figurettes award-winning sales representatives, and we attended a banquet where she won awards. She worked the job in the evenings for two or three years.

It was just after the start of this job when Hellen began sexually abusing me in a new, perverted way. She called it, "enema night."

I remember her saying, "Trust me, I'm a nurse, and I know what's best for you."

Hellen claimed to be a nurse for over 30 years, but she had no formal schooling, training, or certifications, it was just her word that she was. She wasn't even trained or certified in CPR.

1969: 5 Years Old

~

Enema nights were frightening and followed a distinct pattern. Hellen would arrive from work and decide that I needed enemas. At first, I didn't even know what an enema was. I was healthy and energetic, and there was no physical reason for them.

It started one afternoon when Hellen walked in the door, her mind made up; from that point on I was not allowed to eat anything until the next day.

In her bedroom, she ordered me to take off all my clothes. I became very scared. The position she made me get into to receive the enema was frightening and humiliating. Hellen began doing weird things to me and it hurt bad. Really bad. She slapped my bottom and said, "Shut up ya big baby, I'm just giving you an enema." It felt awful and I cried.

Then, she made me run down the hallway to the bathroom naked. I begged for something to cover myself with but she wouldn't let me have anything and my stomach hurt so bad, I finally just had to run, to make it to the bathroom in time.

The house had just one bathroom, halfway down the hall from Hellen's bedroom. I was 5, Tracy was 9, and my brothers were 10 and 11. I didn't want anyone to see me naked, and I cried a lot about that.

Once I was in the bathroom, Hellen propped the door open, and she stood in front of me as I sat on the toilet. With a firm grip on my chin, Hellen poured cup after cup, of scalding black tea (no sugar) down my throat. I learned to hold still as she poured the tea into my mouth because spilling the tea caused burns on my bare legs.

As soon as I was allowed off the toilet, she forced me to run (and she meant *run*) to her bed for another enema. The evening included several quart-size enemas. After each one, I'd run naked back to the bathroom, sit on the toilet, and swallow more cups of scalding tea. The inside of my mouth and throat were burned as Hellen forced me to

1969: 5 Years Old

quickly swallow more tea than I could hold. Then she held a trash can for me so I could vomit. Even as a young child, I was surprised when I realized the tea was still hot when it came back up. The times I missed the trash can, Hellen slapped my face and pulled my hair, while she yelled, cussed, and called me names. I felt stupid because everything I did on that night was wrong.

Every single thing.

I begged, sobbed, pleaded, "Why, mom? Why do I have to have enemas?"

Backhanding me, splitting my lip, she spoke cruelly through her gritted false teeth, "Because you're so stupid and ugly, it'll help you, that's why. I've got to come home after working all day to flush the **** (junk) out of you, so maybe, just maybe, you won't be so stupid and ugly when I finish with you."

I would try not to cry–I would try so hard–but I couldn't help it and sobbed each time. The enemas consumed the entire evening, and when Hellen finally stopped, she allowed me to put on a nightgown and get into her bed, without a bath or dinner. I went to sleep hungry, with the hiccupping that comes after extended bouts of anguished crying.

When enema nights began, they were once, often twice a week. Through the years, they followed the basic pattern of that first night, but true to Hellen's escalating perversions, her cruelties escalated as well. I dreaded her arrival at the end of the day, and I lived in constant fear of her and the scary, red enema bag.

~

Since we lived in Phoenix, Hellen's father, my grandpa Bullard, became a snowbird. His leaving Pennsylvania and spending the winters in Phoenix was beneficial for Hellen, too. He was our babysitter.

Grandpa told everyone I was his 'special' girl.' Folks used to say, "Whatever she wants, grandpa will buy for her…he never tells her 'no.'"

I did ask him to buy me a bed of my own. Grandpa was not

1969: 5 Years Old

wealthy, but he had plenty of money to travel, spend, and enjoy. He often bought us toys and treats; the only thing he refused to buy was a bed I could call my own.

When Grandpa visited, I slept with him at night.

Hellen required me to take naps in her bed.

~

Grandpa kept his room clean. He made the bed every day. He often sat in his room to read, and I liked how it smelled of aftershave. He kept a framed picture of Hellen on the dresser; he said it had been taken when she was 18 years old. I asked him why he had a picture of Hellen, and not grandma. He told me that having a picture of grandma wasn't right...since she had died.

Inside the top drawer of the dresser he used, he kept a box of mints. He'd give me one mint a day. But grandpa also had a mean side. He had little patience with my brothers, often yelling at them and hitting them. After he'd backhanded Danny in the face for being 'mouthy,' my brother stole grandpa's box of mints when grandpa was in the bathroom a long time.

I loved crawling into bed with grandpa. He'd cuddle with me, pressing my face against his whiskers, as I smelled his Old Spice cologne. He'd tell me how special I was and hold me while I drifted off to sleep. He didn't like lights on when he slept, but since I was afraid of the dark, he allowed a nightlight in his room. I loved, longed for, and basked in his kind words, affection, and his constant attention.

But...I didn't understand why he'd wake me up in the middle of the night, to tell me that I'd wet the bed. He said I needed to take a bath. I was confused because Hellen didn't say that when I slept in her bed.

We'd go into the bathroom where he'd run the water, help me out of my nightgown and watch me get into the bathtub. I remember crying. I didn't want to take a bath. Grandpa insisted and he also got undressed. I thought he was going to get into the bathtub with me,

1969: 5 Years Old

but he never did. Though I was sleepy and cranky, I felt even more confused watching grandpa. I didn't understand what he was doing, or why. I felt uncomfortable because, in the middle of the night, he was different from the grandpa I knew in the daytime. I didn't like the nighttime grandpa. He scared me. After a while, he'd help me out of the bathtub, watch me get into another nightgown and we'd go back to the bed to sleep (each time, the sheets were dry on the bed...).

~

Grandpa made no secret that he preferred me over his thirteen other grandchildren. I was a grandmother before I could explain what being his "special girl" involved. I don't know how long grandpa molested me. But he did abuse my trust, my love, and my body. Instead of seeing him as a dirty old man, I saw myself as a dirty little kid.

Throughout my life, whenever the memory of his abuse crossed my mind, I'd cry, reliving the sight, smell, and confusion of those nights.

~

Conflict was a major component of my childhood. Grandpa was the only man in my life, my only grandparent, and his actions created confusion and troubled my mind.

He never hit me or spoke unkind to me. I was sad when he died. I missed feeling I was special to someone, but I didn't miss the confusion of the middle-of-the-night baths.

~

Enema nights continued to worsen. I didn't know what I did to make Hellen decide one was 'necessary,' or what I could do to make them stop. I thought maybe grandpa could make Hellen stop the enema nights, but I was wrong. I don't remember a time when he tried to intervene. Since grandpa didn't stop her, I reasoned I must deserve them.

Hellen said they were because I was stupid and ugly, and I believed her. I so wanted to be smart and pretty. I learned to eat 'normal,' not showing pain from the burns in my mouth and throat from the scalding tea. I was in pain, yet I was afraid to ask for a baby aspirin from the medicine cabinet, so I never did.

I lived in terror of the woman I called mom.

It was perplexing to me that on enema nights, the rest of the family appeared to enjoy a typical evening. Tracy, Hugh, and Danny did homework, ate ice cream, and watched TV. It was as though they were unaware of what was happening down the hall. Perhaps they had grown accustomed to Hellen and me 'fighting.' That's what they called it.

~

Enema nights caused me to feel separate from other people. I believed I was the weird one–the one who caused the trouble. In my mind, I taught myself to 'leave' to get through those long, awful nights. I learned and experienced the difference between what I called shutdown and total shutdown.

In shutdown, I could see and hear what was happening but refused to let it affect me. In my mind, the shutdown was like a glass garage door. I could close off the situation or person with my eyes, and separate myself from reality. I learned fast to separate myself from everyone, especially Hellen.

Total shutdown was like closing a black garage door in front of my eyes; my vision went dark, my hearing silent, except for the pounding of my heart in my chest. It's where I went in my mind during the sexual abuse.

The mechanism of total shutdown had one weak link. There was one place it failed me. I discovered that no amount of shutdown could keep out Hellen's sickening touch, or putrid smell. I was crushed with disappointment when I realized that shutdown would not turn off my sense of touch or smell. That discovery was devastating.

~

It seemed whatever I expressed a desire for, Hellen made sure I

1969: 5 Years Old

would not be allowed to have it. I desperately wanted to have my own bed, but I still had to sleep with her. I clearly remember deliberately referring to the bed as, "her bed" and *never once* calling it, "my bed."

∼

Hellen required me to wear Tracy's old underwear. Sometimes Hellen bought me underwear at the Salvation Army Thrift Store. The worst part was that she wouldn't take the underclothes to the laundromat before I had to wear them. I hated the thought of wearing someone's dirty clothes. I didn't believe I deserved new clothes, like Tracy.

∼

I loved and memorized every word of the song, *Casper the Friendly Ghost,* and played the record constantly. Casper was happy and could disappear. That's how I wanted to be: happy and able to disappear.

After a week or so the record disappeared.

I had loved Casper too much.

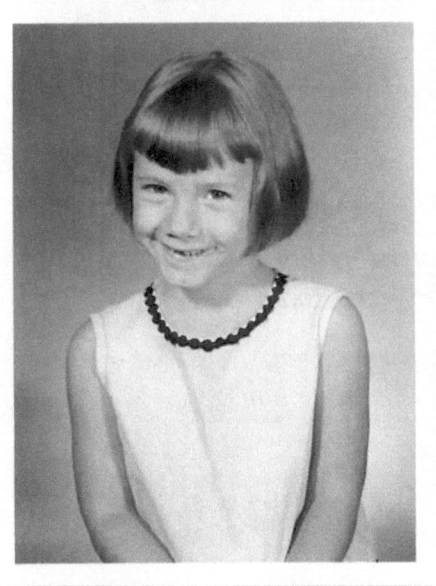

Hellen had this outfit made in the Figurettes pink and black color theme for a banquet.

She received the Top Sales Award.

Hellen cut my hair (crooked as usual) right before leaving the house.

Some of my front teeth are still missing from jumping out of the car when I was three.

1969: 5 Years Old

Phoenix, Arizona – 1969

*Enema nights started in this house
on Mountain View Road.*

*Later, when I was seven,
I ran away from this same house.*

1969: 5 Years Old

~ Counseling Notes ~

Only a few family members–but many friends and acquaintances–acknowledge that Hellen was a closet lesbian *and* a child molester. Decades later, Hellen lived in an open lesbian relationship, years before it was socially accepted as a lifestyle.

~

I was too young to understand that Hellen's ignited fantasies caused her to start the enema nights when I was 5 years old.

The counselors said, "Hellen crossed a very distinct line with the enema nights. She went from being sexually abusive to committing acts of sexual torture. The enforced silence and nudity she required, was part of the dehumanizing many abusers do to their victims. Also, from the details you've explained, she was apparently experiencing sexual gratification on those nights as well."

~

I asked about grandpa and the contradiction between his declaration of 'love' for me and his abuse.

The counselors said, "There are two types of molestation: manipulative, gentle and 'loving' (though it's traumatic and hurtful), and violent, cruel torture, which leaves much deeper scars. Your grandpa's molestation caused conflict and confusion because he didn't use violence, cruelty, or threats as

Hellen did. Unfortunately, you were accustomed to violent sexual abuse, so you didn't recognize what he did as bad, though it troubled you at the time."

Phoenix, Arizona – 1969

Hellen Proietti – 38 years old

Figurettes Banquet
Hellen receiving a Top Sales Award

1970: 6 Years Old

The only man who never makes mistakes
is the man who never does anything.
~ Theodore Roosevelt

The Times

In 1970, the first commercial 747 aircraft went into service, Automatic Bank Tellers (ATMs) became available, and I joined and quit the Brownie Girl Scouts.

September mornings in Phoenix are warm, and my first day of school, at age 6, was no exception.

The morning was busy as we rushed around getting ready. Hugh and Danny laughed at my excitement. "You will like it, Wilma. You will learn a lot at school." Hugh said.

Danny chimed in, "Yeah, you're excited now…but give it a few days. You'll wise up, like me, and start looking for any excuse to stay home!"

That morning, I went from happy and excited to puzzled. Hellen insisted I wear a blouse and skirt of Tracy's instead of my own clothes. Tracy, now 10 years old and starting fifth grade, was significantly taller than me and a bit pudgy. I was short and underweight; her clothes hung on me. Her blouse had to be folded over between my shoulders, and Hellen crudely fastened it with a large safety pin on the outside, so that it would stay on. Tracy's skirt draped my ankles, so Hellen folded and safety pinned the fabric at the waist, the way she had adjusted the blouse. I hated that my new friends at school would see the safety pins. I wore the only pair of socks I had–white ones that had turned dirty gray.

My shoulder-length brown hair was filthy. Hellen had recently cut my bangs and they were crooked. Two big knots poked out of the strands at my neck. I couldn't comb them myself, and everyone was too busy to help me. I hadn't counted on starting school wearing Tracy's clothes and my hair being a knotted mess.

I hoped my new classmates wouldn't notice.

They did.

~

Mrs. Jones, my teacher, was a stern older woman with a large stomach, and skinny legs. I thought, *she looks like a big fat hen.* I was excited when I met first met her, but turned nervous when I heard Hellen say, "Now Mrs. Jones, Wilma is not like my other kids. You will have to keep a heavy hand on her to make her behave. This one's gonna make you sorry you ever chose to be a teacher."

Mrs. Jones replied, "Thank you, Mrs. Proietti. I'm quite sure I'm capable of handling Wilma."

Soon I discovered that the other children in my class had gone to kindergarten. They laughed when I didn't know the morning routine.

Mrs. Jones began that day by teaching us her rules of the classroom. There were so many, I wondered how I would remember them all. While Mrs. Jones was talking, a girl sitting beside me said something I didn't hear.

I turned to her and asked, "What?"

Mrs. Jones walked over with her hands on her large hips, and said, "Put both hands on your desk."

Naturally curious, I did as she instructed, wondering why she had stopped teaching to look at my hands. To my surprise, she slapped my knuckles with her ruler.

1970: 6 Years Old

"No talking in class!"

The other kids laughed as I cried. I didn't know I would be slapped at school, too.

~

When it was time for recess, I ran to the swings. My pace was slowed by Tracy's long skirt. By the time I got to the swings, they were taken. I thought about going down the slide, but I couldn't climb the ladder because of Tracy's skirt.

Standing on the playground alone, I met a girl named Lynnette who was kind to me. I noticed she was clean and had beautiful clothes. The kids began forming a circle, pointing at my big clothes, dirty hair, and socks. The group had grown to about 15 kids when someone yelled, "You're the Playground Pig!"

I didn't know what to do. Lynnette didn't either but she slowly backed away.

I looked around and everyone was looking at me.

The kids began chanting, "Playground Pig, Playground Pig" in a singsong manner while pushing up their noses and making oinking sounds. Their faces looked ugly when they did that.

Mrs. Jones blew the whistle, and the kids formed a line by her. I didn't understand that recess was over, so I went to an empty swing and jumped on it. I was relieved the kids had left me alone.

Happily, I pumped the swing higher and higher as I watched Mrs. Jones continue to blow her whistle. Then, I realized she was blowing the whistle at *me*. Dragging my foot, I slowed the swing and slithered off the seat. When I got close to the line, Mrs. Jones said, "Wilma! When I blow the whistle the first time, everyone including you is expected to line up immediately."

School was harder than I thought it was going to be.

~

After a few weeks, I still desired to fit in with the other kids. I begged Hellen to let me join the Brownie Girl Scouts. On the final day of registration, Hellen let me join.

I looked forward to Scout meetings after school, but after a few weeks, I realized something was wrong and I was uncomfortable.

I noticed the other girls had their uniforms and Brownie socks. I was still wearing dirty clothes, or Tracy's clothes, or some of both. I asked every day for a Brownie uniform.

Crafts were one of the things I loved about Brownies. The girls brought their crafting supplies in pretty boxes that held glue, scissors, and crayons. I had no uniform and no box of craft supplies. The girls didn't share their craft supplies with me, but they did share them with each other. It puzzled me that they would share their glue or crayons with someone who already had glue and crayons. Because I didn't have supplies, and the girls didn't want to share, I sat silently and watched them make their crafts.

I dreamed of having a craft box, but I couldn't imagine the luxury of owning scissors.

Even though I pestered Hellen to buy some supplies for me, she always said, "I don't have money for junk like that."

Each week the Brownie Scout leader asked if I had my dues for that week, and the prior weeks as well. I didn't have any of it, so she smiled in a kind way and gave me a note to give to Hellen.

I tossed it in a trash can when I left the meeting. The other notes had just made Hellen mad anyway.

As the fall months passed, attending scout meetings became unbearable. I didn't have my Brownie dues, I didn't have snacks for the troop, and I didn't have my craft supplies.

And, I didn't have a uniform like the other girls.

School days started and ended with the constant singsong taunting of the kids: "Playground Pig, Playground Pig."

I believed that if I got a scout uniform, I would be like the other children.

1970: 6 Years Old

~

During school's recess over the winter holidays, Hellen found a Brownie uniform for me at a thrift store. I was excited and wore it, unwashed of course, all day.

When school resumed, I wore my uniform the day of our Scout meeting. It was the first time I felt like one of the kids, but I was surprised when the kids continued to call me names. I hated it when they pushed up their noses and made oinking sounds. They looked so ugly when they did that, and I felt ugly, too.

The Brownie Scout leader was pleased I had the uniform and asked if I had also brought in all my dues.

I had to say, once again, "No, but maybe next time my mom will have the money."

She then asked when I would be able to bring in my craft supplies and provide snacks for the troop.

"I don't know."

I'd already learned that asking for those things made Hellen angry. It was easier to do without, and by February, I realized the scout uniform couldn't fix the problems I faced at school and in Brownies.

I realized that it was I–the person, not the clothes, nor the lack of ability to participate in Brownies–who was different from all kids. The problem was me. No uniform, crafts, dues, snacks, scissors, or pretty boxes could make me be like other children. I was different.

I didn't fit in anywhere.

One evening in the early spring of first grade, after crying alone, I got up the courage and asked, "Can I quit Brownie Girl Scouts?"

Hellen said, "Well, I sure saw this coming. A brat like you doesn't belong with kids like that. Couldn't tell you that, though. This is the way your whole life is going to go. Trying to fit in where you don't belong. You're a quitter, a loser, and you're always gonna be, but will you listen to me? Nooo. You'll have to learn the hard way. I'm not surprised."

"I don't have to quit. It's okay. I'll be okay. Never mind."

"Oh no!" Hellen replied. "You made your bed; now you'll lay in it. You want out and out you'll go. Should've told me before you spent the whole fall whining for a Brownie costume or whatever you call that ridiculous thing. I wouldn't have wasted my hard-earned money. Oh well, you can wear it to school anyway. No sense wasting a good school dress. Tell 'em tomorrow you're a quitter. They probably know it already, I figure."

I don't know why I thought she'd understand.

Oh well, I thought, *at least I wouldn't have to attend any more Scout meetings.* I had no way of knowing it then, but Brownie Girl Scouts was the last club Hellen would ever allow me to join.

~

After some evaluations, officials at my school decided I needed speech therapy. When I brought the permission slip for Hellen to sign, she threw the paper on the floor.

"You can talk right; you just don't want to. You slur your words for attention. That's all. You think it's cute to get attention by not talking right, you big baby. Well, guess what? I'm not giving you attention until you speak right. How do you like them apples? Huh, baby? Huh?"

I wanted to talk right, but I still had no front teeth. And I sure didn't know what apples had to do with it. I didn't even like apples, since she asked...

After her scolding, I was completely surprised when Hellen signed the permission slip.

I loved speech therapy but doing the exercises didn't allow me to talk any different.

My teacher was young, tall, and pretty. She was kind to me. One thing about her captivated me: she had huge, white teeth that

1970: 6 Years Old

looked like the piano keys at church. I stared at her teeth constantly. I wondered how she grew them so long. I wondered if I had to have a toothbrush to grow teeth that perfect. Hellen didn't allow me to have a toothbrush, but I wanted one even more than ever before.

Smiling, the speech teacher would say, "Now listen carefully, Wilma. Sally went to the seashore to pick seashells on Sunday. Now, you say that for me."

Basking in her attention, I'd repeat, "Thally went to the thea thore to pick thea thells on Thunday."

She would frown, sigh, and start over again, pointing to her mouth to show how she formed the words, but all I could see were her bright, white, piano teeth.

~

The first year of school changed me. I knew I was different from my siblings, but realizing I was different from the kids at school brought a flood of disappointment.

I began to question and wonder if Hellen was right, *am I stupid? Am I a loser?* I knew I was different. After a lot of thought I reasoned, *if I could change enough, my life would get better.* I thought, *maybe I can even get a bed by my seventh birthday. My speech will get better when I get my front teeth.* I challenged myself to try harder in second grade so everything would get better.

And that persistent thought, *maybe then the kids will like me.*

Except–and there was always an exception–even I could see I was different. *The kids at school have not even met Hellen, and they don't like me. So, on those points, I am stupid and a loser,* Hellen must be right. That's how I reasoned in my 6-year-old mind in June of 1970.

1970: 6 Years Old

~ Counseling Notes ~

I asked about what goes on in the mind of an abuser like Hellen, regarding making me wear used, dirty clothes, and cutting my hair crooked.

The counselors said, "It was all about dehumanizing you. It's about constantly devaluing you, making sure you were worthless in your own eyes; not worth anything compared to your siblings. She was sending the message loud and clear to you and your siblings that you were not worth new clothes, or even clean clothes.

It was also about isolating you. She worked consistently to show a separation between you and your siblings. They could go to school; you couldn't. They had beds; you couldn't have one. You 'needed' enema nights, they didn't.

She made it clear that your siblings were worth the things she withheld from you. You were not good enough, yet. That is a powerful message in a family dynamic.

Hellen kept the meaning of 'good enough' vague, constantly manipulating you with her disapproval, so it was impossible to achieve your sibling's status. As a result, it was just a matter of time until the other children would 'naturally' see a difference between themselves and you as well. This is an example of a mother who is cruel and abusive emotionally, mentally, and physically. It's too bad the authorities weren't alerted to her abuse and cruelty."

~

I asked why Hellen let me join the Brownies and then refused to help me with supplies, snacks and troop dues. What was the point?

The counselors said, "Hellen deliberately set you up to be different from the other children at school. She insisted you wear Tracy's clothes, then later your own dirty clothes, and cut your dirty, knotted hair crooked. Hellen made sure you wouldn't fit in. She manipulated the situation ensuring that she'd be validated.

Also, by that time, she had begun systematically controlling your world. To accomplish that over the long haul, she had to keep you isolated. That is what happened with Brownie Girl Scouts. Isolation was critical to keeping you under her manipulation and control. She had to make you fail at scouts and she did.

She also never let you join another club again, making a point in your mind that you'd fail if you did, so she was 'helping' you, by not 'allowing you to fail *again*.' That creates long-term, unparalleled pain. Hellen was sick."

1971: 7 Years Old

I would tell her:
It's okay to cry. You aren't too sensitive.
Those things they say about you? Don't believe them.
They are just afraid of your light, as it reminds them of
theirs that was dimmed long ago.
You aren't unlovable, you aren't a mistake.
I know you fear life without them, but one day that will change.
Keep going.
~ Courtney Burg

The Times

In 1971, Intel introduced the first computer chip, the voting age was lowered to eighteen, Amtrak began operations, and I made a bad decision.

At the age of 7, I was very troubled and wanted to get away from Hellen. I was still sleeping in her bed; the beatings, sexual abuse, and the enema nights were painful and ongoing. I was desperate to do something. I just didn't know what.

I was curious about my dad, but I never heard from him. I wondered if my father was smarter than Hellen and had gotten away from me when I was still a baby.

Sometimes I wondered if he even knew our address since we moved so often, and always in the middle of the night. I didn't know

1971: 7 Years Old

his address, or even what city he lived in.

We had some old pictures of him in the house. I wondered, *if I did find him, would he even want me?* Hellen said he didn't want me. I figured, *she must be right, or he would contact us, wouldn't he?*

I also wondered if he had died and no one had told me. Hellen said he was 50 when I was born, and I kept track of his age by my age.

My longing for my dad went far beyond curiosity, though. I wanted someone who would approve of me. Someone like I read about in the *Little House on the Prairie* books.

~

One day Hellen said, "I don't want you, I never wanted you, and I'd get rid of you today if I could. I'd wipe my hands free of you in a heartbeat if the opportunity presented itself. Don't kid yourself. I'll praise God the day I unload the burden of you outta my life."

Her words hit hard and left me speechless. When she saw the hurt her words caused, she repeated them often. I thought all moms adored their kids. I didn't know how to hide the hurt. She said she loved me, but yet she didn't want me?

~

My desperation grew and I felt like a failure because my mother didn't want me. I didn't know if anyone wanted me. I always tried to be good, but it seemed I messed up every time.

When Hellen talked about unloading me, I felt afraid. I wondered, *will she leave me at the welfare office downtown?* I didn't want her to, and yet, I was scared of her at the same time.

I hated sleeping in her bed and was ashamed of the things she said I caused her to do. She said if I was a good girl, I could have a bed. Despite my efforts to pick up her shoes and the few toys I was allowed to have, I still didn't have a bed.

It seemed I was always in trouble and I sensed a growing anger inside. I didn't know what to do, but I had to do something.

1971: 7 Years Old

It was time to make a decision.

So, I made one. The wrong one.

Thinking my family would be happier without me, I decided to run away.

I left early one afternoon with no plan. Desperate to get away from Hellen, I packed a small bag and started walking.

I realized I had nowhere to go, so I hid a couple of houses away in some giant oleander bushes. I sat in the neighbor's yard and played with a stray dog. The dog was content, and so was I.

There were no fences between the backyards of the houses and I watched throughout the afternoon as my siblings (who were supposed to be watching me while Hellen was at work) searched for what seemed like hours, calling my name. I watched as they talked amongst themselves, but I couldn't hear them. I walked over closer to our yard, staying out of sight, easily hidden by the thick bushes. The dog followed me.

I sat for a long time until I heard Danny say to Tracy, "Hugh's gone to call mom."

"What's he calling her for?" I heard alarm in Tracy's voice.

"He's going to tell her that we can't find Wilma and see what she says." Danny looked worried. Usually, Danny could turn anything around and make it funny. He wasn't turning this around.

Hugh didn't call Hellen at work unless it was an emergency. Otherwise there was "hell to pay," as Hellen liked to say.

When Hugh slumped out of the house, Danny and Tracy turned towards him.

"What did she say?" Tracy asked.

"She's on her way."

Silence.

"This is bad," Danny conceded.

I had gone too far, and I was scared. Hellen was leaving work. Hugh was in tears. I had never seen him like that. There would be no easy way out of this.

1971: 7 Years Old

The sun went down, and afraid of the dark, I was terrified. The stray dog, my afternoon companion, abruptly stood up, looked around and trotted off, as if dinner was waiting for him elsewhere. Right when I needed him.

Hellen was going to make me pay for this

I watched as my brothers and Tracy continued to look for me until Hellen arrived.

She cussed at them and said, "I count on each of you to be responsible for Wilma, so I can go to work and earn *your living* and provide a roof over *your heads*. It seems to *me* that the very *least* you could do is to keep an eye out for your little sister while I'm out earning a living, since your good-for-nothing father isn't here to do it. Look around; do you see your father providing for you? Huh? Huh? Of course not! That's why I'm here, working, and the very *least* you can do is help out by watching that little brat. If I have to call the police to help find her, they'll know I don't have the money to pay for a proper sitter, and they will make me quit my job to take care of you, and we'll lose our house, and we'll all have to live on welfare. And all because you kids couldn't help me out while I was at work! I cannot afford to be leaving work early to look for this little snot. You're going to have to keep a closer eye on her. You hear me?"

Even though the back-porch light was dim, I saw them nod their heads.

"Now, where was the little snot when you last saw her?"

They all start talking at once, and I couldn't make sense of what they were saying. It didn't matter. I felt awful.

Watching from behind the tall oleanders, I felt utterly stupid. I'd messed up everything. I couldn't even run away right. The more she yelled in the backyard, waving around a flashlight with batteries that were about to die, the worse I felt.

I have blown it. I am so stupid.

I had hoped Hellen would call the police. I thought the cops could

1971: 7 Years Old

find a home for me where I wouldn't get into trouble. I had thought the police would help me.

I made another decision as I watched Hellen stomp around the back alley searching for me, repeatedly calling my name, and cussing at Hugh, Danny, and Tracy.

I came out of hiding.

When Hellen saw me walking out of the bushes, she stood very still. Instinctively, I knew that was not a good sign.

Calmly, in a quiet, stern voice she demanded, "Where. Did. You. Go?"

Looking her in the eye, I swallowed hard and said, "I ran away."

"Get in the house. Now," she ordered.

~

Once we got inside, Hellen beat me with my brother's belt, her slipper, and her fists. Then, cussing and yelling, she dumped a lot of junk into a heavy suitcase.

"You want to run away? Here, I'll help you. You don't appreciate the good, godly mother you've got, then, by cracky, you won't have her anymore. GET OUT!!"

She shoved the suitcase and me out the front door. Then slammed the door, locked it, and shut off the porch light.

~

Standing outside alone in the dark, my body bruised and beaten, I sobbed, too scared to remain outside, and too afraid to ask to go inside. I tried to lift the suitcase and walk away, but I couldn't lift it. I tried dragging it and only got a few feet before realizing I was dragging the doormat underneath the suitcase. I sat down in the dirt and cried.

Running through all my options, I realized I had none. I knocked on the door.

"What do you WANT?"

"To come in the house."

1971: 7 Years Old

Hellen jerked open the door, reached through the doorway yanked my arm, and pulled me inside.

Dragging me down the hall to her bedroom, she beat me until I thought I'd die. She wailed on me using a strap, extracting promises with each blow that I would never, run away again.

"You disgusting troublemaker. I should have never given birth to you. I've cursed the day you were born. You are nothing but trouble to me. You've cursed my life. What did I ever do to God that He stuck me with you? What? What? Answer me!"

"I don't know."

"Of course, you don't know. You're too stupid to know. You've got it made here, and you decide to run away. That's stupid. You're stupid. You're so dumb we gotta watch you like a little tiny baby! Watch out, the baby might crawl outside and get hurt… Everybody watch out for the wittle, stupid, idiotic baby."

Taking a moment to catch her breath, she railed on. "Promise me, right now, that you will never cause me trouble again. That you will never open your fat-trap mouth again."

I stood there, silent and afraid.

"I said, promise me."

"I promise."

"Promise what?"

"I promise never to cause you trouble again."

"Cute. You forgot the other part, stupid."

Trembling, I couldn't remember any other part.

"You don't know do you? Oh God, why do I have to put up with this? Now, promise me you will never open your fat trap mouth again!"

"I promise I will never open my fat trap mouth again."

She took a deep breath and walked out of her bedroom.

I thought it was over.

Then came the worst part.

1971: 7 Years Old

A short time later, I had to go to her bed. Her anger made the sexual abuse more frightening.

Phoenix, Arizona – 1971
Hellen Proietti – 40 years old.

~

My decision to run away was not worth the few hours of freedom. Later when Hellen got into more extreme torture emotionally, physically, and sexually, I never again tried to escape. Instead, I ran away in my mind. Shutting down worked and I was quite proficient in going there.

I accepted Hellen's abuse as the discipline she said it was and the consequence of failing to meet her standard of good enough. I believed that if I could just be a good girl, Hellen wouldn't have to do those horrible things to me.

At 7, I was ashamed of myself. I was a failure as a daughter.

~

Second grade was easier. I was enrolled in another year of speech therapy, and I loved my second-grade teacher, Mrs. Wiseman. She was patient and kind and I looked forward to each day. She had a gracious way about her that touched me. My hair was always a mess, and sometimes when Mrs. Wiseman was speaking to me, with a gentle push she'd move strands of dirty hair away from my face to tuck it behind my ears. It was a small thing, but her kindness created a sweet memory. I felt important to her, and I didn't feel that way with anyone else.

The kids still called me the Playground Pig because of my dirty clothes and hair. But Lynette was my friend despite my unkempt appearance.

Although more good things happened for me in school during second grade than first, life in Hellen's house confused and scared me.

~

Hellen continued her food games. Often, she would make me eat weird foods or go hungry. Then, when my siblings were present, she'd give me portions I couldn't possibly finish, usually large plates of spaghetti or orange squash. I'd sit at the table for hours, *literally, hours*, and get yelled at for not finishing my food. Orange squash does not hide well in a glass of milk. I tried.

When I couldn't clean my plate, Hellen would put the uncovered plate in the refrigerator. That was all I was allowed to eat for days, until I finally finished the stale, cold hardened food. I hated eating cold spaghetti or cold squash.

Most of the time, Hellen preferred to let me go hungry. She told my siblings she was worried I had juvenile diabetes because I was so thin. I had to go without food because I was 'bad.'

I was too afraid of Hellen to complain about my hunger, but I preferred hunger over cold squash.

Hellen's food games seemed small compared to enema nights and the sexual abuse, but I hated being hungry. Hellen lying about me being a juvenile diabetic was just another manipulation of our ignorance of medical issues, manipulating my siblings to see me as separate and different from them.

1971: 7 Years Old

~

From my earliest memories, Hellen had a close friend named Scharlie. She was one of Hellen's weird handful of friends who had nothing in common with her, yet somehow held the elevated position of counselor in her life.

Scharlie was a tall, chubby woman, a gossiping old maid from the church we attended. She played the piano for Wednesday night Bible study, then waved and jangled her keys, and her arm fat, promptly at 9 p.m. as a reminder for the pastor to dismiss the service on time.

Scharlie claimed to be a true spinster. She publicly bragged about being a 60-year-old virgin. "I'll save myself for heaven."

I did not understand that.

She believed she was gifted with beauty, even wearing a ring on the third finger of her left hand so men wouldn't "proposition" her.

I saw her as a wrinkled, aged woman, with rolls of fat popping out from chin to ankle. She'd spent way too much time in the sun, and far too much time looking in the mirror. She wore tight, form fitting clothes accompanied by spike heels. She carried an extra 40 pounds and belittled anyone that 'let themselves go.'

She didn't need the ring. The propositions weren't coming. Ring or no ring.

Though she never married, she counseled the married couples at church.

I didn't understand that either.

Scharlie was clean and health conscious. She talked endlessly about being a teetotaler, often saying, "I will save my liver."

I wondered if she was saving that for heaven, too.

I was puzzled by Hellen and Scharlie's friendship. They were polar opposites in cleanliness, health, and life experience.

Scharlie would occasionally host barbecues for the church kids in her backyard, all eight of us, but not allow us inside her house to "muss it up." Each time, she served burgers, chips, and brownies along with soda outside on her patio, while she advised us on proper etiquette.

"Sit up straight. You look thinner that way."

"Fold your napkin on your lap like this. No, don't wipe your mouth. A proper lady or gentleman pats the mouth gently around the lips."

We'd look away from her and roll our eyes.

"Now, now. Don't tip the soda can up. You can drink it like a lady by sipping it in a slightly tilted manner. Very good. I can teach you children proper comportment because I'm wise concerning such matters."

She drove us crazy.

Then, as we left her barbecues, she'd pull Tracy and I aside to give us advice. "Now girls," she'd begin, leaning forward making eye contact, "you mustn't allow yourselves to imbibe on soda, burgers, chips, and brownies or it will cause you to remain repulsively fffaatt, and you do not want to be unhealthy, like your mother. Just a word of caution and advice before you leave tonight…because I care, and it's only wisdom to take care of your body which is the temple of God, you know. You must have wisdom."

When saying the word 'fat' her bottom lip seemed to hold on to the 'f' drawing out the word in an occasional stutter. We'd nod and say thank you. Then we ignored her. I figured, *if she is right, then she needs to stop eating her own food.*

Scharlie was a real thorn to Tracy and I throughout the years we were growing up. She gave the dumbest advice. I could never understand her motivation. I did not like being around Scharlie or going to her house. I never trusted her.

~

Starting when I was only 5 years old, Hellen insisted I learn her adept way of snooping through other people's personal belongings. I hated it when she required me to do that.

1971: 7 Years Old

When we'd visit someone's home (her co-workers or people from the church), Hellen would distract them and then she'd give me what I call the "hairy eyeball" to spring into action.

Under the guise of needing to use their restroom, I had to prowl through their bedrooms, nightstands, medicine cabinets, and dressers as quickly as I could. I hated snooping through people's stuff and worried I'd get caught.

Hellen specifically wanted to know what type of underwear they had, their prescribed medications in the bathroom cabinets, and the personal items in their nightstands. Remembering the long names on the medicine bottles was difficult, but the more information I could provide, the happier she was.

~

Hellen had an unusual interest in Scharlie's home and I was required to snoop each time we visited her house.

I had no interest in Scharlie's miracle wrinkle creams. *They weren't working*. Or in her collection of phony wedding rings, *why did she need more than one?* Or her assortment of partial and full-length girdles, *was it okay to be partially fat sometimes and not others?*

As a skinny kid, I wondered *why does a woman with all those girdles care if I eat a brownie?* I knew it wasn't good to ask or she'd know I'd been snooping in her "bee-ureau drawers."

I hated snooping for Hellen, but I was too afraid of her to disobey. I knew if Scharlie found out, she would tell everyone at church. She was the main geyser for the church gossip fountain.

I'd never live it down.

~

When I was 7 years old, I began to steal from every store where we shopped. I thought that if I could get things for Hellen for free, maybe she would be happy with me. I soon discovered that I enjoyed the challenge of not getting caught.

1971: 7 Years Old

As we walked into a store, I'd wander off to the candy and trinket aisles. Watching for store personnel, I'd load my pockets with anything I thought might please Hellen and my siblings. Later, when we got to the car, they'd be excited to see what I had for them. They would say how much they liked the free stuff and tell me what to get next time.

Each time I stole things for Hellen, she'd smile. I couldn't get a good grade in school or wash a sink full of dishes to get a smile like that. Nothing I did, other than stealing, made Hellen smile at me like that. So, I stole everything I could. I would've stolen anything she wanted if I thought she would have been happy enough to give me my own bed.

I had one big problem, though. Stealing bothered my conscience, but I didn't know how to stop. It made everyone happy but me.

Hellen allowed it to go on for several months.

One evening after shopping, when I pulled the stuff out of my pockets, Hellen said, "All right. That's enough. Come with me." She opened the car door.

I froze.

"I said, enough. Now come with me."

Slowly I stepped out of the car.

"Listen here. You're going to march right back into the store and you're going to confess your sin of stealing right in front of God, the store manager, and everybody. It's high time you pay for your sinning. They'll probably call the police, so you better expect it."

"The police?" I asked as we walked through the main entrance.

"Oh yeah. You're looking at handcuffs and a ride to juvenile hall. And don't look to me to stop them. Folks don't tolerate thieves. After you get smacked around at juvie hall, you'll get a new appreciation for how good you got it."

My knees and hands were trembling. *Police? Handcuffs? Juvie? For stealing candy bars?*

1971: 7 Years Old

I was mortified as we walked into the store.

"Hello, we need to speak to a store manager please," Hellen said to the first clerk she saw.

"Of course, ma'am, but is there perhaps something I could help you with?"

"No, no. This is a matter for the store manager. Now if you'll just get the manager, I don't have all day."

"Yes, of course."

When the manager approached, he asked, "May I help you?"

"She has something to show you." Hellen said.

I stood there, hands in my coat pockets, barely able to look at the man's knees.

"Go ahead. If you're big enough to do it, then be big enough to fess up."

I burst out crying.

"Go ahead, crybaby. Tears won't save you now."

"I…I…I stole this stuff from your store." I said, looking up as I handed him the candy bars and small toys.

The manager said, "Well…okay. Thank you for returning the items and talking to me."

He shifted on his feet as if he were unsure of what else to say.

"I'm sure you're going to have to call the police, maybe she'll even have jail time, but don't worry about me. I won't stand in your way," Hellen said.

I looked at her shocked and betrayed. How had she enjoyed the candy for months, even putting in requests for her favorite Hershey bars, and then do this to me now?

The manager looked surprised and said, "Oh, I…uh…for today, we'll let it go. I won't call the police this time. Just don't let it happen again, okay?"

Crying, I nodded.

1971: 7 Years Old

In a condescending tone, Hellen said, "These days, I'm appalled at what this child will do. What with all the time I've spent training her, and yet I can't turn my head for a second. God only knows where this child will end up."

The manager frowned, shifted uncomfortably, and said, "Well, let's consider this the end of the matter, shall we?"

"It sure as hell better be. I won't have a child of mine disgracing me. Next time, and believe you me, there *will* be a next time, I'll let the officers haul her off to juvie hall. Teach her a few good lessons."

"Well, that is certainly not necessary today."

Kneeling down to look into my eyes, the store manager said, "There, there, no need to cry anymore. It took a lot of courage for you to walk back in here and tell me what you did. Everything's okay now. Friends?" He put his hand out and I hesitantly shook his hand.

Hellen watched with her arms folded across her massive stomach.

As we left the store, Hellen said, "That'll teach you. I have to break you like a wild horse. Oh well, God requires me to be a good mother, whether you like it or lump it."

When I got back into the car, Hugh, Danny, and Tracy were quiet and staring at me. I wanted to die or disappear, anything but sit in Hellen's car feeling like The Idiot of the Universe.

Although I never told anyone, I was relieved that it was over. It was challenging in the beginning, but it had become a duty, and I didn't know how to stop.

~

I wondered for years why Hellen didn't just tell me not to steal anymore. After all, I was so afraid of her, I would have complied. I also didn't understand Hellen's apparent enjoyment of public scenes, which she was known for throughout her life.

As an adult I realized, public scenes provided Hellen with a personal stage. She was the star in her own self-directed show.

1971: 7 Years Old

~ Counseling Notes ~

Running away was an awful decision and I paid dearly for it. I asked why I thought that would help.

The counselors said, "Choosing to run away was following the behavioral pattern of a traumatized child. It was when Hellen gained full control of your mind. It was the point when fight, flight, or freeze was primarily taken from you. It was after this point that you began to escape in your mind. Running away is where you physically buckled under the abusive load. It's where you caved. You never physically tried to escape Hellen again."

~

I didn't understand the conflict I felt when I stole and enjoyed Hellen's approval *and* felt guilty for stealing. Then her betrayal and public scene.

The counselors said, "Also, it is normal that you felt betrayed when Hellen made you take back the stolen candy. After all, she encouraged it and enjoyed the things you brought her.

However, public scenes are often a method abusers use. Throughout your childhood, Hellen used public scenes to establish herself as an upstanding mother and citizen. In the event that you ever reported her physical and sexual abuse, she would need character witnesses throughout the community, church, and at your school.

1971: 7 Years Old

It's important that you understand how abusers craft a defense at the same time they are abusing. They cannot risk abusing without the safety net of public disguise."

I still hate public scenes.

1972: 8 Years Old

*People don't care how much you know,
until they know how much you care.*
~ Theodore Roosevelt

The Times

In 1972, former President Harry Truman died, Computerized Axial Tomography (CAT) scan technology was introduced, and screening passengers and luggage became mandatory on all U.S. domestic flights. And, I learned to never tell Hellen I had an ear infection.

When I was only 8, Hellen thought it would be fun to take us kids to see the movie called, *Everything You Always Wanted to Know About Sex* But Were Afraid to Ask*, a movie based on a book of the same name by David Reuben, M.D. The movie was rated R: Restricted for children under age 17 unless accompanied by a parent. Tracy was 12, Danny 13, and Hugh 14 years old. While standing in line, several moviegoers confronted Hellen for allowing us to see the movie.

Hellen laughed, "Ah, that's stupid. How are the kids supposed to learn if the parent doesn't let them see a few things in life? I'm their mother; I know what's best for them."

The people shook their heads in disgust. One of them said, "Somebody ought to *do* something. Those poor children shouldn't be exposed to this film. What kind of mother is she anyway?"

While the film played on the screen, I watched people's faces. I wondered why they wanted to see it and why they thought it was funny. I was embarrassed by what I saw. I thought it was gross and embarrassing. Hellen thought it was hilarious, and my siblings laughed. I didn't want Hellen to know I didn't understand it, so I pretended to laugh too.

Later, as adults my siblings expressed how crazy it had been for Hellen to take us to see the movie.

~

In June, grandpa got sick with emphysema and went to the hospital. Hellen acted worried but told us he would be fine.

Late one night, a few days later, the hospital called with news of his failing condition. Hellen woke us and left us alone while she went to the hospital.

Awake in the middle of the night, we all understood this was serious. Danny, ever the clown, decided to cheer everyone up. He went into grandpa's room and brought out a box of chocolate mints. He said, "Hey guys, lets scarf down the entire box!"

When we questioned him, he said, "Aw c'mon. Grandpa will understand. It's 2 o'clock in the morning, and we are four worried kids. What are we supposed to do? Candy fixes everything!"

The chocolate mints in the box disappeared one by one.

When the candy was gone, Danny looked at it as if he were shocked. "Oh no!" he said, "Grandpa's gonna kill us! I didn't mean for us to take 'em all! Here, quick, let's put the empty box back. Maybe when he comes home from the hospital he'll think he ate them. Maybe with the medicine they're giving him, he won't remember that it was almost full. That's what we'll tell him, right guys?"

We all agreed that the box had been empty when he went to the hospital. Danny ran and stashed the candy box in grandpa's drawer then rejoined us…relaxed, as though he'd been waiting in the same place on the couch for hours.

1972: 8 Years Old

When Hellen opened the door, I could tell she'd been crying.

"Grandpa's gone."

Gone where?

After several minutes of listening to Hellen explain what happened, she told us to get dressed. She was going to take us to the hospital, so we could see him.

This added to my confusion and I thought, *see him?* before I said to her, "You said he'd be okay."

"Well, I thought so too, but the good Lord took him home tonight."

I didn't understand, but I kept my thoughts to myself. *Home? Wasn't that here, home, or had he gone to Pennsylvania?* I tried to make some sense of the situation while Hellen drove us through the dark streets to the hospital downtown.

The officials at the hospital allowed us to see grandpa. I thought it looked like he was sleeping, but he was cold. I wondered, *why didn't he have a blanket?* That's when I realized, grandpa had died, and I cried. I was inconsolable.

Later, she dropped us off at the house and left on an errand.

Danny called us all around, and said, "Psssst. You guys. Come here. Hey, it looks like we're not gonna get in trouble for eating the mints after all. So uhh....well...I took the box and put it in the bottom of the garbage can, so mom wouldn't see it and spaz out. You know, save her all the trouble we can...it's a rough time and all for her, okay?"

I thought Danny was clever. Hugh and Tracy laughed.

~

The funeral was in Pennsylvania. Hellen left for a week and arranged for Tracy and me to stay with Pastor Murphy and his wife. Another family kept my brothers.

It was the most peaceful week of my childhood.

We loved staying at the pastor's house. Pastor Murphy was kind to me; but his wife found me annoying. Mrs. Murphy loved Tracy and was kind to her. She fussed over Tracy's every need; the two cooked together and talked between themselves a lot.

I wondered why she was so grouchy when I was around.

On cleaning day, Mrs. Murphy gave me a list of chores to do. I was happy and eager to help. I wanted to please her and show her I was not lazy. I had fun helping because she became kind when she realized my willingness to work.

Most of the time we spent at their home, I spent outside. Mr. Murphy had a ride-on tractor when no one else had one. They owned acres of land and a large orchard. He let me ride the tractor with him every day. He laughed a lot and seemed to enjoy my questions and my constant curiosity of how and why things worked the way they did. He was patient and explained how fruit grew on trees, why he had to oil the tractor, how irrigation worked, why he didn't irrigate every night, and everything else I could think to ask.

He often commented, while chuckling, "You're one curious little girl. You're smart too."

When he said that, it prompted me to ask more questions. I loved his kind attention and spending time with him was a real joy. I was sorry when the week was over.

~

When Hellen returned from her father's funeral she was depressed and grumpy. Our typical summertime lives in Phoenix resumed. We were home by ourselves all day while Hellen worked.

~

Hellen worked at an Italian restaurant/grocery store during the day. Each week the owners sent large batches of garlic home with her and we all would spend the whole evening peeling garlic for the restaurant the next day. I loved it because I was allowed to use a real knife. We had to do a good job, making sure there were no skins left in the fresh garlic when we were done. If we did well, the owner sent home two large pizzas as payment for our work. We thought we were getting the good end of the bargain. I enjoyed those evenings around the kitchen table, all of us talking and laughing. Hellen was usually in a good mood and I felt part of the family.

I also thought it was wonderful because if the owner sent home bags of garlic with Hellen, I felt safe from enema night. And I always was.

~

Though the enema nights had continued during the winters grandpa stayed with us, they changed dramatically when Hellen returned from his funeral. Hellen's sexual perversions escalated at an alarming speed. She became more violent, physically brutal, and emotionally cruel. The intensity was frightening. Hellen could drag an evening of enemas on for several hours with me required to be naked and run up and down the hall the whole time. The physical pain lasted for days. There are no words for the demeaning humiliation I experienced.

I simply did not know *what to do.*

I wondered what I had done, or failed to do, to make things worse. Until that point, I had never known Hellen to be as scary and cruel as she was after his funeral. I didn't know the words to say to anyone about the things she did. She said she loved me. But I didn't feel loved.

Still, it troubled me enough that I finally tried to talk to her about it.

When questioned, Hellen said little (or nothing), and gave me just a long, mean stare. Then, she 'communicated' by making me 'pay' during the next enema so severely that I'd get the message–loud and clear–that Hellen was not one to be questioned. She would be so intensely brutal during the enema, that I would be sore for days afterward. Often, I was still recovering from the enema when it was time for another one.

At the time, if someone would have asked me if I was being abused, I would have told them no. She had completely convinced me the torture '*had* to happen' because I was bad.

1972: 8 Years Old

One thing I did know for sure: I wanted, *I needed*, my own bed more than anything.

~

My grandfather's death had upset Hellen in a peculiar manner. I wouldn't have a glimpse as to why until the spring of 2011, when the family secret was disclosed to me.

This is the Grandpa I knew in the daytime.

I was his 'special' granddaughter because I was the only one of all his children and grandchildren that had his dimple.

It took me years to get past the pain of being his 'special' girl.

I may have gotten his dimple, but I'm sure glad I didn't get his ears.

~

I was in third grade and loved school. I didn't want to miss a day. Any day at school was better than one at Hellen's house. I was still called the Playground Pig, but I had a good teacher and reading was the highlight of my world.

Reading was my escape from reality. I went everywhere Laura Ingalls Wilder took me through her book series, *Little House on the Prairie*. I was consumed with reading everything I could get my hands on. When reading, I could tune out the taunts of the kids, get caught up in

1972: 8 Years Old

a story, and forget about my own life. Reading saved me on lonely days.

So...I read a lot, because most of my days were lonely.

In third grade, when the cafeteria ladies saw me in the lunch line, they scooped extra mashed potatoes or whatever they were serving on my tray. Daily while I sat at the lunch table, the janitor slipped me an extra carton of milk. I always drank it, but I especially loved it when he gave me chocolate milk.

~

One cold winter morning, I noticed frost on the cars as I rode my bicycle to school. I was wearing a sky-blue windbreaker jacket. It had big holes under the arms, and stains down the front. The zipper was broken. I was cold.

Just after the pledge of allegiance, the school secretary came to the classroom and asked our teacher to excuse me for a few minutes. I was nervous. I was afraid Hellen had shown up at school. I left my desk and walked out of the room with the secretary.

She smiled, took my hand, and asked, "How are you doing this morning?"

Hesitantly, I answered, "Fine."

"Well, I think I found something that might fit you when I was packing up the Lost and Found yesterday afternoon."

I just looked at her, not understanding.

"Every year, after the classroom teachers have a chance to go through the Lost and Found, we box up the remaining items and donate them to the local charity. I was boxing them up yesterday and saw a jacket that might fit you. We had walked to the cafeteria by this time, and she'd walked over to the one cardboard box that was open. "Come over here," she said. "Let's take a look."

I wanted to ask what a charity was but decided not to.

She reached into the Lost and Found box and pulled out a bright red winter coat with a hood. It seemed brand new. It did not have a child's name written on the inside tag. I was excited because the coat still had the string inside the hood to tighten around my face. I stood still with my arms sticking out as she zipped it up, put the hood on my head, and tied the string under my chin. It fit me perfectly. My heart pounded. A new coat? For me? I swallowed hard. I felt like I was going to cry.

I smiled and said, "I feel like Little Red Riding Hood."

Holding my face in both her hands, she smiled back.

"And you look like Little Red Riding Hood." She stood up, took my hand, and walked me back to class.

Just outside the classroom door, I stopped her before she turned the knob.

"Thank you." I said, wrapping my arms around her waist.

"You're welcome. You're so very welcome," she replied, returning my hug.

I treasured that kind lady, that kind moment, and the new red coat. The red coat was a special gift, and as an adult, I realized the school personnel had purchased it for me. I wore the coat until it was uncomfortably too small.

When I showed Hellen the new coat she said, "It's about time my tax dollars benefit me."

~

In the summer, Danny and I both got swimmer's ear. By the time Hellen decided to treat the infections, it had developed in both of my ears.

"I can't afford to be running you kids to the doctor all the time." Hellen said, and then she told us about an old home remedy that would take care of our problem.

Hellen heated evaporated milk on the stove and poured the warm liquid into Danny's ear. He lay still for about 15 minutes, and then turned over. White, milky stuff drained out of his ear and onto a washcloth. Everything seemed okay. He appeared to find the warm milk soothing.

1972: 8 Years Old

Then it was my turn.

Hellen yanked on my ear lobe as she poured in the now steaming milk. I screamed from the intense pain.

"Oh stop!" she yelled, and a string of curse words followed before she explained, "I accidently let the milk boil instead of just warming it a little, that's all. Shut your whiny mouth."

It hurt so bad. The hot milk mixed with my tears and ran into my eyes.

Hellen slapped my head and hit my ear. I cried even harder from the pain.

When the time came to pour the boiling milk into my other ear, she ordered Hugh and Tracy to help her. "Help me hold her down," Hellen instructed them, "she's being such a ridiculous baby. She cries when I try to help her. I can't win with this brat. I just meant to heat it up, so it wouldn't be cold, and I accidentally let it boil." She poured the hot, foamy milk into my ear.

I screamed and writhed in the bed as my head felt like it was on fire.

Hellen stood back, still holding the pan. "Oh, for God's sake, it wasn't that bad. Danny didn't scream and cry like an idiot!'

Hugh and Tracy kept silent as they watched Hellen and me. She turned to them and said, "Don't look at me like that! I'm a nurse! I know what I'm doing! She's just crying for attention. You didn't see Danny act like that, did you? Huh? Huh?"

When they shook their heads no, she said, "Of course not. This one just wants attention. And if she doesn't shut up, I'll give her something to cry about."

I forced myself to stop crying. The pain continued for days. I never complained to Hellen about an earache again. Ever.

1972: 8 Years Old

~ Counseling Notes ~

I asked why any parent would take children to see that movie like Hellen did.

The counselors said, "When Hellen took you to see, *Everything You Always Wanted to Know About Sex* But Were Afraid to Ask,* she deliberately introduced inappropriate sexual content into your heads. Abusers often do unusual things like that for a reason. The motive being that if the child expressed any comments that would alert another adult to the sexual abuse, the abuser could 'fall back' on the 'funny movie' and the child's 'grand imagination.'"

It's easy to believe Hellen had motives, because everything she did had motives.

~

I described the swimmer's ear and long-term effects.

The counselors said, "Pouring hot milk into your ears was nothing shy of emotional, mental, and physical torture. Making Hugh and Tracy help hold you down, essentially participate, was abusive and cruel to them as well."

A medical doctor said, "I've never heard of such a thing. The bacteria alone could have caused a life-threatening infection in the surrounding tissues in the ear canal and brain, and it's a miracle that there wasn't more damage than there was."

I have scars from being scalded and minimal hearing loss.

1973: 9 Years Old

Do what you can, with what you have, where you are.
~ Theodore Roosevelt

The Times

The Pet Rock fad started in 1973, and I had one. The song, *Tie a Yellow Ribbon Round the Ole Oak Tree,* became a national favorite. The American Psychiatric Association revised its categorization of homosexuality; it was no longer considered a mental disorder. And, I defied Hellen's order to snoop for her.

One afternoon, just before I turned 9, I stood in the doorway of Tracy's room and stared. Hellen had purchased a brand-new, four-poster canopy bedroom set for Tracy from the Ethan Allen store. Tracy's bedroom had the matching dresser, chest, vanity, upholstered vanity stool, mirror, and nightstands. Her bed also had a frilly canopy and bedspread that matched. It was the most beautiful furniture I had ever seen. Tracy seemed so happy. I was happy for Tracy because she deserved to have it.

Yet, in the pit of my stomach, I hurt. I still wasn't allowed to have a bed. As I looked in Tracy's room, Hellen walked up behind me, filling the doorway.

"I would like to have a bedroom set like Tracy's someday." I said quietly.

"You can, if you can ever learn to be good and clean like Tracy," Hellen snapped.

1973: 9 Years Old

I didn't know what to say, so I said nothing. I assumed I was getting Tracy's old bed, so I was happy. I wanted to ask where Tracy's old bed was, but Hellen's mood was off, and I couldn't gauge it.

Over the next few days, I didn't see Tracy's old mattress anywhere, and wondered, *surely, I was getting her old bed...right? I understand I don't deserve a bedroom set. I can't imagine being worth enough to deserve a new bedroom like Tracy. I just want a bed. A mattress of my own.*

I need a bed.

~

I decided, *I have to try harder to be good.* I looked around the house and increased my efforts. *I need to do more,* I thought.

As one of my efforts to please Hellen, I used white shoe polish with the sponge on the end of the bottle for Hellen's nurse's shoes. Even though she wasn't a nurse, Hellen worked nights at different nursing homes all over town as a nurse's aide.

Hellen could never find her hairbrush. I was the one to find it for her because I knew where it was. It was always in her bed.

Sometimes, I'd wash the dishes using warm water. Hellen made me re-wash them. She made me use very hot water, so my hands would burn while I worked.

Any time I thought it might work, I smiled at her, as I saw Tracy do. Hellen would not smile back at me.

I amped up my housekeeping efforts by making her bed every day. It was hard because Hellen didn't have a blanket or bedspread, just urine-stained sheets. Everything about her, and everything she used or touched...reeked. Everything. Including me. I lived in disgust of her odor, every day, and especially, at night.

I couldn't pick up her dirty clothes and put them in the hamper because she wore them over and over. She just hosed them down with spray deodorant and an off-brand perfume. Then, she'd yell at Tracy to iron them, and fly out the door to work or church, trailing a stinky imitation-of-Chantilly-perfume, body odor and urine cloud.

I could always breathe better after she was long gone.

After all my efforts to earn a bed, I was speechless when I learned that Hellen had given Tracy's old bed away.

I was devastated.

I'm not even good enough for Tracy's garbage.

I wept for weeks. Literally weeks.

~

On the first day of fourth grade, I walked into Mrs. Thomas's class. Right in front of the other students she said, "Oh dear me, not another Proietti child, oh, please God, not another Proietti child." I was embarrassed to be the last of Hellen's kids to rotate through her classroom.

Fourth grade was the beginning of homeroom, with the changing of classes throughout the day. As it turned out, Mrs. Thomas taught math, and I struggled with math. Hellen, of course, was very good at math.

Mrs. Thomas was the first one of several teachers throughout my school years who openly admitted to being fearful of Hellen. If Hellen didn't like something a teacher did, she bypassed the principal and went straight to the school superintendent's office. Whatever the problem, it became a humiliation for the teacher, principal, and support staff, because Hellen refused to deal with it on a reasonable level.

She screamed, cussed, and yelled, "discrimination." She accused everyone of discriminating against her because she was a single, divorced mother. She was an embarrassment, leaving her nasty odor wherever she went.

Regardless of how terrible my math scores, as long as I tried, Mrs. Thomas put happy faces on the paper and I passed with flying colors and smiling faces. I didn't understand math or Mrs. Thomas, but I didn't care. There were many things in life I didn't understand.

1973: 9 Years Old

When Hellen saw my school papers, she glanced over them in seconds, throwing them on the floor. The times she really focused on the math papers, she cussed and berated me for hours at a time. I often 'lost' my math papers.

~

Enema nights continued whenever the mood struck Hellen. After four years of continuous enemas, the nights were emotionally and physically devastating. Fearful of Hellen's endless demands, I'd sob, run naked down the hall to the bathroom, drink the scalding tea, and silently beg for God, someone, *or anyone* to rescue me. The enemas were so degrading. I felt so powerless, so worthless and so defeated afterwards. My siblings were now in their teens, and I didn't want anyone to see me naked, not Hellen, not Tracy and especially not Hugh or Danny.

I had long ago quit fighting her. I learned if I cooperated, the soreness in my mouth and the pain in my bottom resolved within three or four days. I felt resigned and hopeless during those tortuous evenings. The enema nights were effective in silencing me. I felt dead inside afterwards.

I was nine years old, and after an hours-long evening of total nudity, humiliation and Hellen's brutal degrading enemas, I was completely defeated and there was *nothing* I didn't comply with. Perhaps that was Hellen's motivation. When the enemas were over, I felt hollowed out and had no fight left in me. Mentally and emotionally shattered, physically weakened, I'd lie in Hellen's bed limp, quietly sobbing as Hellen played out her sexual fantasies and perversions on my body.

Most nights, Hellen cuddled up afterwards saying, "Oh, stop crying. You know I love you."

I didn't feel love. I felt hate for my body that brought such horror to my life and such thrill to Hellen's. I felt blame and shame, because my body was making bad things happen to me.

1973: 9 Years Old

Memories of enema nights remain difficult to talk about. Those nights left damage to my mind, body, and emotions.

The enema nights robbed me of all dignity even though back then I didn't know what dignity was. I didn't know the word or that the concept even existed. I didn't know I had a right to tell anyone what she was doing to me.

At the time, I despaired that they would continue until I was old enough to leave her house. I felt total, utter despair, and it tore me up inside.

I've said little to my siblings regarding enema nights since it is a difficult subject for all of us. They deny that Hellen did it to them, and I am relieved they didn't suffer like that. Whatever the case, I place no blame on them; they were just kids. They too, were growing up with an evil, abusive mother. We did not live in a loving, supportive household.

Hellen was fat. She stood 5'6" and her weight fluctuated from 250 to 300 pounds. None of us kids were capable of stopping her from whatever she decided to do. She covered up the abuse as caretaking; none of us dared challenge that label.

Enema nights remain some of the most traumatic memories of my childhood.

I wish I could have known then, that enema nights were almost over.

~

Hellen liked to brag about 'all' her friends, though she only had two or three. And she especially loved going to their homes so I could continue to snoop for her.

One of the hardest things I did as a child was stand up to Hellen about the snooping, and I was so proud of myself when I did. One evening we were visiting Scharlie's house and I'd been instructed to snoop once again while Hellen distracted her.

I was grouchy and didn't want to snoop through Scharlie's girdles, stockings, or assorted wedding rings. There are few things I hate more in life than a snoop. No doubt that is result of Hellen being one and forcing me to snoop for her. I hated when Hellen went through my stuff.

But, being fearful of the consequences if I disobeyed, I went down the hallway to follow the routine.

~

I was almost inside Scharlie's bedroom when I felt something inside of me propel me around. I stood outside her bedroom thinking, *it's like Hellen wants me to be just like her, and I will never be like her. I will never be like her. I'd rather die.*

I did not enter the bedroom. I walked towards the living room. I decided I was done. Beating or no beating, I made up my mind that I would never snoop again. When Hellen saw me, a look of surprise was on her face. I had only been gone a minute. There was no way I could have searched Scharlie's room.

Later, as we drove away from Scharlie's house, Hellen asked, "So, what'd you find in her room?"

"I didn't go in her room." I was shaking.

"What? What do you mean you didn't go? I told you to, didn't I?"

"Yes."

"Then why in God's name didn't you do what I told you?"

"I hate snooping through people's stuff, and mom, it's not nice. I don't like it when people do that to me."

"So, you're gonna play the Pharisee card, are you? Well, when I tell you to do something, you're supposed to do it. The Bible says, 'Children obey your parents.' That's not obeying God, you self-righteous smart aleck." Hellen was cussing, and I expected her fists and slaps to start flying. I regretted sitting in the front seat.

It had seemed so smart not to snoop, but now facing the consequences, I figured I had made another stupid decision.

I heard Hellen laugh. A ridiculous, mocking laugh. "So...you think you're gonna do what you want and not do as you're told. You're more stupid than I gave you credit for. Absolutely retarded."

Then, such painful words…

She cussed again, and then said: "What did I ever do to God to be stuck with a lousy excuse for a daughter like you? Huh? Huh? And what makes you think you can disobey the Bible? Huh? Answer me, huh?"

"I don't know."

"I donnn't knnnooooww," she mocked.

"Well, you'd better know if you're going to stop obeying me and God. You better know, or you'll go straight to hell. You're gonna bust hell wide open. Dumbhead…you won't listen to your own mother, even when I show you the Bible." Hellen heaved a weary sigh of exasperation.

Wow, I thought. *The Bible says I have to obey her? She didn't show me that. Where is that?*

I hurt. I felt that I'd failed God. *So much for making a good decision about not invading Scharlie's privacy. I mess up everything.*

I was surprised that Hellen did not beat me for refusing to snoop.

As punishment, she started ransacking my belongings about twice a week. I'd come in from school and what few things I was allowed to own had been dumped out of my dresser drawers and thrown all over the room.

When I'd discover the mess, Hellen simply said, "Clean up your pigpen."

It was a small price to pay to not snoop for her anymore.

1973: 9 Years Old

~ Counseling Notes ~

Years later, Hellen died still waiting for me to "stop being stupid." I was never good enough, or smart enough, in her eyes, to merit her love.

In counseling, I tried to talk about Hellen giving away Tracy's bed without crying, but I broke down describing my absolute despair as a child.

The counselors said, "It was emotionally abusive for Hellen to deny you a bed of your own. It is a dehumanizing mechanism she used to strip your identity by denying you a basic need she willingly provided for your siblings. Hellen was consistent to manipulate the environment to make you separate from your siblings…so that they saw you as different.

There is no way that she didn't notice when you wept for weeks after she disposed of Tracy's bed. Even Danny mentioned you 'cried all the time.' Hellen knew she was getting to you. Her methods were working, and how could they not? You were a normal little girl, with normal needs, expressing them in a normal little girl manner. You asked, you hoped, you rushed around trying to clean, and please Hellen. And when you failed, or what you perceived as your failure, you cried. You were a normal little girl, facing a monster."

~

The enema nights dragged on, causing long-term

1973: 9 Years Old

physical and emotional damage. They are some of the most painful and humiliating memories of my early years. I asked why Hellen started and continued them on a regular basis.

The counselors said: "Hellen firmly established her domination and control over you with the enema nights. After the first one, you learned to obey or suffer serious pain. Her methods of literally stripping you of your dignity, scalding your mouth with the hot tea, and more enemas in one evening than is safe for an adult, overwhelmed your five-year-old mind. That was her intent. Once she established control, she was well on her way. It appears the bonus was she then had her way sexually, as you were exhausted emotionally and physically afterward, so she could do to you whatever she wanted sexually without any resistance. She was a very evil woman, and it's a shame the authorities weren't able to stop her."

～

I asked, why could I refuse to snoop at Scharlie's and not refuse other orders from Hellen?

"Hellen requiring you to snoop for her was part of her determination to make you just like her. She was attempting to make you do what she wanted, when she wanted, and for how long she wanted. All kids try boundaries and that time, you got away with it without the beating you feared. It was risky, but you paid for it, *for years,* as she ransacked your room weekly until your rescue. It's possible her constant ransacking of your room was just enough to keep you afraid of refusing other orders. Because

1973: 9 Years Old

she was constantly amping up the abuse and finding new ways to torture you, at some point, moving forward with resistance could only happen in the mind, as you were in survival mode. Still, your refusal showed resilience and courage in the face of her manipulation and attempts to control you."

1974: 10 Years Old

*The trouble ain't that there is too many fools,
but that lightning ain't distributed right.*
~ Mark Twain

The Times

In 1974, the 55-mile per hour speed limit and the Child Abuse Prevention and Treatment Act (CAPTA) were enacted. I watched on television as Richard Nixon resigned, rather than be impeached as President of the United States. I turned 10 years old, and Hellen's sister moved to Phoenix, so we packed up and moved to California.

My tenth year of childhood marked the start of six years of a dark downward spiral into unspeakable anguish in Hellen's house.

I was troubled and did not know who to talk to, or where to find comfort. As a young girl, I had seen a diary for sale with a lock and key. I was fascinated by the concept that I could write things down and lock them up. I had no money to purchase the diary, so I began writing on notebook paper and it seemed to relieve the pain inside. After writing my thoughts and feelings, I tore the paper into tiny pieces and flushed them down the toilet. I figured the California sewer system was the safest place to store my thoughts because Hellen would not be able to find them. Flushing my writings down the toilet was a wise choice at the time, and encouraged me to write my thoughts openly, confident that no one could ever read them.

I also began writing poetry and branched out, trying different styles and I wrote often. Unfortunately, all of my early writing was lost, or rather, flushed.

Writing continues to center me when I am overwhelmed and need a safe place to sort my thoughts. Writing provides clarity and I still write often.

~

We settled in Hawaiian Gardens, California in a rental house Hellen found a few weeks before Thanksgiving. One afternoon we went to the grocery store, and someone was sitting in front with a box full of free puppies. I begged Hellen to let me have one. Of course, she said no. I kept begging and my siblings joined in, telling her it would be a good idea now that we had a house. Hellen hesitated and surprised us all when she said yes. We picked out a little black puppy, and I got to carry him into the store. My siblings picked out the puppy food. I was so proud to have my own puppy. Everyone kept asking me his name, and I didn't know what to name him. Finally, we all decided to name him Herbie, after the movie, *Herbie Rides Again*, part of Disney's *Love Bug* series and one of our family favorites.

I loved Herbie and took care of him without complaint. I woke early in the mornings before school to look after him, and I ran the three blocks home after school in a rush to spend time with him. I had never had my own pet before, and I spent hours holding him, rocking him, wrapping him in a blanket, walking him in the yard and running all over with his ball and whatever makeshift toys we came up with. I experienced true puppy love.

~

We were expecting visitors for dinner that Thanksgiving weekend and Hellen had prepared a lot of food. Our guests were Hellen's friends from Phoenix, Ilene, her new husband, Doyle, and their daughters Lola and Susie. The visit by Doyle and Ilene was unusual. Hellen rarely invited anyone into our house, and even considered a visit from the landlord to be intrusive. She didn't entertain guests, so for her to cook and make a big deal of their visit was out of character.

Ilene was a tall, thin woman with a loud mouth, big opinions, and quite conceited. She had a large, hairy mole on her face, and she ate with her mouth open. I didn't like her at all. Although we knew Ilene from Phoenix, neither my siblings nor I had met Doyle–we only knew he was Ilene's fourth or fifth husband.

Doyle was over six feet tall with long arms and legs, big hands and feet. I remember he was dressed well, in a proper way with dress shoes and dress clothes. He seemed to smile a lot with the same kind of false looking teeth that Hellen had. Doyle was big, but he wasn't fat like Hellen. He was just really tall. What Hellen called a gangly person. As soon as I met him, I didn't like him. I didn't know why.

Lola and Susie were rowdy kids who played rough. After play dates with them in Arizona, I always ended up with injuries: bruises, scrapes on my arms and legs, a swollen ankle, a bump on my head. The girls were bullies and I was afraid of them.

When my siblings and the girls went out to play, I chose to stay in the house with the adults. Hellen, Ilene, and Doyle had been visiting for a few minutes when I joined them. I sat down in a chair in the living room. Something felt odd to me, but I didn't know why I felt that way. I sat quietly, not speaking, just listening to the adult guests, and wondering why I felt so ill at ease.

Ilene went into the kitchen to help herself to the iced tea. I could see her.

Hellen stood quiet; her arms were folded across her chest. She watched Doyle as he sat on the couch.

I wondered, *why is mom just standing there?* Normally she would have been busying herself getting them something to drink.

Doyle smiled at me.

1974: 10 Years Old

I didn't smile back. I looked down at the floor, then up at Hellen. Doyle patted his thighs and said, "Come here and sit on my lap."

"No." I said quickly.

"Oh c'mon. I won't bite."

"No." I was uncomfortable. I was too old to sit on a man's lap, especially a strange man.

Still standing silent with her arms folded, Hellen watched the exchange. Finally, she spoke.

"Go sit on his lap." It was a clear order.

"No, mom." I felt brave. I shook my head 'no.'

"He's our guest. Go."

"Nooo, mom. I don't want to." I was shocked and now terrified.

"C'mon, I don't bite. Just sit here on my lap." Doyle smiled, patting his legs. His smile creeped me out.

Hellen said, "I said, *get up* and *sit* on his lap. *Now.* You're being rude to our guest."

She was growing angrier by the moment, yet I pleaded with her.

"No, mom, please," I begged. "I don't want to." Searching for an out, my thoughts were scrambled and I tried to bargain. "I'll go outside. I just don't want to sit on his lap. I don't even know him! I'm ten. I'm too big to sit on his lap."

While I was pleading with her, she unfolded her arms and pointed to Doyle. Speaking through her gritted dentures, "You're back-talking to me, which I will *never* tolerate from you, and you're being rude to our guest. I said to get up and do as the man asks. *Now!!*"

I couldn't believe it. How bad would it be for me after they left? My despair and regret ran wild, as I reluctantly made the few steps to his lap.

He smiled when I drew near, and then suddenly scooped me into his lap. I felt foolish sitting sideways on his lap.

At that moment, Hellen left the room. I was beyond scared.

Without a word, Doyle put his big hand on my chest, forcing me back until I was laying down in his arms, then he shoved my right arm back behind him around his waist and started tickling me. In that startled moment, his left hand wrapped around my left wrist pinning it down under my left hip. Lying back on his lap with my arms pinned down, his big right hand tickled me all over my body. It wasn't funny and he wasn't tickling.

Stunned, I couldn't seem to react fast enough. I couldn't free my arms. He was stronger than I was and he had my arms pinned back.

I went crazy with terror when his hand went inside my clothes.

I had been kicking and squirming, but then I flailed, kicked, and screamed crying, "Mom, help me! Mom! Quick! Help me!"

I could see her. Hellen stood in the small kitchen leaning on the counter, watching me scream, watching Doyle molest me.

Still kicking and fighting, I turned to my left as far away from Doyle as I could, making eye contact with her, crying, "Please mom! Moooommmm! Help me!"

Hellen watched me fighting the big creep, crying for her help, and for a moment, just a moment, she and I...made perfect eye contact.

Then, as Doyle's fingers probed my body, she turned her back and walked away to have tea with Ilene.

I was shocked when I saw her turn on me while I flailed wildly at the hands of that nasty, perverted creep.

As I continued to fight Doyle, biting his shirt as he fondled me inside my clothes, he laughed a big, horsey laugh at my attempts to free myself.

~

When he decided that he'd finished with me, he shoved me off his lap onto the floor.

I scrambled away from Doyle as soon as I hit the floor, straightening my clothes as I went.

He stood over me, straightened his clothes, and said, "Ilene, dear! I'm ready to go."

Ilene said, "Are you sure, dear? Hellen and I were just catching up over tea, and I was really enjoying myself."

"I said, 'Let's go!'"

It seemed he had changed his mind about having dinner with us.

Then I ran down to the bathroom. I only stayed in there a second, because I wanted to keep my eyes on the big creep.

I watched as he casually wandered out the front door with his hands in his pockets, as if he'd had a relaxing day. I felt awful, but I followed him out, keeping him in view, but at a distance at all times.

By the time they had corralled Lola and Susie into their car, I felt frozen.

As we watched them explain the change of plans to their bratty kids, I thought that whatever he had just done to me, he was doing to Lola and Susie. I didn't understand what had just happened, but I knew it was wrong. I felt violated, dirty, and angry.

As Doyle backed his Buick out of our driveway, I said to Hellen, "I don't ever want that man to touch me again." It was a brave thing to say, as I was never allowed to speak my mind.

Hellen looked at me for a long moment and said, "He won't."

The next day, I had bruises on my chest, both wrists and legs from fighting him, and on my heels from kicking the arm of the couch.

~

Hellen was breaking her normal pattern the day Doyle molested me, and I sensed it. It was odd for her to invite people into her house. I knew something felt odd to me and deeply regretted not acting on it.

I couldn't sleep that night, or for weeks afterward. I was so angry at myself for not being able to get away from that creep. And I felt so betrayed that Hellen could watch him hurt me and not come and help me. *How worthless of a child must I be, for her to skip my screams and have tea with her friend, eight feet away?* When I did manage to fall asleep, I had nightmares of Doyle's big, giant hands inside my clothes, while I screamed, making eye contact with the only person in the world who was supposed to love and protect me, but wouldn't–my own mother.

It was several weeks of lying in bed next to Hellen in the middle of the night, tears rolling, heart pounding, knowing there was only one person to blame. Me. *The whole thing happened because I was stupid. Stupid garbage. Poor Hellen. Stuck with stupid garbage.*

I never saw Doyle again. I hoped he was dead.

I don't know if Hellen ever felt guilty about watching Doyle molest me. She never mentioned Ilene or Doyle to me again. It was as though it had never happened.

~

A few nights after Ilene and Doyle's visit, as my siblings were going to bed around 11 p.m., Hellen called me into the kitchen. "Get your stupid puppy and get in the car."

The evening had gone remarkably well, so I was puzzled. I scooped up Herbie and walked to the car. Something about Hellen's order frightened me. Then I realized I'd forgotten my coat. Herbie nestled in my lap, snuggling for warmth. It was cold, but I was afraid to ask to go back in and get my coat when Hellen came to the car.

"Where are we going, mom?"

Hellen heaved an exaggerated sigh and began scolding me, as she weaved her way through the neighborhood streets.

"Never mind. If I needed to ask you, I would have. I will tell you this much, though. I'm fed up. Fed up with your irresponsibility and how you're so unreliable. I've known from the beginning I was going to have to do this. You're predictably unreliable and irresponsible. That poor dog." She was also cussing a lot. That was never a good sign.

Worried, I sat shivering while holding Herbie's head, so he could see the Christmas lights out the passenger side window. I kissed his head.

1974: 10 Years Old

"You are so irresponsible. I don't know what God is going to have to do to you to make you wise up, but I hope He does something soon. I sure as hell can't seem to do anything. You just don't think. People are going to have to think for you all of your life, because you're so stupid! I've never had to intervene on situations with the other kids like I'm required by God to intervene concerning you."

Then she mumbled, "God requires me to take action as your mother, and by God that's what I'm gonna do. I'm not gonna shirk my duties. Nope, not me. I'll be clean when I stand before the Lord."

Her scolding didn't make any sense to me. What was she required to do? Knowing what she did to me in her bed, my fears overwhelmed me on that car ride. I was wondering where we were going and what she planned to do to me and why she had to take me away from my brothers and sister to do it. I felt sick to my stomach.

I held on tight to Herbie as I brought him closer to my face and searched through recent memories for anything I could have done to upset her. I couldn't think of anything. I had been taking good care of Herbie. Each day I spent time feeding him, cleaning up after him and playing with him. He was such a joy in my life.

I was doing well in fifth grade, even making straight A's. Oh, but it was stupid that I'd sat in the front seat. Often, as she drove me around, Hellen beat me when I sat there. When I did choose the back seat, she'd yell that she was not my "chauffeur." So what else could I have done?

After we'd been driving for about fifteen minutes, Hellen turned down a long, dark road. At the end, a big cul-de-sac opened to a large apartment complex. Parts of it were still under construction. Turning the car around in the cul-de-sac Hellen's tone changed and I was alarmed, but I did not see what was going to come next. "Open your door and put the stupid mutt in the street."

I couldn't believe it.

"Now! Don't sit there and look at me like an idiot. Open the door!"

I opened the door and wondered why she wanted to leave Herbie and me out there. What was I going to do? I'd forgotten my coat.

"Now! Put. The. Mutt. In. The. Street! Do I have to spell it out for you, too?"

"Why mom? I love Herbie!"

"Do as I tell you, NOW!"

"No, Mom, c'mon, please. Pleeaase no, mom." I sat with the car door open, still holding Herbie, looking at him in disbelief. We were both shivering. Cold or fear? Probably both. I didn't see her fist coming. She backhanded me. My mouth was bloody. My lips were swelling.

In a stern, deep voice she reserved for moments when she meant business, and with cuss words flying, she hollered, "I said NOW! Put that mutt in the street. Do as you're told for once in your life."

The blows kept coming. She hit my left shoulder, ear, and the side of my face. Herbie was yelping. I wondered if she had hit him, too.

Defeated and powerless to change her mind, I leaned out of the car and braced myself with my left hand on the car door. With tears clouding my vision, I set Herbie down on the cold, dark asphalt. Hellen hit the gas and sped off so quickly I almost fell out of the car. Sobbing, I watched with the car door still open, as Herbie barked and tried to run alongside the car.

"That's what happens when you're unreliable and irresponsible. Maybe the stupid mutt will find a better home."

Knowing better than to say one word, I stayed silent and shut the car door.

Hellen continued to scold me for the rest of the drive back home. "At least I did my duty by God and intervened when you failed again. If you had half a brain, just *half*, then you would understand that *you* forced me to drive the stupid mutt to a better home. *You* forced my hand at this. *You* made this happen. You, and you alone. If you can't take care of a dog, then by God I'm required to do something about it. At least God won't hold me responsible for not recognizing your stupidity and doing my job as a good mother. That's another thing. God gave you a wonderful mother and you don't have the brains to recognize what a gift I am in your life."

That drive took a long, long time, maybe forty minutes or more. Obviously, she took the long way back so she could give me a good scolding.

Finally, we pulled into our driveway. Exhausted from crying and having to abandon my puppy, the very last thing I wanted to do was crawl in bed with Hellen, but I had no choice.

I still didn't have a bed.

Lying in bed with Hellen, I felt hatred with an intensity I didn't know was possible.

I lay awake for hours, crying as Hellen snored. I went through every checklist I could think of and couldn't recall any way I'd ever failed Herbie. Hellen's scolding was the first I had heard that she thought I wasn't properly taking care of him.

Before drifting off to sleep in the wee hours of the morning, I concluded that, *I am only a child and mom is the adult. Mom knows where I failed, and I just don't know. I am wrong for hating her. She was just doing her job. I feel awful that I have messed up so bad that my puppy is crying on a dark street alone because of me. I pray, God let someone good find him and love him. Herbie had to go away because I am bad. Herbie is cold and alone because I blew it again.* I cried myself to sleep.

The next day, I felt like I should tell mom I was sorry.

But I didn't. I couldn't. I didn't know why. I just couldn't.

~

After moving to Hawaiian Gardens, Hellen made a practice of cooking meals for us; something that I don't remember her doing before. Angelo and his sisters had taught Hellen the old-world style of

Italian cooking and she cooked well. I liked her cooking and looked forward to dinnertime.

Someone bought this dress for me and I loved it.

Hellen cut my hair–crooked again.
(It was always my fault that it was crooked.)

On the back of the picture, I wrote:

"This is the last time I let mom cut my hair."

We were on welfare and food stamps, but Hellen worked part-time on a graveyard shift using Tracy's social security number. She'd figured out how to show up for all the welfare appointments in the daytime, and she bragged about how much smarter she was than the stupid men who made the welfare rules. We had plenty of food because Hellen told us that she was smart and could provide for us better than our dad.

After she'd watched Doyle molest me, Hellen made new rules for the food games she'd subjected me to. Instead of withholding food as she'd done in the past, she now pushed large portions of food my way. I didn't understand why, but I decided to enjoy it while it lasted.

Until Ilene and Doyle's visit, I had been an underweight child. Just four weeks later at Christmas time, Hellen had to buy me clothing made for chubby kids. I had gained about ten pounds.

~

By Christmas Day, I could not ignore an undeniable buildup of hatred inside of me for Hellen. My mind constantly replayed the awful moments I spent trapped in Doyle's arms. The replay stopped at the same place every time: when Hellen and I made eye contact and she turned her back and walked away. I hated her for ignoring my screams. I hated myself that I had been stupid and stayed in the living room, getting myself molested.

I felt as though I couldn't trust anyone, especially myself.

Life went on, but the memory of what Doyle did to me would not go away. I wanted to believe that Hellen was protecting me because Ilene and Doyle never visited us again. But she didn't seem to have to do that for Tracy, Danny and Hugh.

I wanted to tell Tracy about what Doyle had done to me, but I didn't want her to know how dumb I had been. I was afraid she wouldn't want me around her if she knew.

~

Over the next few months, I continued to try to sort through the painful memories of that day. I was ashamed of what Doyle had done to me. Yet, I felt weak because I had been unable to get away from him. I didn't know what to do about the constant replay in my head, and finally decided that it was dishonest to blame Hellen for what happened. I concluded that the real blame was mine for not having the brains to find something else to do that day, for not going outside to play with the girl bullies…I should have gone to Hellen's room to read a book. I should have trusted that odd feeling I'd had and done something about it. I blamed myself. The facts were clear; if I had been smarter, it wouldn't have happened. It hadn't happened to my siblings, and they were smart. I had messed up again. I wondered where the limits were to my own stupidity.

I had a lot of anger inside of me with no place to vent, and I started cussing and getting into fights at school. If another student said something to me or maybe nothing at all, I would explode. Even I didn't know why. I pretended I didn't care, but I did. School had been my refuge, and now I was messing up that, too.

The school administrators suspended me a few times until Hellen went to the office and said she wouldn't allow them to go that far. Since they were afraid of her, they reversed the suspensions, and I kept cussing, fighting, and having angry outbursts.

∼

The enema nights ended the same way they had begun five years earlier: with no explanation. I didn't realize they were over, I just noticed that she threatened me with them, but didn't follow through on her threats. It was a huge relief, though I remained terrified that she would go back to them at any time. The abuse wore me down emotionally, mentally, and physically. I felt different from my siblings and totally alone in life.

I lived in constant terror of Hellen.

1974: 10 Years Old

~ Counseling Notes ~

It blew a circuit breaker in my mind when Hellen turned her back on me while Doyle molested me.

The counselors said, "You need to understand the situation for what it was. You were not guilty in any way. You were an innocent child and your mother committed an act of betrayal so big, you couldn't wrap your mind around it. It is common for molesters to run together. You said the house was small, approximately 900 square feet. It is also common for an abuser to make their victim available, in the event the victim ever reports the abuser. All three adults there that day should have been prosecuted for child molestation, or failure to report child molestation. It's inexcusable that Hellen and Ilene didn't intervene. They both deserved prison time for not intervening and not reporting Doyle.

Also, we have heard of situations like you've describe many times. What happens is the parent that is abusing makes a deal to pimp out their child. It's highly probable that Hellen was paid by Doyle to molest you and that would explain why it happened so quickly after they arrived, and why Hellen watched. It also explains why Hellen put up no argument for them to stay for the dinner she worked so hard to prepare. Likely Hellen didn't like 'sharing' you and so she never pimped you out again. It's sick, but we have heard of this type of thing many times before. It's a type of voyeur thing that she no doubt got paid for."

~

I questioned the sudden weight gain that followed within the next four weeks.

The counselors said, "Hellen deliberately set you up for weight gain when she changed the food games and started allowing you to eat regular meals and food you liked to eat. She stopped pushing orange squash and those things she knew you hated, and allowed you to eat like your siblings. You had the normal reactions of a hungry child–to eat while you 'had the chance.'"

Later, Maria Iannone commented regarding the years I struggled with weight problems that directly followed the molestation from Doyle.

Maria said, "It's not who Doyle was, it's how he made you feel about yourself and your body. He made you feel powerless, worthless and dirty. Doyle made you feel that small was vulnerable. Small was stupid. Small was bad. Small was easily hurt, but small was none of those things. Small had nothing to do with any of that. Doyle was a predator and size had nothing to do with that. You were nothing to him. You were still going to be hurt by him. You were still going to suffer because it was planned for him to hurt you before he ever laid eyes on you. You were set up. You were powerless then. Completely powerless. But you are not powerless now. You can heal through this."

1974: 10 Years Old

~

I asked about the motive for making me abandon Herbie.

The counselors said, "No doubt initially it was to distract you from the trauma Doyle caused. But it was more than that. Hellen forcing you to abandon Herbie was about power. It is about not allowing you to love anything, enjoy anything, be attached to anything; it is part of stripping you of your identity, dehumanizing you. The primary thing with this is that the abuser is essentially saying, 'You will not love anything or be affectionate towards anything except me. Anything that gets in the way of me, I will remove from your life. I have the power to do it, and I will. I can abandon the puppy and not be bothered by it. I can abandon you.' It was all about her power over you. It was meant to instill fear in you and it did. What a traumatic thing for a little ten-year-old girl. She was horrifically cruel."

~

What made Hellen abruptly end enema nights after five long years?

The counselors said, "Likely, Hellen stopped the enema nights because you were approaching puberty. Her sexual interests had begun a more perverted and violent turn. The result is that you suffered in a much more horrific manner than you did with the enemas. As we've said, Hellen crossed a very distinct line with the enema nights. She went from what we call 'normal' sexual abuse to committing acts of sexual torture. The enforced silence and nudity she required, was part of the dehumanizing many abusers do to their victims. It helps the abuser to place the blame on the victim, while gaining more control of the victim's mind. Also, from the details you've explained, she was clearly experiencing sexual gratification on those nights as well. You have no blame or guilt here whatsoever."

Pastor Sawyer said, "When carrying guilt for what happened, you cannot believe anything else. It's one or the other."

1975: 11 Years Old

Denial, perhaps, is a necessary human mechanism to cope with the heartaches of life.
~ Richard Paul Evans

The Times

In 1975, mood rings became popular, and I had one. Word processors, staple guns, and disposable razors went on the market, and in response to the energy crisis, Daylight Savings Time commenced nearly two months early in the United States. I turned 11 and tried smoking cigarettes.

My brother Danny hurt his eye with a pocketknife. He was trying to open a latch that was placed up high on a screen door. The knife almost released the latch, but slipped out of his fingers, falling blade-first into his eyeball. He lost his vision.

The doctors advised a set of specialized surgeries, and Hellen searched for the best surgeon available.

The surgeon believed he could restore Danny's vision. Anxiety and nervousness settled on our house before each operation. The hospital had rules forbidding children under the age of 12 from visiting patient rooms. The hospital was hours away, so while the rest of the family was packing for the first surgery, I worried about where Hellen was going to leave me, or if I would be staying at the house alone.

Hellen arranged for one of her co-workers to house me for a week.

It seemed odd to me because I'd never met her co-worker. I wondered why Hellen hadn't asked any of the folks at our church for help–at least I knew them.

Hellen's co-worker's name was Patsy and she was very nice to me. Hellen was fat but I had never seen such a large person before I met Patsy. In her home, she had a special chair with wheels on the legs. She used it to scoot around so she didn't have to walk.

In private, us kids called her Fatsy Patsy.

Perhaps Patsy suffered from some type of illness that contributed to her size. Meeting Patsy helped me to realize that she had normal feelings regardless of her size. Up until that time, my siblings and I laughed at people like that thinking they were all constant snackers like our mother. Meeting Patsy made me feel ashamed of that kind of laughter.

Patsy's mother lived with her; she was an old woman with no teeth, thin and very frail. When she smoked a cigarette, it looked as if her cheeks were meeting at the middle of her mouth. She was what Hellen called a 'chain smoker.' I had never seen a chain smoker before, but I stared at her fascinated, as she lit each new cigarette with the old one she'd been inhaling. I was impressed that she didn't have to light a match every time.

Katrina, Patsy's daughter, was close to my age and we got along well. She was fun to be with because she shared her games and dolls with me. Patsy was kind to me and that week was memorable. Though I had moments of concern for Danny, I loved every peaceful, relaxing minute at Patsy's house. Patsy made sure Katrina and I had plenty to eat and more treats than I could imagine. We could watch as much TV as we wanted, and we played many board games. There was no yelling, cussing, or hitting in that home. Everyone seemed content to just be together and be happy. Staying there was my first glimpse that life might be different in other peoples' homes. I liked their house so much better.

1975: 11 Years Old

Patsy often asked me, "Is there anything you need? Anything I could do to make you more comfortable while you stay with us?"

I was grateful. "No, thank you. I'm just fine. Thanks for being so nice to me."

"Well, if you think of something, let me know. I know you're worried about Danny, and I just want you to be as comfortable as possible."

The truth was that I wasn't all that worried about Danny. I thought the nice doctor was taking good care of him, and because of that I got to enjoy life more than ever. It was amazing to me how good I felt when I wasn't afraid.

~

There was one thing I wanted that Patsy didn't offer.

I wanted to try smoking.

I talked Katrina into helping me steal cigarettes and matches from her grandmother. She distracted her grandma while I went into the old woman's bedroom and stole the cigarettes and matches. Being that neither one of us was a chain smoker, I was proud of myself that I remembered to grab the matches.

We went down the alley and tried the cigarettes. Katrina coughed, choked, and doubled over. I didn't and that surprised me. After sharing the first cigarette, I smoked most of the second one. I enjoyed smoking so much that it scared me. I wanted more and realized how quick it would be for me to become addicted. Those two cigarettes scared me so much that I have never smoked again. It was a good lesson that I learned without Hellen screaming, cussing, or beating me. Though Hellen was a smoker herself, I was afraid that if Hellen found out, she'd kill me.

The freedom I had at Patsy's was wonderful. I felt safe there. I was glad when Danny healed, but sorry I had to leave her house.

~

Not long after my stay at Patsy's, Hellen decided it was time for us to move. She insisted we move in the middle of the night again. It was hard to move everything when we all had to whisper so we wouldn't wake the neighbors. Hellen explained that night was the best time to move because the weather was cooler.

We moved into a big apartment complex in Cypress, California. The apartments were clean inside, the landscape was beautiful, and there was a nice playground. For the first time I could remember, it was a pretty walk to our front door every day. There were beautiful flowers and lush grass and I loved the well-tended garden appearance.

Hellen hated that apartment. It brought to the forefront her racial prejudice. She felt smothered on all sides by the "Blacks and Mexicans." She was nervous they would be a bad influence on her kids and she muttered racial slurs as we walked past them.

Her behavior was the "bad influence on her kids."

I found Hellen embarrassing and wondered, *how is it their fault that they were born with their skin color? I didn't choose mine, and who decided their color was bad?* Inside the growing hatred I wrestled with towards Hellen, I questioned her reasoning. As young as age 11, I knew racial discrimination was another area of my thinking that made me different from Hellen.

~

One winter night after we'd moved to the apartment, I developed the flu and suffered a high temperature. At 2:30 in the morning, I grew weak as the fever continued to rise.

Hellen devised yet another home remedy.

"I'm gonna give you a bath to bring that fever down."

"I don't want a bath, mom."

"If you don't let me give you a bath, then I'll have to take you to the hospital."

I didn't believe her about the hospital or the bath, even as she began to run cold water in the bathtub.

1975: 11 Years Old

"You need a cold bath to bring that fever down, and that's what I'm gonna give you."

"I'm not taking a bath, mom. I'm too sick."

"I said I'm gonna give you a bath, you little snot! If I take you to the hospital, some man doctor claiming to know more than I do, is gonna make you get naked and put on a dinky paper gown, then the pervert is gonna give you a shot in the butt. Is that what you want? Or, are you 'too sick' for that, too?"

I didn't want that, and I didn't want her yelling, cussing, threatening me or calling me names, either.

When I said once again, "I'm too sick to take a bath, mom," Hellen exploded with anger and flew into a rage. She slapped me, punched my head, pulled my hair, then ripped off my nightgown and panties and shoved me towards the tub.

In the struggle, I fell onto the bathroom floor. Terrified that Hellen would give an enema now that I was naked, I went crazy with fear. Crying, screaming, and not caring if the neighbors heard, my screams woke up Tracy and she came running.

After she listened to Hellen's explanation and saw her insistence about the bath, Tracy whispered, "I'll help you."

Shivering, still crying and naked, I begged my sister, "Please, Tracy. I'm sick and mom won't leave me alone."

"Ssshhh," she said, while helping me get into the tub, "I'm right here with you. I won't leave you."

Out of options, I trusted her and let her help me into the tub.

The water felt freezing cold to my feverish body. My teeth chattered. True to her word, Tracy knelt in front of the tub and held my hands as I cried in the cold water.

Hellen stood back, crossed her arms over her massive body, and observed her daughters. She rambled on as she leaned on the doorframe: "I don't know why you're such a baby. You had to wake up the whole household. I'm a nurse, if you happen to recall, and I know what's best for you, even if you don't have the brains to know it. The real problem here is that you're so fat, stupid and ugly, that my life would be better if you'd change, and start cooperating when I tell you to do something."

Then, pointing to different parts of my body, Hellen taunted, "Look Tracy. See where the fat deposits are settling in on her body, and she's only 11. My God, Wilma, are you *really* gonna be fat, stupid and ugly all your life?"

Still holding my hands, Tracy squeezed my fingers, the only way she could communicate comfort to me. Tracy made no comments, not even glancing sideways toward Hellen. Instead, the love and concern showed in her eyes as she focused her gaze into my eyes. She looked sad, and I thought I saw some tears in her eyes, but I wasn't sure. I was humiliated and still crying too much to see with clear vision.

After a while, my fever went down and Hellen allowed me to get out of the tub. Tracy let me crawl into her bed and I fell into an exhausted sleep. I was so thankful for Tracy's help. I don't know how I would have made it through that bath without her. She was of great comfort to me that night.

The next day I felt stupid about my hysterical crying and waking up Tracy. I thought about how dumb I had been not to let Hellen watch me take a bath. After I fought with Hellen, two people watched me instead of just one. Once again, I wondered if there were any limits to my stupidity.

I hated my body.

To this day, I don't know why Hellen insisted on the cold bath, (or why she did most things) but I did my best to fight it. Though Hellen won, it is significant that I tried to fight her.

~

Through the years, Hellen pointed out that things would be better

1975: 11 Years Old

if I was a 'better' child. I believed her because I didn't see the same things happening to my siblings.

The result, I believe, was that Hellen decided if she was going to keep me quiet about the ongoing sexual abuse, then she had to control me better. Over time, her manipulation, domination, and control worked. The message Hellen wanted me to get was that fighting back just made things worse.

It was stupid to even try. I got the message.

Loud and clear.

Over the next several weeks, I thought about the bath and wondered, *how can Hellen criticize my weight when she was nearly 300 pounds.* I also wondered, *why is it that Hugh, Danny, and Tracy don't have to be stripped and bathed when they develop a fever?*

A cauldron of anger was boiling just under the surface and it was becoming more difficult for me to contain it. I hated everyone including myself.

Everyone, that is, except Tracy. I loved Tracy.

Before 1975 ended, Hellen decided it was time for another middle-of-the-night move. We left the lovely apartment in Cypress for a rental house in Orange, California.

Danny's term for these moves was, "another one of Mom's midnight specials."

1975: 11 Years Old

~ Counseling Notes ~

Danny's eye surgeries were significant events and Hellen's concern puzzled me. After Hellen died, I discussed with Danny his memories of that time. His perspective was that Hellen seemed concerned because of his limitations of partial blindness, and because of her narcissistic patterns, she didn't want to have a 'handicapped child,' one that had to depend on her in adulthood. We both remember Hellen saying that she'd bless the day when she was "finally free from all you kids."

The surgeries were successful, and Danny regained his sight.

I did not use counseling time to discuss why Hellen sent me to Patsy's house instead of someone in the church that I knew. My thoughts are that perhaps Hellen was concerned I would say or do something that would cause the church folks to have suspicions about abuse going on. Whereas, if I was stayed with someone I did not know, I'd be less comfortable and more shy, which I was. Hellen could easily manipulate me because I was a normal little girl, with normal emotional needs.

~

In counseling, I spoke about Hellen's racial prejudice and my private disdain for her actions.

The counselors said, "Your resilience shows many

times as you were growing up. Your understanding that you were different from Hellen regarding racial discrimination is just another example. At a young age, you understood you were different than her, and were wise enough to keep quiet and not argue the point with Hellen. On some level, you understood that you would not change Hellen, but only make your life harder."

~

I asked why Hellen would rip off my nightgown and force a bath. Why the scathing assessment of my body during the bath? What was the purpose to be so cruel?

The counselors said, "The forced bath is just another unfortunate example of Hellen's brutality. If she was going to conceal the ongoing sexual abuse, she was going to have to control you better. What better way than to beat you down when you are already struggling under the stress of Doyle and having just abandoned Herbie, when she blamed you for both?

So, you get the flu and she makes you take a bath your siblings don't have to take when they are sick. And what happens when you don't want it? She gets violent, rips your nightgown off in the middle of the night and you're in trouble for waking Tracy. You can't win. When you do find solace in Tracy helping you, Hellen can't bear that, so she demeans your body during the bath, causing further humiliation. No woman with a mother's heart could do that. Not a real mother. She was evil. She was not concerned

1975: 11 Years Old

for your health that night. She was operating on her own agenda, as always. You fought her as best you could, even though you were sick."

1976: 12 Years Old

*He who will not reason is a bigot, he who cannot is a fool;
and he who dares not is a slave.*
~ William Drummond

The Times

The Viking 1 Spacecraft landed on Mars and sent the photographs of the planet's surface back to Earth. It looked lonely. We lived in Orange, California, just east of Anaheim and Disneyland. Ironically, I lived near the "Happiest Place on Earth." Yet, life became even lonelier for me.

We settled into the house in Orange and Hugh, Danny, and Tracy were in high school, driving, participating in school clubs, sports, and working part-time jobs. Hellen had changed the birth year on each of their birth certificates so that they could start jobs the day they turned 15 years old.

Hellen got a full-time job and spent a lot of time away from the apartment.

I stayed outdoors most nights after the sun went down. It was a nice neighborhood, but when the other kids were called home at dinnertime, no one was around to call for me. I sat under a streetlight (because I was still afraid of the dark), with my bicycle lying on its side. I could smell dinners cooking and so wanted to have parents call me into a house for dinner. The other kids seemed annoyed when they were called in, but I didn't think I would be upset by it.

The year brought a lot of changes. The enema nights were over. Hellen didn't even threaten them anymore, though the sexual abuse continued. I had no warning then, but Hellen's rage and perversion was escalating, and I had no idea how much worse my life was going to get.

~

Hellen became increasingly violent as my body developed and entered puberty. She crudely expressed her excitement about the changes she saw in me. I loathed the changes, and was very uncomfortable around her.

I was still required to sleep in her bed.

I didn't know how to handle Hellen's rules about my personal hygiene, or what I could do about it. I wanted to ask, *what brought this on?* But, fear always stopped me. Asking meant loose front teeth and busted, bleeding lips. Asking meant explaining at school that I'd run into the door jamb on the way to the bathroom in the middle of the night. Asking just wasn't worth it. Asking resulted in my questions still unanswered and more pain and even more punishment.

I grew more troubled each day. By now, I didn't just want my own bed; I was consumed with wanting my own bed. I prayed. I begged God for one. I told Him I would do *anything* if I could just have my own bed.

But, I still had no bed of my own.

I worried that maybe God was mad at me, since Hellen told me He was. I messed up everything. I wondered if God had forgiven me yet for abandoning my puppy, Herbie. I continued to sleep in Hellen's bed and shutdown my mind while she did her weird sexual stuff to me.

One evening, under the streetlight, alone, I admitted to myself that I didn't have parents like other kids, and I decided it was my fault. I felt that God had given me the life I had because I was garbage. *Whatever is wrong with me, is what caused my mother to hate me, and my father to abandon me.* Hellen told me I was God's garbage. That evening I figured, *she must be right.*

1976: 12 Years Old

~

I now had another new school to navigate. Sixth grade brought changes and I got into a lot of trouble from the moment I enrolled. The school was small and I did not fit in with the other children. The kids made fun of my clothes, my hair, my shoes, my speech problems, and my emotional outbursts.

Mr. McFarly was my teacher. I thought he was odd because he wore a macramé necklace with granny glasses attached. He said he had made the necklace himself. It was so ugly, I wondered why he told people that, and why he wore it. Behind his back, some of the kids called him Mr. McFartly. I thought it was a funny name, though I seldom laughed at anything.

Instead, I worked hard to stem the growing anger inside and to hide from the world the angst I lived with each day. It seemed as though I could manage to get through a few weeks at school with no problems by hardly speaking to anyone. Then one inconsequential thing could happen, and I would blow a gasket.

One day Mr. McFarly refused to give me a pass to the restroom, though I repeatedly asked. Frustrated, I went berserk, yelling, calling him names, and threatening him in front of the class. It was an awful, humiliating scene and I knew I was out of control. He immediately tried to calm me, but I could not seem to calm myself down.

I stormed out of the classroom without the pass, went to the girls' restroom and cried. I had blown it and was stupid again. I was disgusted and disappointed in myself.

When I returned to class about 20 minutes after the explosion, Mr. McFarly was standing over a large stack of blank writing paper. There were approximately 50 pages and he was attempting to staple them together with his big stapler. It didn't work, so he put a rubber band around the big stack. He walked to my desk and plopped down the stack with a loud thud.

"There are two sentences at the top of the first page. They are, 'I will not yell at Mr. McFarly, call him names, or threaten him. I will not walk out of class without Mr. McFarly's permission.' You are going to write these two sentences on each line, both sides of the paper, and you will turn them in to me first thing tomorrow morning."

I looked at the stack of papers, then looked him in the eye and said, "I ain't doin' it."

"It's due in the morning, or I will call your mother."

"Call her. I ain't writing one word on your stupid papers!"

"It's due in the morning. Now, back to our classwork."

Mr. McFarly stayed calm, never raising his voice, though his face was red.

I knew I had lost it in front of everyone before I stormed out of class. I was embarrassed and mad. Mad at the teacher and mad at myself. Emotionally, I was buckling under the load from Hellen's abuse, and it showed on the outside.

I was not able to hide the growing anger inside of me.

When class dismissed for the day, I hauled the big stack of papers all the way back to the apartment. We lived one and one quarter miles from the school, and I did not have a backpack. The closer I got to home, the more scared I got. I couldn't predict how Hellen would respond to this homework project or my failure to do it, and I was truly scared.

That evening, I told Hellen about the blow up in the classroom. When she asked for more detail, I embellished the story by saying my need to go to the bathroom was urgent. I cried while telling her the story...and I was shocked that she believed me.

"Well!" She declared, "Ain't no man in hell gonna prevent my kids from going to the toilet. I hated that when I was in school and it's why I've got bladder problems today."

I held my breath. It was her pattern to go over the heads of the teacher and the principal and barnstorm the district office when she didn't agree with something. This was barnstorming material. I was trembling.

"You ain't writing one word on any of those papers. Throw the whole stack in the trash."

I stood and picked up the stack of papers, but Hellen interrupted my walk to the garbage. She reached out her hand and said, "Here. Hand me the top paper, the one that he wrote on. If he wants sentences, he'll have to settle for what I write to him instead."

The top sheet was wrinkled. It had gotten wet from the tears I'd cried while walking home. Below Mr. McFarly's handwritten sentence, Hellen scribbled in her little tiny handwriting:

> *No child of mine will ever be refused permission to go to the bathroom. That's against the law, need I remind you? I am proud that I taught Wilma to not take nonsense from anyone. She will not be writing one sentence you require her to do for a punishment. It's a stupid punishment for doing nothing wrong, and I made her throw away the stack of paper you sent with her. If you have any problem with this, I'll meet you at district headquarters, and we'll let the superintendent of public instruction remind you that you broke the law.*
>
> *Hellen J. Proietti.*

I held onto the note throughout the evening, hoping Hellen would take it no further. If she found out I had embellished the story to save my hide, I was afraid she'd beat me to death.

The next morning, I walked towards Mr. McFarly's desk casually waving the single piece of paper as my classmates watched. Looking over his reading glasses on the tip of his nose, he waited in silence as I approached his desk.

After reading the note he simply replied, "Well enough then. Take your seat, please."

Over the next several weeks, I tested him and asked to be excused to go to the restroom often, even when I didn't need to. He was quiet and kind and remained that way throughout the rest of the year.

As the school year progressed, Mr. McFarly spoke softly to me, going out of his way to be patient and considerate. When he corrected me, he was gentle and explained why my behavior was inappropriate.

When I saw his kindness and that he wasn't going to make me pay some other way, I backed down. I felt bad for being disrespectful towards him. He didn't deserve the threatening note from Hellen. The truth was, I had lost it when he had simply told me 'no.'

I felt ashamed about my emotional outburst, especially since he had taken the brunt of it. Worse yet, I lied to Hellen to protect myself. I feared the wrath of Hellen more than I feared God. I hoped God would understand. I believed He would. As far as I know, for the rest of the school year, Mr. McFarly never attempted to contact Hellen.

~

As the school year progressed, I realized I was the only kid in my class who didn't have a dad and I was embarrassed. I feared that if the other students found out, they would know that even my dad didn't want me. Troubled, I scrambled to find a resolution, a way to deal with it before I was forced to.

In an effort to be like the other kids, I'd include a reference to my dad in the few conversations I had with the other students: "Oh, my dad took us all to Dairy Queen last night," or, "After my mom made dinner, dad took us to the park." Trying to sound real, sometimes I'd say, "My dad was such a grouch last night."

I went through that school year playing the 'dad' games.

Mr. McFarly knew the truth, but he never said anything.

The fact was, I still didn't know where Angelo lived or how to contact him. I had no memory of the sound of his voice or what he looked like as he grew older. I wondered, *does he ever think about me? Is he still alive? Would anyone tell me if he had died.* I had no one to ask… and, no way to find the answers.

1976: 12 Years Old

~

Another problem was simply eating lunch. The grade school was unusual in that it had no cafeteria. Each day the students brought their lunches and ate at picnic tables outside our classroom. The custodian delivered milk cartons to our room just before lunch. This system presented a dilemma for me. In every school I had attended before, I had been on the free lunch program. Since this school didn't even have a lunch, all I got was a free carton of milk. Most days I had nothing to eat, because I had no food to bring to school.

Once in a while, *if* Hellen happened to be in a good mood, she would give me some change from the bottom of her purse. The only store I passed on the way to school was a liquor store. The owner opened early each morning while he stocked the shelves. He got used to me wandering in there trying to buy something for my lunch with just a few coins. Often, all I could afford was a big dill pickle in a plastic bag. Although the pickle didn't go well with the free carton of milk, it was better than nothing. A few times, the owner gave me a sandwich that had passed the sell-by date and I asked him to put it in a brown paper bag. I felt proud to carry the bag to school and have a real lunch like the other kids.

Most days though, I simply went without food. I'd start the day walking to school without breakfast; at lunch I'd drink the free milk, then I'd walk back to the apartment feeling very hungry.

After the restroom permission incident and note from Hellen, Mr. McFarly brought extra food in his lunch bag two or three days a week and offered me his 'extra apple,' or 'half a peanut butter sandwich.' On many days, the food he shared with me was all I had to eat for the whole day.

Mr. McFarly was kind and made a genuine effort to help me on his own…and he did.

~

1976: 12 Years Old

My yearning to fit in was noticed by other teachers. Mrs. Leonard was our sixth-grade music teacher. She was petite with dark hair and I liked her. I went to her classroom after school two or three times a week and she found projects for me to do. Mrs. Leonard encouraged me to participate in a several-month rehearsal for a bicentennial concert in the spring. I was excited about the program and the afternoons I spent working with her were fun. She acted as if she couldn't put the program together without my help. In my innocence, I believed her. I felt important and basked in her attention.

To be in the program, Mrs. Leonard told me I needed to have a red, white, or blue blouse, and a long skirt with any sort of red, white, or blue print. For months, she asked me if I was going to be able to get the outfit together for the concert.

I often asked Hellen and Tracy about the skirt and blouse and they both assured me that getting them would be no problem. But the week before the big concert, I asked if we could go to Goodwill to find the clothing I needed, and Hellen said, "No."

The night before the concert, I cried to my sister because I did not have the clothes I was required to wear. Tracy gave me one of her white blouses and she talked Hellen into driving her to a fabric store. We got there 10 minutes before they closed. Tracy bought some thin cotton fabric in red, white, and blue. I thought she was the greatest person in the world.

When we returned to the apartment, Tracy began to measure the fabric for the skirt. Hellen watched her for a few moments, and then barked, "There's plenty of time to work on that nonsense tomorrow. Knock that baloney off now!"

I went to bed worried that Tracy wouldn't have time after school and work, but there was nothing I could do.

The next night, Tracy sewed the fabric to create a long tube. She put elastic in one end to make a waistband. The skirt was not yet hemmed or ironed, but it was time to leave for the concert. I held back tears as Hellen drove me to school that evening. I knew if I cried, she'd beat me. Tracy sat in the back seat and fashioned the crude un-ironed hem with masking tape. She finished just as we pulled into the school driveway. I changed into the wrinkled skirt in the car.

Hellen dropped me off and said, "The paper says this shindig is supposed to be over at 8:30. I'll pick you up then. Meet me here and don't make me hafta wait for you."

It was then I realized, *none of my family will be attending my concert.*

I was crushed. We all went to Hugh's and Danny's games, Tracy's plays, and other extracurricular events. We ate at the fast-food restaurants where they worked.

None of them can come to my concert?

"I thought all of you were going to be here," I said. "What are you doing instead?"

"We all want to go to church." Hellen said.

I knew she was lying. They looked for every feeble excuse to get out of going to church every chance they could.

"Mom, I've been working on this for months!"

"So? We haven't. Meet me here at 8:30 sharp, and don't make me hafta come looking for you."

The cars behind us were honking their horns for Hellen to move, so I got out and went inside the auditorium alone.

Mrs. Leonard had been so proud of all the work and commitment I had invested in the program that she had me stand in the front row of the chorus. We sang many patriotic songs, and I hoped that no one noticed that my skirt had a masking tape hem and wasn't ironed.

I hadn't considered there would be people taking pictures, but flashbulbs were lighting up in the audience. While singing, I worried that someone would notice that I didn't have a slip under the thin cotton skirt Tracy had sewn. Standing in the front row, there was nothing to do but keep singing.

Throughout the concert, I watched the other students' parents creep up the side aisles to get a better view and snap pictures.

I wondered, *why isn't my family here?*

Thoroughly disappointed, tears ran down my face while singing, *You're a Grand Old Flag.* How odd that must have seemed to the audience.

When the concert was over, I went outside and waited for Hellen to arrive. I cried as I stood under a tree watching my classmates receive hugs and congratulations from their families. I told myself, *it's not important that my family didn't attend, because I'm not an important kid...like the other kids.*

When the auditorium cleared out and the parking lot was empty, I was surprised I wasn't scared waiting there alone. I wondered if Hellen had forgotten about me. *Should I walk home in the dark?* I decided to wait a while longer. It was 9:45 p.m., well over an hour after the concert ended.

Just when I thought, *maybe I should start walking to the apartment,* she pulled into the driveway. I wiped my eyes and pretended that everything was okay.

I was excited as I began to tell her how nice the concert had been and how I remembered the words to all the songs.

Hellen interrupted, "I don't want to hear about your stupid evening."

I stopped talking and knew Hellen's mood signaled trouble. I tried to scoot closer to the car door. I hated being in the front seat when she was like that.

Hellen began: "In truth, Wilma, you frankly ought to be ashamed of yourself. I certainly am ashamed of you. Putting a worldly school event ahead of the house of God. Dear God, what *am* I *ever* going to *do* with you? I was humiliated to have to tell the church folks that you were attending a stupid worldly concert instead of being faithful to the house of the Lord where you belonged. Your priorities are way out of whack. My God, when are you gonna get your priorities in order? No, don't even tell me about your stupid evening. I don't want to hear about it. I will *not* partake in your sin. I'll be clean when I stand before the Lord."

What?

Seeing my crestfallen face, she continued, "Don't look at me with that pout! I'll slap you silly. I'll knock that fake innocent look to kingdom come! It's my job as the good mother I am, to point out the error of your ways, especially when you're in full-blown sin."

I got past the surprise and shock to say, "Sorry, mom."

She then quoted scripture: "Seek ye first the kingdom of God," and, "Choose you this day who you will serve."

I had my priorities out of whack, and she was proving it by quoting the Bible. As she talked, I wondered why she'd chose that time to tell me I was doing wrong–she had driven me to the performance, and she hadn't said one word in all the months I was working on the program after school and in rehearsals.

Why now?

Well, maybe she had just learned those scriptures at church tonight? I felt bad, and I went to bed afraid that God wouldn't ever give me a bed, since I had my priorities out of whack. I felt dumb, and believed, *in my stupidity, I just delayed the day when I'll finally be allowed to have my own bed. I can't believe how stupid I've been–again.*

~

Hellen's moods dictated the rules she made up. Doing things for me at the last minute was her pattern. She wouldn't allow me to get a skirt for the concert because she enjoyed watching me panic and beg, for the skirt, for a ride, for food, a bed, or whatever I needed. Waiting was my reality and making me wait was her power trip. Making me wait until there were no cars left in the parking lot after the concert. Always waiting. Waiting to be good enough for her to love.

Waiting for my basic needs; love, food, and a bed. Waiting for her approval.

Always waiting.

~

The concert changed me. I became angrier inside. Hellen was a master at being cruel. She manipulated my fears, emotions, hopes, dreams, my innate need for her approval, and crushed it all by refusing to attend the performance, and then scolding me as she drove me back to the house. Everything I touched was bad, because I was bad.

There is simply no hope for me.

~

Unbeknownst to me, Hugh, Danny and Tracy started having conversations wondering why I hated Hellen so much. They couldn't make sense of it, especially when Hellen was kind to me in front of them.

When we were adults, Danny said, "We used to ask each other, 'Why does Wilma hate mom so bad?' We couldn't figure it out. Now it all makes sense."

I had no idea my feelings had been so transparent. I thought I was hiding my hatred better than that. I lived in a whirlwind of Hellen's abuse, and I was angry. I had been stumbling through the storm, unaware my angst was so obvious.

~

Hellen took me to yard sales in Orange on Saturday mornings. She spent time teaching me to examine an item to make sure I wanted to buy it and then coached me on how to negotiate the price. The kindness and interest she showed felt wonderful. For a few hours, I felt normal and not like a stupid, worthless disappointment to her. She was never mean to me on those trips, even when I bought something

1976: 12 Years Old

flawed, or if I failed to negotiate as she had taught. She'd pull me aside, and with a patient, quiet voice show me how I had missed the flaws, or, she'd point out how the sellers were easily negotiating with others. She smiled often. Her generosity and kindness confused me.

Once we got back, we'd show my siblings the treasures. Sometimes Hellen would tell them how well I had done and it felt good to hear her brag about me. It was so rare for her to be proud of me for anything.

By late Saturday afternoons, she had switched back to her old self. I treasured Saturday morning yard sales with Hellen because she was kind, patient, and she smiled at me. Each time, I felt like I had failed when she switched back to her old self.

~

On a breezy Friday evening in mid-April of 1976, Hellen and Danny got into a big fight. Hellen claimed Danny had been rebelling against her rules for a while: ignoring curfew, smoking pot, and had a girlfriend that Hellen called "Slut." I don't know what his girlfriend's real name was.

I watched the yelling, cussing, and calling of names and I cried.

At one point, Hellen got so angry she grabbed a lamp that was turned on, jerked it off the table, ripping the cord out of the wall in the process, and threw it at Danny.

Hugh interceded and tried to negotiate a peaceful resolution, but Hellen and Danny were too angry to be swayed by his high school level reasoning.

By 2 o'clock on Saturday morning, the argument died down and Hellen announced we'd be moving back to Phoenix on Monday morning. Hugh pleaded with her to wait and let all of us finish the school year, but she said we had to move before Danny ended up fathering a child or going to jail, or both.

Danny didn't have a transmission in his car, so Hugh worked all weekend helping Danny put his car back together.

1976: 12 Years Old

We left on Monday morning.

∼

Hellen claimed to hate Phoenix. She called it 'Egypt.' I didn't understand why we were moving back since she hated it so much. There were so many cities to choose from, why Phoenix?

Years after I was married, a family member disclosed that Hellen moved to Phoenix in 1976 to meet or reunite with a lesbian lover. The relationship lasted from April 1976 until January 1981. The family member and another relative knew about Hellen's relationship, though they weren't sure what caused the relationship to end.

Yet, Hellen blamed Danny for having to move us back to Arizona.

∼

Hellen chose to settle us back into the same neighborhood, church, and schools we'd left 18 months before. We unpacked our belongings in a run-down, two-bedroom apartment.

On my first day back at my old school, I hoped the kids wouldn't remember me. Of course, they did, and had a great time laughing at how much 'uglier' the Playground Pig had become. I was thankful that school would be out for summer break in just a few weeks.

At the Phoenix apartment, Hellen's behavior became significantly more unpredictable. She would go into a rage at the smallest irritation. The beatings she inflicted on me took on a painful new viciousness. Often, she clenched her false teeth as she pounded me with her fists. I wondered if they would break from her clenching them so hard. She was careful to leave bruises only where they wouldn't be seen by hitting me in the chest, lower back, and hips. I had large purple bruises under my clothing most of the time.

I got into some fights at school and I'd often ditch during my lunch hour. The principal didn't discipline me for the fights and I was never caught crawling in and out of the hole in the schoolyard fence.

In Phoenix, things got worse for Danny, too. Hellen became meaner

1976: 12 Years Old

towards all of us, but especially toward Danny. At 17, Danny was big and muscular, and he had no qualms about hitting Hellen back after she'd hit him. By now, she was 44 years old, a severe diabetic and weighed approximately 280 pounds. She was no match for Danny's height, youth, strength, or rage.

One hot afternoon in May, they took their fight out into the back yard. Tracy and I watched through the patio door. Hellen and Danny were out of control with anger. Hellen picked up a metal garden rake and used it to hit Danny in the face and head. Danny pounded Hellen with his fists. She screamed in pain. Tracy and I should've called the police, but we were too scared. We were sobbing. Tracy and I both referred to the fight as "the day mom tried to kill Danny."

Sometime during the night, Danny ran away.

I thought, *when Danny ran away, he must have been feeling both rejection and torment. When your mother attempts to kill you, what choice is there? Fight, flight or freeze. He ran. I understood rejection.*

When Hellen realized he was gone, she ordered Tracy to leave with her and drive to California to find him. I begged Hellen to take me, since Hugh worked and went to school full time. We had no food in the apartment.

She refused.

A few days later, they brought Danny back. The California State Police had given him the choice to go with his mother or go to juvenile hall until he turned 18. He agreed to return to Phoenix.

~

After Danny returned, Hellen worked to put more separation between me, my brothers and sister. Hellen got a job working nights at a nursing home and made me go to work with her. I hated it and begged to stay with Tracy. Hellen would argue, "No. You're just too important to me to leave you with those irresponsible, selfish kids."

I'm important to her? My siblings are irresponsible? Since when?

1976: 12 Years Old

When we arrived at her job, she would tell her supervisor, "I had to bring my baby girl with me tonight. She was just too afraid to stay alone. I'll have her sleep on the couch in the front lobby. I know you'll understand."

I'm afraid to stay at the apartment alone? That was the first I'd heard of it.

The nursing home reeked of urine and I hated trying to sleep on the uncomfortable vinyl couches in the lobby. When I wasn't trying to sleep, I went on nightly rounds with Hellen. I witnessed firsthand the large amount of drugs she stole. The cabinet with the residents' medications was unlocked at night and the supervisor would give Hellen two sleeping pills to give to a resident. As we walked to the resident's room, Hellen put both pills in her pocket. When we left the room, the pills remained in her pocket. She'd smile and wink at me. When the resident continued to have a restless night, Hellen would report to the supervisor, "The resident in room 23 is gonna need another sleeping pill to settle down tonight." Busy with stacks of patient charts, the supervisor would then instruct Hellen to take another pill to the resident. Hellen would slip two pills from the bottle and give the patient one.

Over the course of one shift, Hellen stole several sleeping pills and tablets of Valium.

I often saw Hellen grow impatient with male residents, most of whom she said she couldn't stand. Not following orders, she'd give them one of the stolen pills to 'shut them up.' She laughed at how easy it was to do. As young as I was, I wondered if the medicine conflicted with their other health conditions.

There were other times, however, that the way she treated her 'special' residents deeply disturbed me. I worried about what she was doing to them alone in their room. The special ones were always female and I was not allowed in their room when Hellen 'saw to their needs.'

1976: 12 Years Old

On slow nights, when things were especially quiet, I watched her give her favorite female residents two, and often three, of the stolen sleeping pills. Then she'd send me back to the visitor's waiting room to sleep on the couches. As they drifted off to sleep, Hellen told me she'd massage their legs and backs with lotion. I thought what Hellen was doing was odd, since they hadn't complained about cramps in their legs, having a sore back, nor had they asked for a sleeping pill or a massage.

~

As an adult, I realized Hellen wanted me to see her steal drugs and give them to people who didn't have these medications prescribed for their use. She wanted to show me that she had the power to drug people at her will, and there was nothing I, or anyone else could do about it. She was proud of her cunning theft and drugging of the helpless, elderly folks. I had no idea at the time Hellen was showing me her power over my vulnerability, for in the future, she would use her power to drug me and take advantage of my vulnerable age.

~

We didn't own a washer or dryer and we lived miles from the closest laundromat. Hellen would take us there only once every few months. I had very few clothes and I wasn't allowed to wash them out by hand. If she caught me hand-washing clothes, I was severely beaten. I was already beaten for other unknown reasons; I couldn't risk anything else so I wore dirty clothes every day.

~

When I started seventh grade that autumn, Hellen restricted the showers I could have. At first, I wasn't allowed to shower or wash my hair for a week. Soon, the restrictions lasted four to six weeks. At school, I was teased because my hair was dirty and greasy, and I smelled bad. Like the physical beatings, food restrictions, and sexual abuse, the shower restrictions worsened as time went on. I hated this new punishment. I hated being dirty like Hellen.

1976: 12 Years Old

Hellen told me, "You can forget about wasting my money to take showers or wash your hair. Until you straighten up by God, you'll go without. You don't need to be wasting water anyway, especially when you're not obedient to me, or God himself. No one wants to be around you anyway, so quit pretending it matters if you go a few days without a shower. You're no princess."

Hellen had an endless stream of ideas to punish me, each being worse than the one prior. I hated wearing dirty clothes and going for weeks without showers. I was too afraid of Hellen to disobey her, and I cried many nights over the new punishment. With the onset of puberty, the lack of proper hygiene became a humiliating problem.

~

I had no one I could talk to. On rare occasions, I'd wonder, *why is this happening to me, since all I do is go to school and clean the house? Why do I deserve such cruelty? I don't have a boyfriend, I don't listen to unapproved music, and I do obey Hellen. What am I doing to cause the beatings, and the other punishments?* But they were just fleeting doubts, and rare moments of question.

My world grew darker by the day. I lived each day scared of Hellen, scared of her cruelty, her brutality, her perversions. Always trying to gauge her mood, often failing, always afraid. Fear was my constant companion.

I was sure it couldn't get any worse.

I was so, so wrong.

1976: 12 Years Old

~ Counseling Notes ~

One of my greatest sources of anxiety was being denied food, clean clothes, and the basic things I needed in life.

The counselors said, "Once again, Hellen continued her pattern of separating you out from your siblings. You didn't 'need' to be provided lunches at school on a regular basis, your siblings didn't have to 'shop once in a while with change' for their lunches at a liquor store, your concert wasn't important but their plays, concerts, and sporting events were, etc. She was consistent in making you different from them, so as they grew up you *would* be different from them, in *their* eyes. That kind of separation is difficult, if not impossible, to ever heal or reconcile. That is unparalleled cruelty."

~

I asked about my angry outburst towards my kind, soft-spoken teacher, Mr. McFarly.

The counselors said, "It was just a matter of time until all the angst you were holding surfaced and it did that day. It is not surprising that you had an outburst towards a male authority figure. Somewhere in your subconscious you knew you could get away with it due to Hellen's hatred for men. It was a risky gamble, because Hellen could, and did, turn on you, like when you stole the candy. It worked for you this

1976: 12 Years Old

time, and it sounds like this teacher was kind and compassionate."

~

The concert was a huge disappointment to me, but my family didn't seem to notice. I asked why this eight-month project could so easily be dismissed?

The counselors said, "Hellen made you wait until the last minute for your outfit for the concert. She made you wait in the parking lot alone in the dark for over an hour after everyone else had left. You were only 10 years old. No parent in their right mind would deliberately leave a child waiting alone at night. Her manipulation was about making you worthless in your own eyes and your siblings' eyes. You didn't matter, that's how the concert was so easily dismissed.

Then it was all your fault, again. It's possible your siblings had become numb to your disappointment. They were busy with high school and working. Hellen was able to fool professionals; of course, she could snow your siblings. The key point here is that Hellen chose to pick you up alone to scold you. Who knows what Hellen told your siblings? Likely, it was some completely different lie. The bottom line here is Hellen used the concert to crush you, and she did. She was intensely cruel."

~

I asked why would she be so kind to me for those few months, when we were going to yard sales?

The counselors said, "Hellen also followed a typical pattern for abusers regarding the Saturday morning yard sales. Very often a parent that is molesting their child will do kind things for the child. The reason is to cause confusion in the child's mind, as it did in yours. However, if you will look back, you will likely see a predictable pattern. That is, that the kind actions were done when someone in the community, the church, or the family was able to witness it. It is more about strengthening the parents' defense should the child ever tell, than it is about actually being kind to the child. The abusers often use kindness to manipulate, dominate and control their victim, simply because it works."

~

After we moved back to Phoenix, Tracy and I watched as Hellen tried to kill Danny with a rake in the backyard. I asked about the day Hellen tried to kill Danny.

The counselors said, "Danny was 17 and Hellen hated men. She was a 44-year-old, morbidly, obese diabetic. She had no business trying to take his youth and strength on. All four of you kids suffered in that hellish environment. Danny ran away that night. You ran away at seven years old. There was no way to live in Hellen's house and leave unscathed. It's just a matter of where the pain manifests in an individual's life and if they get help for it."

As an adult, Danny told me, "Mom put me through hell for running away. Those were the worst days of my life."

None of us deserved her brutality. Though we survived, we all bear the scars.

~

1976: 12 Years Old

I hated the awful nights when Hellen took me to her work. It made it so hard for me at school the next day and I was already struggling with my grades.

The counselors said, "The manipulation and control Hellen used in separating you from your siblings by insisting you spend nights at the nursing homes was abusive. And it likely caused guilt for your siblings since she accused them of being 'selfish and irresponsible.' Also, there is no way to gauge how it affected your school day after getting little to no sleep the night before. Again, this was another way of publicly showing how 'caring' of a mother she was, and privately separating you from your siblings, strengthening the you/them difference.

It was at this time she began the shower and hair washing restrictions for you, but not for any of them. Why? Because she wanted to again reinforce that you were nothing, you were worthless and you deserved whatever she handed out. She was setting up a possible defense so if they were ever asked, they could say she had never withheld from them the things you might say she withheld from you. She was aligning her defense along the way. She was preparing in case you ever spoke up you wouldn't have been believed. And you wouldn't have been."

~

I asked about the shower restrictions that Hellen started and the increase in beatings.

The counselors said, "The shower restrictions were about Hellen's manipulation, dominion, and control. She had to up the angst, defeat and compliance in your mind to control you. She wanted you to be just like her. Dirty, stinky–and who knows how far she intended that to go? The beatings were about controlling you and keeping you literally beat down, defeated in your mind, physically in pain, unable to focus. She should have been in prison."

1977: 13 Years Old

Trauma mocks language and confronts it with its insufficiency.
~ Leigh Gilmore, Author
The Limits of Autobiography: Trauma, Testimony, Theory

We literally do not know what to think about it. The unlinkable is unthinkable and all we can say to ourselves is 'there are no words.' I do not know what to do with that. I don't know where to put that.
~ Meg Jay, Author, *Supernormal*

The Times

The novel, *Roots*, by Alex Hailey, won the Pulitzer Prize. Elvis Presley, Charlie Chaplin, and Bing Crosby died, and I entered my teen years going through each day on autopilot.

I didn't fit in anywhere.

At school, I was still called the Playground Pig.

At church, I was scolded for not appreciating the good mother God had given me.

At Hellen's house, I was the target of Hellen's daily brutality and her nightly perversions as I slept in her bed.

I felt so alone.

Distanced from regular life, normal people, and even the idea of hope, I lived in shutdown mode in an attempt to protect myself from the nightmare of life in Hellen's house.

1977: 13 Years Old

Shutdown mode worked, so I stayed there.

Life in shutdown was necessary for my daily survival. I've heard different terms for what I've called shutdown, but I've stayed with the term because it succinctly describes the 'garage door separation' I felt between myself and the rest of the world.

~

I was 13 and too old to have to sleep with my mother. I resigned hope of ever having my own bed.

I worried that the kids at school would find out that I still slept with my mother. Just the thought made me panic. My sister and brothers went to high school with the siblings of my classmates. While I felt that Hugh, Danny, and Tracy would do nothing deliberate to hurt me, just one off-hand joke or one out-of-context remark could've been enough to sink whatever shred of dignity I had left.

Though I kept handwritten journals and wrote poetry (and hid them), I confirmed my memories with my brother Danny after we were adults. We discussed the long wait I'd endured for a bed, and we walked in memory through each house where we'd lived. Danny was outraged as he realized the many years Hellen had delayed my hopes for a bed.

~

School was a constant nightmare. The kids were cruel from the moment I set foot on campus, until I pedaled my bicycle away in the afternoon.

I had a locker on the bottom row, in the middle section of a corridor of lockers. When I knelt to open it, some kid would sneak up behind me and pull hard on my shoulders, causing me to fall backwards. Then they'd run to the water fountain to wash the 'Playground Pig's germs' off their hands. Falling backwards never made my clothes any dirtier than they already were, but it was still embarrassing.

Sometimes the kid who snuck up on me surprised me and didn't knock me down. Instead, the kids challenged each other to see who

1977: 13 Years Old

could kick the hardest. They devised some sort of rating system, competing to win the 'kick of the day.'

They aimed their feet at my lower back and I often had difficulty catching my breath after suffering the blows. The kids didn't know–and they couldn't have known–that they were kicking bruises I already had from beatings from Hellen. After they left me alone, I would find a bathroom stall where I could cry until the pain subsided.

I was often late for class.

The kids kicking me at my locker was painful, but compared to everything else in my life, it was a small thing. I was beat down and entered the downward spiral into a dark depression–one that I would not be able to rise up out of by myself.

I would need to be rescued.

~

One morning during the fall semester, I was half a block from school when I decided to try riding my bicycle with no hands. I pedaled along just fine but then decided to close my eyes.

Seconds later, I slammed into the back of a pickup truck and camper. I lay on the street, tangled in my bicycle, feeling stunned and stupid. Slowly, I untangled myself and picked up my bike.

An elderly couple, Mr. and Mrs. Layton, were sitting on their porch. They witnessed the crash and came over to help. They insisted I come up on their porch for bandages. I declined, but they insisted, so I parked my bicycle on their driveway and stepped onto the porch. Only then did I realize I had bloodied both elbows and knees. The Layton's rushed about, getting peroxide and doctoring my injuries. Mr. Layton called the school and told them they were helping me after a bicycle accident and I would be a little late.

Mrs. Layton cleaned my wounds and prepared a large mug of hot chocolate with whipped cream. I stayed outside on the porch, never stepping inside their home. After a short time, I was calmed down and the hot chocolate was gone. I thanked them and left on my bike towards school.

The accident was the beginning of a sweet relationship. At their encouragement, I stopped by the next morning for hot chocolate and a muffin. They wanted to know how I was healing from the accident.

Breakfast with Mr. and Mrs. Layton became a daily event. I looked forward to breakfast on their porch and left early so I could spend time with them. Over the course of the next four months, they asked me about my family, school, my teachers, and homework. When I had a test, they remembered and asked how it went, and what my grade was. I basked in their undivided attention as I willingly answered their questions.

~

One morning in late February, I was drinking hot chocolate with Mr. and Mrs. Layton when they asked, "So, where did you say you live?"

"In a two-bedroom apartment. It's really crowded."

"I would imagine so," said Mrs. Layton.

"My mother is looking at a four-bedroom house, but she doesn't know if we can buy it."

"Is your mother working?" Mr. Layton asked.

"She works two jobs."

"That's a lot for one person. Why doesn't she think she may not be able to buy the home?"

"I don't really understand it. My mom just said that the owner has to carry it, whatever that means."

"Oh. Where is this house your family is looking at?"

When I told them, they looked at each other.

"Do you know the house too?" I asked.

"Uh, yes, as a matter of fact, we own that house," Mr. Layton told me.

I was surprised, but it was time for school, so I finished my hot chocolate and left.

Within a week, Hellen had approval to buy the house. The owners were willing to carry the loan.

1977: 13 Years Old

I felt stupid for wrecking my bike, but I believe meeting Mr. and Mrs. Layton was Divine intervention. Though the house they sold to Hellen was where the most violent abuse occurred, it was also the place from where I was rescued, years later. I believe God allowed Hellen to buy that home because it kept all four of us kids in a stable place until we could get out or be rescued. It put a stop to her dragging us all over from rental to rental.

~

It was early in the spring and one day after lunch, I went to home economics class and was assigned to work with a group of six girls. The classroom was outfitted with several kitchens. I felt nervous because this group of six girls teased me all the time. Eleanor Maynard, the meanest one, was part of the group. Throughout the class period, they ignored me, though we were supposed to be working together on a recipe.

Near the end of class, I noticed that the dishwater in our sink was dark and grease was floating on top. We had a big bottle of dish soap to use and I wondered why the girls hadn't changed the dirty dishwater, but I didn't say anything.

The rules required us to only work on the specific tasks the teacher assigned to each student in each group. The teacher was very strict about that. I was assigned oven duty, not dish washing. I turned away from the nasty dishwater.

Moments later, I was covered with it.

The girls had poured the dishpan over my head. It was disgusting. I burst into tears as I realized what had just happened and why. My hair and clothes were soaked. The first person I saw was Eleanor. With her hands on her hips, she said, "NOW maybe you'll come to school with clean hair!"

The other girls doubled over with laughter.

The teacher rushed over, scolded the girls, and instructed them to mop up the water on the floor. I was sent to the school nurse, Mrs.

Rill, who listened as I told her about the incident through my tears.

Handing me a tissue, she said, "You sit right here honey. I'm going to make a phone call or two and get you everything you need."

I was afraid she was calling Hellen at work.

She didn't call Hellen. Instead, she called the custodian to unlock the bicycle rack, then handed me a bottle of shampoo and sent me home early to take a shower.

I walked to my bicycle looking at the ground. I didn't want the custodian to see me with wet hair and clothes, but there he was, at the entrance of the bike rack, having unlocked the gate for me.

I unlocked my bicycle and pedaled several feet when I burst into tears. I couldn't hold the anguish any longer. I wept with giant humiliated sobs as I pedaled my bicycle through the city streets. I couldn't see the road, and I didn't care.

I was relieved that Hellen's car was not in the driveway. She was probably at work. I was terrified that she would come home and discover me taking a shower and breaking her rules, but I still took a long shower and washed my hair with the nurse's shampoo. Afterwards, I hid the bottle in the back of the cabinet under the sink. My clean hair felt good.

The last time I'd had a shower or washed my hair...well, I couldn't recall when it was.

I didn't tell anyone what happened to me at school, not even Mr. and Mrs. Layton. I figured it was my own stupid fault anyway.

The thought of facing the kids the next day was dreadful. If there was ever a day I didn't want to go to school, it was that day, but I knew I had to go back sometime.

The next morning, I arrived in the bike rack just before the bell rang. I had expected the kids to tease me, but I was unprepared for what they had planned.

The story of the 'home ec hair washing' had spread through the school. Crowds of students lined both sides of the hallway leading

1977: 13 Years Old

from the bicycle rack, as I walked towards class. They were laughing, pointing, and jeering; some were saying things like, "Finally, your hair is clean!" and, "So…did you wash your stinky clothes?" and "Hey, Playground Pig, did you take a shower, too?" Most of them chanted: "Playground Pig, Playground Pig" in singsong tones mixed with oinking sounds. I was so embarrassed and also hurt and surprised by some of the kids that participated in the crowd.

~

The shower and hair washing restrictions Hellen imposed on me caused untold humiliation. True to Hellen's patterns, the restrictions worsened over time. The 'home ec hair washing' was one of the most humiliating moments of my school years, including high school, where I had classes with those same girls. I am thankful that the school nurse gave me that bottle of shampoo and allowed me to retrieve a sliver of dignity. Maybe her decision couldn't work under the laws and guidelines in place today, but it was the best decision at the time.

Years later, I met and spoke with the home ec bullies when we attended our 30th high school reunion. Eleanor was the one who'd dumped the water on me. I approached her and told her it was good to see her. It truly was, for I was not the broken, dirty, depressed girl she'd bullied.

She didn't recognize me until I told her my name. Then, her expression hardened and she told me that she'd been married three times and had seven children.

Still smiling, I went on to introduce myself to the other bullies because I was not who they thought I was then.

Two weeks later, I received a phone call from one of the bullies. She told me that after the reunion, the women wondered why I'd spoken with them, and why I'd been nice to them.

I told her I held no grudges, and I was kind to them because that's the only way to be.

The woman persisted. I thought perhaps she didn't believe me. She asked, "So why where you nice when the *one chance* you had to really let us have it…you didn't. Why?"

"Because I'm not like any of you." Then I explained that I was living in an extremely abusive situation while the girls were bullying me, and there was no way they could have known that.

I did not expect her to tell me her own history of abuse, but she did. I recommended to her the counselors who'd helped me with my healing process. Greg and I offered her our guest room if she traveled back to Phoenix for counseling. She was stunned and thanked me saying, she'd 'give the offer consideration.'

∼

In April 1977, we moved into the four-bedroom house the Layton's owned. The enclosed carport was set up as a small apartment, so Hugh and Danny made it their shared bedroom. With all the room the new house provided, there was no excuse for me not to have my own place to sleep. I got my own bedroom, and finally, my own bed.

After years of having to sleep in Hellen's filthy bed, my own bed was a relief beyond measure. God had answered my prayers.

I asked Hellen if she would paint my room pink, and she did. She took me to the store and let me pick the perfect pastel shade. She furnished my room with a desk and a doll lamp from a yard sale. For a few days, I thought that I had started to be good enough that she could love me and be nice.

But I was wrong

After I got my own bedroom, I suffered from constant bouts of colds and allergy symptoms. Hellen wouldn't ever allow me to see a doctor. Instead, she decided there was something wrong with the carpet in my bedroom. She asked Tracy to help her rip out the carpet, and when they did; it created a huge cloud of dust. I was surprised to see almost an inch of dirt underneath. It took quite a while for them to sweep and mop up the mess, but there was pretty linoleum underneath the dirt.

1977: 13 Years Old

Hellen wouldn't let me help; she was concerned that I would get sick again. After the carpet was taken out of my room, my respiratory infections ceased.

~

After we moved back to Phoenix the year before, Hellen had rejoined the same church we had attended prior to moving to California.

The pastor was kind, but his wife tended to be moody.

Hellen loved the church and felt important because she played the clarinet on the platform during the music service. She lifted the clarinet high and played it like a trumpet. She wouldn't spend money on reeds, so she produced a lot of squeaking noises through each song. She was such a spectacle. I would've given anything to be able to disappear when she was playing. People snickered at her playing.

Tracy and I found her to be a constant source of embarrassment. She also had a horrible singing voice. I wondered if she'd even been asked to sing by the church officials; if they did, they had to be desperate for singers. Sometimes, Hellen sang special songs as solos, and she preferred, *Sheltered in the Arms of God*. She added a lot of drama while singing. She jerked her head around, twisted her face, squeezed her eyes shut, and slammed the podium with her fist at big moments in the song. Sometimes she got so dramatic, I worried her false teeth would fly out, but they never did.

I kind of hoped they would.

Tracy and I used to imitate her singing when we were alone. We would laugh until we doubled over. Sometimes we'd imitate her for so long that we'd get sore throats from hitting too many of Hellen's high notes.

~

With the fearful strain that is on me night and day,
if I did not laugh, I should die.
~ Abraham Lincoln

~

1977: 13 Years Old

Hellen was upset when Hugh and Danny quit going to church in their late teens. She thought it was tragic they were going to miss seeing God use her music and singing to bless everyone. I didn't see it and I was there.

~

Hellen often put her arm around me when we were in public, saying, "I love my baby girl so much. My baby is so important to me." Then she'd smile and kiss me with her nasty garlic breath.

Vomit rose in my throat each time as I was overwhelmed with repulsive thoughts. I couldn't stand her touch for even a moment, so I'd jerk my body away from her grasp. I felt confident she wouldn't backhand me in front of everyone.

Hellen would laugh off my reaction, saying, "Oh, baby. You know I love you."

As a matter of fact, I didn't know or understand her 'love.'

I hated the whole, public, phony baloney.

~

Hellen kept me isolated so I could not develop any close friendships. Yet, on rare occasions, she did allow me to go home with two girls from church. During each visit, I hoped Hellen would die while I was gone. I felt guilty when I thought about what a relief her dying would give me. I hated living in her house.

At the girls' house, I found it difficult to relate to their conversations. They had clothes, a dad, perfume, and even toothbrushes. I didn't fit in.

Hellen told me, "Everyone can see what a sorry person you are." So, I wondered, *why do these girls include me?* I feared, *if they knew what kind of person I really am, they wouldn't invite me back.* I wondered, *what have I done to make God mad because I don't have what other kids have— parents, food, clothes, grandparents, family vacations, or a toothbrush?*

~

By nature, I am curious. As a young teen, I watched with interest as my siblings grew and launched into adulthood. They were smart, and I believed, on a different, higher level in life and in God's eyes. I wished I could be like them. Hellen chose their career paths and expected that they would all be college graduates and pay for their own education. No exceptions. Hugh would be an attorney. Danny would be a diesel mechanic, and Tracy would be an accountant. Hellen even chose the schools from which they would 'graduate with honors.'

There were two problems with Hellen's plans. Hugh, Danny, and Tracy had no interest in Hellen's career choices for them. The second problem was that there was never any mention of me going to college.

I was too stupid.

~

By the summer of 1977, Hugh and Danny had both graduated high school, were working full time, and attending community college. I rarely saw them even though they still lived in the apartment at the house.

Danny began to have trouble with the eye injury he'd sustained as a young boy. The surgeries had helped, but when he entered adulthood, his vision began to blur.

Tracy worked full time as a waitress at a popular coffee shop, and she continued to work through her senior year of high school. The regular customers and staff loved her. Often, customers waited for her tables, even when others were available. When she came home from her job, I stayed up late each night to count her tips. We rolled the coins together.

I loved Tracy. Many times, she used her tip money to make sure I had something to eat. I made her bed and did parts of her homework for her…at least, the ones that I could understand. I read books for her and wrote her book reports. We were close, but I couldn't tell her about the things Hellen did to me. I believed Tracy would be disappointed in me for making Hellen so mad that she had to punish me. I didn't want to disappoint Tracy. Life was hard enough.

At night, in my bed, I would tremble, terrified that at any moment Hellen would call me into her bedroom. When it got to be too much,

I'd tiptoe into Tracy's room, and tell her that I was cold. She had a heated, twin-size waterbed, and she'd throw the covers back and I'd crawl in next to her, watching her face as she slept. In those moments, I felt that Tracy was the most perfect person God ever created. With tears running onto the pillow, I'd beg God to remake me, so I could be like her. I felt safe only when I slept in her bed. When I was in Tracy's room, Hellen never called me into her room. It took constant diligence to get to Tracy's room before Hellen called.

My fears were not idle. For years, Hellen threatened to wake me up by yanking me out of bed by my hair in the middle of the night if she thought of something I'd done wrong. Before going to sleep every night, I'd take a thorough mental inventory of the day. I went to sleep for years being afraid I'd overlooked something important.

Always, always afraid.

One night, Hellen woke Tracy by dragging her out of her bed by her hair. I don't know what Tracy did, or if she had done anything, but it was the only time I know of that Hellen got physically violent with Tracy.

~

I gained a degree of independence in June 1977, when Hellen allowed me to attend a week-long Bible camp 90 miles north of Phoenix. It was a life changing experience. The camp counselors said God loved me and would listen to me if I prayed. I believed them, so I tried it. I discovered I liked praying and the peace it brought to me.

Then, they said God would fill me with His Spirit and always be with me, if I wanted. I wanted that, too.

One evening after a church service at the camp, I stood alone on a dark, seldom used bridge, and wept. It was a cleansing cry, as I asked, *God, why would You love a bad girl like me?* With tears streaming down my face, I thought about the bad things I did at home, how I'd abandoned Herbie, my constant stupidity, how I messed up everything, and how I hated my mother.

1977: 13 Years Old

I wondered, *God, if You could love me, why would You want to? What's in it for You? You could love good kids and not have to work at it.*

While crying alone on that dark bridge, I asked, *God please forgive me for being stupid, for messing up everything, for the bad stuff that happens in Hellen's bed, and for abandoning Herbie.* Sobbing, I poured my heart into one simple prayer, *please God, help me not to hate my mother.*

The night was cool, and as the breeze shifted in the pine trees, I felt a sense of calm settle over me. I stopped crying, but hiccupped. Inhaling the scent of pine trees, I stood there feeling real peace for the first time in my life.

The tears began to flow again, but this time in gratitude. I couldn't imagine why God would help someone like me, but that night I knew He was. The happy tears felt good.

I left the camp a changed young girl. I had been able to let go of the hatred and some of anger I felt towards Hellen. The experience with God gave me hope for the first time. I began to read the Book of Psalms and found comfort in it. I read that David, the young shepherd facing the giant Goliath, cried–and God helped him. I read Psalms over and over, hoping that God would see my tears and help me, too.

I innocently believed my experience at camp would help me be better. I thought, *now I'll have God to help me be good.* I felt a definite strength that I hadn't had before, and I believed God was helping me.

Traveling 90 miles to Bible camp and staying in a dorm for a week without Hellen gave me a break from her control and isolation. I needed the time to catch my breath and gain some perspective. I believe God honored my childlike faith in prayer and fasting, though I didn't quite understand the concepts. I believed God would rescue me. At that point in my life, I didn't know how quickly my rescue was coming.

It was going to be soon. If only I could have known...

~

Hellen had been brutal with the abuse before, but after the special time

1977: 13 Years Old

at camp, my life became more difficult. Hellen developed a specific style of beating me that she truly enjoyed. It is still hard for me to describe.

Our house had an unusually long hallway. It led to four bedrooms, two bathrooms, a linen closet, and a large closet for the heating unit.

The beatings usually began when Hellen yelled, "Wilma! Get down here at the end of the hallway. Now! I don't have all day!"

I had to stop what I was doing, even if I was in the bathroom, and scurry to the end of the hall.

Hellen stood at the end of the hall, hands on hips. "Stand up straight against the wall," she ordered. "Make your shoulders, butt, and legs touch the wall." I obeyed as ordered, terrified of what she planned.

"Now. Don't make me repeat myself you idiot. You listening?" Nodding my head quickly, afraid to move it away from the wall, I trembled looking at the long hallway in front of me.

Even after experiencing years of Hellen's cruelty, I was caught by surprise the first time she sneered, "I've decided it's time to beat some sense into your idiotic skull. Bend over, put your head by your knees, hands by your ankles. Don't you dare rear up at me!"

Terror fails to describe my fear as I bent down, hips and legs touching the wall as instructed, my long, brown hair lying on the dirty floor. I wondered what Hellen was going to do.

Taking me by total surprise, Hellen grabbed fistfuls of my long hair, swinging my head in extended arches to the left, then to the right, ricocheting my head with each swing–back and forth, back and forth–hitting one portion of the wall and bouncing across to another. It was very painful, especially when my head rammed door jambs, or doorknobs. Hellen dragged me the entire length of the long hallway, keeping me bent low to the floor, as I stumbled in agony the whole way. Each time I tried to stand up, she'd pummel my head with one fist, while pulling my hair out with the other.

1977: 13 Years Old

When I fell to the floor, I heard my hair ripping out as she yanked me to my feet.

Large clumps of hair fell in heaps to the floor, as I stumbled down the hall. When beating me, Hellen yelled, cussed, and…oddly enough…quoted scriptures.

I was still bent down, doubled over, when we'd reach the end of the hallway. While pounding my shoulders and neck with her fists, she'd shove me to the kitchen floor. Breathing hard, I'd lay there in a heap, sobbing and in extreme pain.

Everything hurt. My mind, body, and soul.

I was stunned the first time she beat me that way. I thought Hellen was done when she threw me to the kitchen floor. Instead, while yelling vicious insults, she poured new strength into hefty kicks aimed at my hips and lower back.

The pain was so extreme, it took my breath away. The blows to my head made the room spin. I was nauseous. I thought I was going to die.

"Get up you sorry excuse for a daughter! You whore! You worthless piece of trash!" The kicks, screams, and cusswords kept coming, blow after blow to my back.

Somehow, I realized she wouldn't quit until I stood up. As fast as possible, I scrambled to my feet. My hair, tangled and matted with tears and snot, stuck to my face, but I could see Hellen's face. It was filled with disgust as she pointed down the hallway.

My glasses had come off when she was beating me in the hallway, so I squinted in the direction she pointed. I thought, "That can't be what it looks like." But…it was–several large piles of hair. My glasses lay near the first pile of hair she'd ripped out.

Hellen pointed, her arm outstretched, fat swinging where a bicep lay hidden. Her breath came in loud gasps, her face deep crimson. Breaking through my bewilderment, she leaned forward and spit in my face. Still pointing, she hollered, "Go sweep up your nasty, godforsaken hair!"

1977: 13 Years Old

Disoriented, dizzy, in pain, and completely terrorized, I looked around, and grabbed the broom and went down the hallway. She stared at me, breathing hard, while I swept the hall and emptied the dustpan in the trash. I was trembling, wondering if she was done, or just beginning.

As soon as the hall was clean, she spoke in a normal voice, "If you weren't so stupid, I wouldn't have to beat sense into you. Can't you see that I just can't put up with your idiocy anymore? You're just too stupid to appreciate the great mother God has bestowed upon you. You really need to be like Tracy. Now there's a winner. Now, I'm going out for dinner before work tonight. Stay here and keep the doors locked. And don't cause me any trouble."

Moments later, she left for work. When I was sure she was gone and not coming back, I limped over to the trashcan. I lifted out the piles of hair. Each pile was about the size of the palm of my hand and there were six or seven of them. I just stared. *That was my hair. What did I do to deserve that? How can she act so normal after that? How can she go out to dinner and leave me with no food in the house? What did I do to upset her?*

I felt dizzy, with a splitting headache. I hurt all over. Touching my head, I discovered my scalp was bleeding. The next few days it remained swollen, and I couldn't brush my long hair. It hurt to lay my head on a pillow. For school, I smoothed my hair to one side and held it in place with a barrette. I hoped the kids wouldn't notice.

They did.

~

The beatings happened once or twice a week, rarely less, often more. They followed the same pattern. I never figured out what made them start or how to make them stop. The only relief was that she always left the house when it was over.

Like the aftershock of enema nights, I felt mute with pain. It was too hard to form words, so I didn't try. I cried myself to sleep every time. Sleep brought small relief from the emotional and physical pain.

1977: 13 Years Old

I believed the things Hellen said about me. I felt bad that I had done wrong, although I didn't know what I did wrong. As much as I tried to never cry, the beatings undid my resolve every time. Like the food games, shower restrictions and sexual abuse, the beatings escalated in intensity and frequency as time went on.

The one thing that stands out in my mind is that though I tried to protect myself from her fists, never once did I raise a hand to hit her back.

I still do not understand why.

~

My body continued its natural development through puberty as Hellen's perverted interest in those changes escalated. I loathed the changes. In addition to her daily lewd comments about my developing curves, she began to grab my body as I walked by her. It annoyed Hellen that her attention and touch repulsed me. The irritation escalated until Hellen decided to punish me for my obvious disgust towards her.

It is an understatement to say–it was horrific.

~

One scorching July day, Hellen devised a new punishment that traumatized and further shattered my world. It is painful to describe.

I was in the house alone with Hellen, attempting to walk past her in the hallway, when she blocked me from passing her. She made obscene comments about my body then reached out and groped me. I was scared and uncomfortable. I tried different ways of handling her remarks. While I slowly backed away, I tried joking with her, pushing her hands away, ignoring her, and getting angry (that wasn't hard), but nothing worked.

Hellen kept on, pawing at me until I couldn't take it anymore. I became angry, but she didn't get angry back. Her lack of response puzzled me.

She abruptly stopped, walked to the end hallway, and in a quiet voice said, "Come in here."

1977: 13 Years Old

I swallowed hard as she walked into her filthy, roach-infested bedroom.

In her room, Hellen ordered me to stand at the foot of her bed, face her dresser, arms at my sides, feet shoulder width apart. My heart pounded in fear. She was too calm. Something bad was about to happen.

Speaking in military-style clips, she ordered me to take off all my clothes.

I was stunned. This was worse than I could have imagined. In an effort to buy time and desperate to find an escape, I pleaded, "Mom!" The horror I was feeling sounded in my voice. I spoke in a high-pitch I barely recognized. My heart was pounding hard.

Hellen had a fierce look accompanying her stern, masculine voice. When she used both, any argument would escalate the situation. Three hundred pounds and towering over me by several inches, she looked me in the eye, and ordered, "I said. Take. Off. ALL. Your. Clothes. Now!"

Keeping my eyes fastened on her, trembling, I slowly began unbuttoning my blouse. She nodded, smirked, saying, "Oh. You want to make a game of it do you? Okay. Game it IS. Now. I. Said. Take. Off. All. Your. Clothes. And. I. Mean. Fast! Hurry up you godforsaken loser!"

Smack! My head reeled to the side with the force of her slap to my face. The swelling in my lips and face began and I had that all-too-familiar coppery taste of blood in my mouth.

I scrambled out of my skirt and blouse, but when I stopped, still wearing my underclothes, she slapped and pounded my head and face with her fists. She cussed as she pushed my hair out of my eyes, (ripping it out in the process), to spit in my face. I tried hard to get the rest of my clothes off, but I couldn't see with my mouth and nose bleeding. My hair was a tangled mess and her spit dripped off my face.

I screamed, "STOP IT! MOM, STOP! OH MY GOD, MAKE HER STOP!!"

1977: 13 Years Old

Abruptly, she stopped. Chest heaving, her breath coming hard, she barked, "Now. Do as I told you."

Sobbing, I removed my underclothes.

"Stand up straight."

Immediately I obeyed, but she reared back, slamming both of her fists into my shoulders, pinning them back. She shoved me so forcefully that I fell backward against her bed, catching myself at the last moment. She laughed that I'd almost lost my balance.

Hellen walked around looking me up and down, inspecting my body. She smiled, as she viewed the changes in my body without the hindrance of clothing.

As tears streamed down my face, my body wracked with sobs, I stood mute while she walked back and forth and scrutinized me.

I felt like a used car for sale as she fondled, pinched, and petted me. When she pinched my body, she'd twist before she released my skin. The painful twists left red marks all over me.

Standing in front of her, humiliated beyond words, I found it difficult to breathe. My face hot with anger and crushing shame, I have never felt more worthless, more powerless, in my life.

I stood there at the edge of hell, facing Hellen.

Indescribable.

After an agonizing 20 minutes or so, Hellen ended her inspection with disparaging remarks about how fat and ugly I was.

"I've seen enough. Get the hell out of my room." She ordered.

I scrambled to grab my clothes. Hellen laughed.

I hurried across the hall to my room. I felt filthy and desperately wanted a shower.

My heart pounded and my mind raced for hours. I couldn't calm myself down as my mind replayed the horror of what she'd done. I was terrified to go to sleep.

Later, I felt unusually sore; it was different from the beatings. When I looked, I had purple bruises all over where Hellen had pinched me.

1977: 13 Years Old

I hated Hellen for making me stand for her inspection. She was evil, perverted and I hated her guts.

Yet, the hate I felt towards her didn't compare with the utter contempt I felt inside.

I hated my body for changing and developing in a way that she enjoyed. I had watched with disgust as the changes occurred.

I felt betrayed not only by my mother, but my own body as well.

I was 13 years old. I absolutely loathed my body and myself.

~

Words fail to describe the devastation the strip searches caused in my mind. Of all the sexual abuse Hellen inflicted on me, the strip searches were by far the worst. The rest of the sexual abuse had its own effects, yet I managed a degree of shutdown, or experienced a drugged fog. For the strip searches, I was fully awake, fully aware, fully terrorized.

Once Hellen realized the terror the strip searches caused, they became a regular part of my world. There was no way I could hide my humiliation and shame.

I learned that showing my anger made any situation more difficult. I felt stupid when I couldn't contain my anger because it made Hellen's punishments so much worse.

How much can I take...before I explode?

I was boiling with anger inside. I was scared that if I started punching someone, I'd kill them.

The strip searches were the hardest thing I've had to endure, survive and eventually forgive. And they are by far the hardest thing to include in this memoir.

~

Years later, after Hellen died, I stood alone in the county morgue looking at her face through the partially unzipped body bag. I went there for one reason alone. I had to see with my own eyes that the torturer I had called mom was dead. Hellen would never order me to

1977: 13 Years Old

the edge of hell again. She was finally dead. I saw her dead with my own eyes and I wept with relief.

I know that I did my best to survive the hellish environment she created. Hellen's fantasies and perversions constantly threw curve balls that I did not have the knowledge or maturity to navigate around.

Writing this manuscript now, 40 years later, I cry. I know God kept my sanity intact. I am so thankful.

Only God, and I do mean *only* God, was able to preserve my sanity. Without Him, I'd have lost my mind.

~

Hellen worked diligently to make sure I knew I had no rights to human dignity. No privacy. Whether she was laughing, angry, violent, or perverted it didn't matter–because I didn't matter.

Hellen had so many twisted sexual fantasies that made no sense to me, then or now. The bruises and swellings after the beatings seemed to arouse sexual feelings in her. Though no detail is warranted here, I continue to mention her sexual abuse because of its constant, ongoing nature. It wore me down, wearied my mind, twisted my emotions, depleted my hope of a brighter tomorrow–of *any tomorrows*.

The drugs, the torture, the strip searches, lying in her bed. The roaches.

I had no dignity. I had nothing left.

I sunk further, if further was even possible, into a dark world of depression.

Death sounded like a picnic compared to life.

I was ready for a picnic.

1977: 13 Years Old

*Phoenix, Arizona
Wilma – 13 years old.*

I have to smile or mom will be mad.

I hope my dirty, greasy hair doesn't show.

*Maybe no one will notice
the big clump of hair
missing above my left ear
...but how could they not?*

1977: 13 Years Old

~ Counseling Notes ~

*We can't hate ourselves into a
version of ourselves we can love.*
~ Lori Deschene

~

I mentioned the embarrassing way I met the Laytons.

The counselors said, "God put the Laytons right there that morning to help you. It was a miracle that God worked to help the family purchase the home. Though horrible things happened in that house, it temporarily stopped all of Hellen's middle of the night moves. It provided stability just long enough for all four you to be able to get out."

~

I asked about the home ec hair washing and what I could have done different.

They said, "It was a nasty prank and seventh-grade girls can be terrible about that kind of thing. The administration appears to have handled it as best they could have considering their known fear of Hellen. Unfortunately for you, she was able to manipulate professionals and you suffered. The school nurse did take bold action that would not be allowed today. And because of the skyrocketing abuse we have now, the laws have changed. I don't know what you could have done differently at the

1977: 13 Years Old

time. You weren't allowed showers. You were under a lot of stress and no doubt suffering depression. The courage you showed then and later at your high school reunion is commendable."

~

Although it was decades later, I still cried when I talked about getting my first bed.

The counselors said, "There is no explanation for her actions. Hellen crossed many lines with the abuse. She crossed the line here into emotional torture regarding a bed of your own. She deliberately withheld a bed from you until you were 13 because she had the *power* to do so. That is cruel and intentional emotional torture. She *gave away many* beds."

~

I asked why Hellen would break her pattern and allow me to travel to Bible camp ninety miles away for a week. She had never allowed it before that time.

They said, "We are not sure, but one of your siblings said that Hellen had plans that weekend and wanted you gone. Whether or not her plans worked out, we will never know. Whatever the reason, God worked it out for you. He gave you time to gain some perspective, meet some friends, and get some much-needed rest. Best of all, He gave you His Spirit and the peace you asked for. You said yourself, that you came back a changed girl."

~

I asked why the sudden, drastic change in the beatings, in the hallway. The severity and frequency was frightening.

1977: 13 Years Old

The counselors said, "I would imagine Hellen saw the change, the peace, the newfound strength, and hated what she saw. I believe that brought a whole host of new punishments, and though you had normal reactions, you did not succumb. You're a miracle. You're a survivor."

~

Though painful to discuss, I asked why an abuser would order a strip search. What was the point? Especially when it was repeated constantly.

The counselors said, "They were horrific. They were mental, emotional, physical and sexual torture. The strip searches alone would have caused your PTSD. All the blame is on Hellen. Any self-hate, self-loathing, self-blame–the root is misidentifying the enemy. These things are done to achieve and maintain control. It is deliberately intended to debase, dehumanize, demean, and to strip the victim of their very own identity.

It is active, intentional torment and torture. When the abuse goes on for a long time, the child is completely powerless to speak about it until it is over. They simply cannot do it. The mind control the abuser has achieved over them is more powerful than handcuffs, and chains, so he doesn't have to use them. That is what your mother did to you. Total mind control, convincing you that you had no choice. That's how she enslaved you. You were dehumanized, literally stripped of your identity, and you did what you had to do to survive. If your mother were sentenced to prison, she would do life. Really, that kind of abuse should get the death penalty."

1978: 14 Years Old

*At such a moment, it is not the physical pain which hurts the most.
It is the mental agony caused by the injustice,
the unreasonableness of it all.*
~ Viktor Frankl, Author, *A Man's Search for Meaning*

The Times

In 1978, American artist Norman Rockwell died, 900 members of Jim Jones' Peoples Temple cult committed mass suicide in Guyana by drinking poisoned Kool-Aid, and I began to wonder if Hellen was truly going to kill me.

Good times were few but one special memory stands out.

One early summer morning, before Tracy went to work, we both wanted to go out and do something. There was not much to do that was free, and we couldn't afford to spend any money. It is hot in Phoenix in the summer, so we quickly ruled out a hike up the nearby mountain. On a whim, I asked Tracy if we could go to the park, just two blocks away and play hopscotch. It was my favorite childhood game. To my surprise, she said yes. We went and the park had painted a hopscotch outline under the shaded roof of the community center. We were happy about that. I don't know how long we played, or who won, but we laughed a lot and had a great time. And it was free and it made my day. Tracy was so kind to me.

But the joy was short-lived when Hellen arrived home.

1978: 14 Years Old

~

I thought we were having a quiet evening. Hellen, Tracy, and I were home and I was in my room, writing.

For reasons still unknown, Hellen went into the apartment that Hugh and Danny shared. After snooping through their belongings, she came into the house cussing and yelling, "I found a joint and a condom. Bless God, my sons will not live in my house with this sinful garbage! I'm a Christian, after all!"

Hellen ordered me to haul everything my brothers owned out into the front yard: their underwear, dressers, clothes, yearbooks, shoes, beds, everything. Hellen watched while I lifted their furniture, but she did not seem to notice how sad I was. When I finished, the front yard was a big mess and the apartment was empty. I swept their apartment and walked into the house. It was 10 p.m. I clearly remember the exact time.

I went to my room. I was afraid of Hellen's mood, and for a moment, I leaned my head on the door jamb, sad about my brothers being thrown out. I felt safer with them around the house.

What a big mistake. I should have closed the door.

Hellen walked past my room and noticed me. Without one word, without any warning, she flew into a violent rage. A rage like I had never witnessed in my life.

In a flash, I was violently thrown to the floor with Hellen's fingers entangled in my hair. Then Hellen dragged me by my hair to the other end of the hallway, yanking me to my feet by my hair and slammed me against the wall. I could barely breathe. I was so scared.

"Stand up straight," she ordered. "I said *straight* you idiot! Make your shoulders, butt, and legs touch the wall. Now!" I obeyed as ordered, terrified of what was coming.

Barking like a drill sergeant in her deep masculine voice, she commanded.

1978: 14 Years Old

"Bend over, put your head by your knees, hands by your ankles. Don't you dare fight me!"

Terrified, I bent down, hips and legs pressed against the wall as instructed, my dirty long brown hair lying on the dirty floor.

Hellen grabbed large fistfuls of my hair, violently swinging my head in arches to the left, then right, ricocheting my head with each swing–back and forth, back and forth–hitting one side of the wall and bouncing across to another. The jerking back and forth hurt my neck, made it snap, pop and later ache. It was very painful, when my head rammed door jambs, or doorknobs. At one point, I cried out in pain as a hard edge of a door and the side of my ear met. My glasses were lost somewhere in the hall, everything was blurry and I was so terrified.

She had beaten me before, but this time was different. I felt as though I couldn't breathe. The pain was extreme and Hellen seemed to gain strength as the beating wore on, while I stumbled and fell more often.

Everything hurt. Hellen was pounding my head with her fist and I could feel her holding my hair tight with her other hand. Bent low, I saw white lights and felt dizzy. The blows to my head made the room spin. I was nauseous. I thought I was going to die.

"Get up you sorry excuse for a daughter! You worthless piece of trash!" The fists, kicks, cusswords and scriptures kept coming now, with the punches to my back and hips.

The beating dragged on and on. Instead of wearing down, Hellen seemed to be *gaining* momentum.

Tracy screamed, "STOP, Mom, STOP! You're hurting her! STOP!" Tracy was sobbing.

I could hear her, but I couldn't see her. She kept screaming but her screams didn't seem to faze Hellen.

I don't know how many times Hellen dragged me up and down that long hallway. It was surreal that night. It was going on so long that I began to notice numbness as my face swelled. The brutality she used as she beat my head and face into the walls and doors, yanked fistfuls of my hair out, and punched and kicked me is beyond explanation or comprehension.

Hellen maintained a constant flow of cusswords, ridicule and scripture quoting as she hauled me up and down the hallway.

That night, the hallway felt five miles long.

Each time I got up after stumbling, she pounded my head with her fist, while pulling my hair out with the other. A few times she pushed my hair out of eyes and spit in my face. (Besides being gross, it was insulting and humiliating. It was compounded because it was my mother.)

Exhausted, I stumbled and fell once again. Hellen kicked my left hip several times and wouldn't quit until finally I crawled back up onto my feet.

This was dragging on too long and too intense. I knew I was hurt but I didn't know how much damage Hellen was doing to my body. I knew my mouth was swollen, parts of it felt numb and I could taste blood. My face was throbbing and swollen by my left ear from the door jamb and I knew my scalp was swollen. My shoulders hurt from being slammed into the doors and walls, and my back and hips hurt from Hellen's fists and kicks. These thoughts raced through my mind like a sporadic kind of inventory...while Hellen continued to beat me in the hall.

When Hellen had beaten me at other times, I had tried not to cry. But tonight, was different in every way. Tonight, I was sobbing, even openly weeping. Outwardly, begging her to stop. Silently, begging for my life. (Even in that moment, I refused to give Hellen the satisfaction of begging for my life. I silently prayed and that is as far as I'd go.)

At some point, I can only say it was near the end, I was beginning to panic. I clearly remember wondering, *is this how I'm going to die?*

1978: 14 Years Old

and seconds later, *is this the **night** I'm going to die?*

It was by far the worst beating I'd ever had.

Tracy screamed, cried, and begged Hellen to stop. But it was as if Tracy was not even there.

Finally, Tracy's screams got through to Hellen.

Hellen stopped, chest heaving, and appeared to notice Tracy's distress.

Breathing hard, Hellen stepped back, red faced. The beating appeared to be over.

~

I lay in a bloody heap. Some hair covered my face; some was in clumps on the floor. My teeth, mouth, eyes, ears and lips felt weird. Swollen and numb.

"Get UP! Don't just lie there, you filthy piece of garbage. Clean up the mess you made, for God's sake."

I lay there for a moment. It hurt to breathe. I thought I couldn't move.

"I said, *get up now!* Or, I'll make you wish you had!"

Hellen began kicking my lower back, shoulders, and head, whatever she pleased with her hard nurse's shoes.

"I said, *get up! Now!*"

I slowly got to my feet. I was bloodied, bruised, several teeth had been knocked loose, and a lot of hair was ripped out, but I was alive. Barely. As I worked to steady myself, I caught sight of the big clock again. It was 10:33. Hellen had beaten me for a full 30 minutes. I reached for the broom and dustpan. My arm moved funny. It felt odd. Sprained and bruised.

I knew what I had to do next.

Then Hellen looked surprised that Tracy was crying. "What's your problem?" she asked. Then she backed up, squinted at Tracy and said, "What in hell's the matter *with you?*"

"Mom! Wilma didn't do anything! Look! Mom! You hurt her!"

"Ah. No, I didn't. And so what if I did? The little snot needs some correction once in a while. Just because she's the baby of the family doesn't mean I can neglect my duties as her mother."

Tracy stared at Hellen, speechless.

Sweeping up the piles of hair in the hallway, I knew Hellen and Tracy were watching me. I tried to hurry, but I was in more pain than ever before. I couldn't focus. I found my glasses just inside Tracy's bedroom. With my glasses I could see better, though the swelling around my eyes was making the cleanup job harder.

My brothers arrived half an hour later and saw their belongings in the front yard. They loaded their stuff into a car as Hellen quoted scriptures, "Be sure your sins will find you out."

Watching them drive away was one of the saddest moments of my childhood.

Hugh and Danny got an apartment together and they almost never visited Hellen's house. I missed them both. I struggled to understand how she could do such a thing to Hugh and Danny. They were smart and good. I was stupid and ugly. *If she could do that to them, what more would she do to me?*

I didn't know the extent of my injuries after the beating that night. I was in extreme pain for several days. It hurt to breathe. We had no Tylenol or aspirin and I didn't dare ask for any. I skipped school and church because I had 'the flu.'

~

Years later, Tracy still remembers that beating; the helplessness she felt as she watched Hellen's brutality taken out on me and her efforts to make Hellen stop.

~

With my brothers out of our lives, Hellen continued the sexual abuse. The large bruises and swellings from the beatings appeared to excite her in some twisted way. Within just three or four days after she threw my brothers out, she began beating me again when I was alone with her. Since I was still recovering from the severe beating that Tracy had witnessed, I was unable to even try to protect myself from anything else Hellen did to me. The pain was unbelievably severe. Even now, 40 years later, I struggle to adequately describe the brutality and force Hellen used when physically beating me.

∼

Even after my experience at camp, I figured God allowed the beatings because I needed them. I repented many times for all my unknown sins. I so wanted to please the Lord, and I recognized that not only was I failing to please Him, I was so incredibly stupid that I couldn't figure out how to be good. I thought surely if I prayed more, I could be a better daughter. I felt like a complete failure in life. Hellen told me that God was on her side and I believed her.

I hated being bad.

I hated being me.

Hellen often looked towards heaven and asked, "What did I ever do to God that He would stick me with a sorry excuse for a daughter like you?"

I never knew what to say, but in my mind, I asked, *what did you do to God that He gave you someone like me?* I wanted to know. I was sorry I was such a burden to her, to God, and to everyone. No matter what part of my life I examined, I found no success, only failure.

I wanted to die.

As far as I knew, with the exception of Tracy, I mattered to absolutely no one.

∼

In May 1978, I was riding my bicycle to school, when I was hit head-on by a car. Thrown over the car's hood, I landed in the middle of the street. A school bus driver witnessed the accident, stopped his bus, and helped me. I was injured all over; my head, shoulder, hip and

1978: 14 Years Old

ankle. An off-duty police officer helped me into his car to wait until help arrived.

Shaking and crying, I looked around for the bicycle and saw it lying in the road, crushed and folded in half under the front of the car. I knew Hellen would be angry.

The officer called Hellen at work, and described my injuries. She refused to allow an ambulance. The officer tried to reason with her, stating that I probably needed x-rays, medical attention, and possibly stitches, but she told him to wait and she would come get me.

I was scared I was in trouble with Hellen, but instead I was embarrassed by the way she treated the officer and me. In a loud whisper, she explained that she could never allow me to go to the hospital. I overheard her and wondered what she was talking about.

The officer seemed annoyed and asked, "What do you mean, ma'am?"

Hellen glanced around as if making sure their conversation was private, then loudly whispered, "She does this stuff all the time for attention."

Of course I heard her and thought, *what...does she really think I did this on purpose?*

I saw the officer shake his head in disbelief as Hellen continued, "Oh, you wouldn't believe the extent this girl will go to for attention. I'll tell you, this girl's gonna be the death of me."

The officer looked at me and I put my head down. I was so embarrassed.

Hellen told him she would take me to a doctor.

He asked me if I was okay with that.

I nodded.

~

I was surprised when Hellen did take me to her family doctor. Hellen said he was a "spineless fellow, a real jellyfish of a man" who was intimidated by her, and he appeared to be. She told him she had already checked me out, but she needed him to document for the insurance company that I had a sprained ankle.

He never looked at my road burns, shoulder, or hip injuries. He did just as she told him. He sent me home with an elastic bandage and said, "Be careful out there."

A few weeks after the accident, I finished eighth grade and looked forward to high school in the fall. I hoped that since it was a bigger school, maybe I could get away from the elementary school kids and their constant taunting. I wanted to have some friends.

By the time Hellen received the insurance settlement money for my bicycle accident, summer was sizzling hot in Phoenix and I was on summer break. Hellen said, "I finally get to have some cash to relax and enjoy a few things in life. Thank God He saw fit to bless me with this insurance settlement."

"Mom? You are going to buy me a new bike, right? I mean…I need a bike to get to school and back."

"Nah. You can walk. God gave you two legs. Use 'em for a change."

Walking would take much longer; I could barely pedal a bicycle to school after a beating. I didn't think I could walk and carry my books when my body was bruised from the beatings. I had to think of something–I needed a bicycle.

"Mom?"

"WHAT!"

"I'm sure you remember, but that wasn't my bicycle that was wrecked."

"What do you mean?"

"It was Tracy's. I don't own a bicycle. Remember? Tracy's been letting me borrow her bike to ride to school."

"Oh. That's right. Well, you sure know how to mess things up! People loan you their nice things and you trash 'em. Well, I'll not stand by and allow that. Now I have to step in and pick up after you once again. I wonder who's gonna do it for you after I'm dead and gone? Really, Wilma, you're gonna have to take responsibility at some point in your idiotic life. You just can't have someone running behind you, fixing every single thing you mess up, and believe you me, you mess up every single thing."

She paused and said, "I'll replace Tracy's bike. Not the fancy expensive thing she loaned you. Nobody has any business wasting money on something like that. That'll teach Tracy a lesson there, but I'll replace it. It's the least I can do. God knows she's helped me bear the burden of you through the years. Tracy will get her bike back."

Hellen bought a cheap bicycle and Tracy was kind about it, never mentioning her own loss.

~

Over summer vacation, Tracy was taking an English class in summer school. English was my best subject. I did her homework for her while she worked full time. I was happy when she received an A for the class.

~

That summer marked a pivotal change in my life. Hellen's punishments were taking a toll on me with restrictions on showering, hair washing, and the inability to wash my own clothes. The food games, the beatings, the strip searches, and the sexual abuse all grew worse by the day. Yet, I worked harder to please Hellen, to make her happy, and to show her I was trying to be good. I tried to obey Hellen's rules, I lied to people about my injuries, I didn't have any boyfriends (I wasn't allowed), I didn't backtalk, and I didn't steal (like she did), even though I was hungry. I attended her church faithfully, I kept the house neat, and I read chapters in the Book of Psalms each day.

Because I'd learned about fasting and prayer at Bible camp, when Hellen deprived me of food, I thought of it as a fast. I prayed fervently that God would help me not to be stupid. I did hide food I'd

1978: 14 Years Old

purchased with my babysitting money, and I did pray. And at times I did sneak a shower and wash my clothes out in the sink. I didn't know how those things deserved the 'discipline' Hellen said they did...but at other times, confused as I was, I figured she was the parent, and she was probably right.

I wondered what was causing Hellen to increase the amount or severity of the strip searches, shower/hair washing restrictions, food games, sexual abuse, hallway beatings, etc.

I lived in daily, constant pain. Every area of my life, everywhere I looked, I felt pain. I didn't know what to do. I certainly didn't think it could get any worse.

I was so wrong.

I cried every day and every night. The despondency dragged me down like quicksand, further into the dark, shutting down of my mind. I felt anger simmering just under the surface, and my biggest fear haunted me day and night.

~

My biggest fear was not of being beaten. My biggest fear was, *what if on the inside I am just like Hellen? Would I hurt my children too?*

~

To pass the long, lonely summer days, I jumped at the chance when Hellen referred me for my first full-time babysitting job. We lived close to an apartment building, and I was offered a job to babysit a 2½-year-old girl. For nine hours of babysitting, I could earn three dollars a day, five days a week. I was thrilled.

When I told Hellen about the offer, she said, "You're going to have to babysit the brat here at the house. Minorities live in those apartments, and I don't want you over there. No telling what crazy ideas those folks will put in your head."

I didn't tell the child's mother why I couldn't babysit at her apartment. I just told her the rules were that I had to babysit at our

1978: 14 Years Old

house. The mother was fine with the arrangement and the little girl and I settled into a routine that we both seemed to enjoy.

I've often wondered why Hellen insisted the little girl had to be watched at the house instead of her apartment. Looking back, I hope Hellen wasn't molesting the child in the early morning hours after her mother dropped her off.

I will never know.

The little girl and I had fun together. I read her stacks of books, we played hide and seek, and we played dolls together. She threw fits sometimes, but I managed to settle her down with a book, a toy, or a treat. I felt proud when I rocked her to sleep for a nap. She seemed happy in my care, and I was happy too. She helped me pass the long summer days and got my mind off the constant pain in my body.

I was proud that I had a job and hoped Hellen noticed that I was working and earning money, like my siblings.

Hellen didn't notice.

Three weeks into the babysitting routine, we had a very bad day.

Hellen noticed that.

~

It is hard to fail, but it is worse never to have tried to succeed.
~ Theodore Roosevelt

~

The morning began when I got up around 5:45 a.m. to the little girl crying and in a cranky mood. Hellen had been with her since she had been dropped off around 5:00 a.m. Hellen left for work a few minutes later.

It was a rough start to the day. I had a terrible headache from a beating the night before and I was in a lot of pain. The little girl threw tantrum after tantrum; her breakfast food went flying, she constantly wet her pants, and hit me when I washed her and changed her. I tried rocking her; it didn't help. I couldn't get her to take a nap, and by

1978: 14 Years Old

the time lunch was over, we were both frazzled. I had no experience handling an upset, cranky child on my own. Her screaming and crying wouldn't stop. I felt like crying, too.

I picked her up and sat her on my lap to calm her down. She flailed and wanted down, so I put her down. Then, she ran towards the kitchen rubbing the tears from her eyes and tripped and fell, slamming her hands and face on the flagstone entryway. Then, she really screamed and cried. I picked her up and checked her face and hands after the fall. There were red marks on her face and hands. I didn't know what to do to help her.

By then, it was two in the afternoon. I realized that she had been cranky, crying, and throwing tantrums for hours. I figured she was tired and probably hungry since she had thrown her breakfast and lunch on the floor. I had never seen her like this, and I truly didn't know how to calm her down.

I'd seen Hellen get stern with little kids, so I got stern. I sat her on my lap and told her to listen to what I had to say. That only made things worse.

As she flailed in my lap, I cradled her against my body. She stiffened and cried.

I'd seen Hellen lightly slap little kids in the face "to get their attention," so I tried lightly slapping the left side of her face, one time. It shocked her, so I did it two or three more times.

Then I stopped.

She screamed and stiffened her body as I continued to cradle her. In just a few minutes, she settled and though still softly crying, she relaxed and went to sleep in my arms. Relieved, I dozed off while still holding her.

Just before her mother was to arrive, we both woke up. I was alarmed when I noticed faint bruising on both sides of her face. I held her fingers and mine against the bruises. They were faint enough that it was hard to tell which one of our hands left the marks. Was it from her fall on the flagstone or my slapping her? Either was possible or both, but I hoped it wasn't from me. I felt horrible and I tried to put an ice pack on the bruising, but she wouldn't let me hold it there.

At first, her mother didn't notice the bruising when she arrived to pick her up at the end of the day. Then, just before leaving, she noticed. When asked, I told her the child had fallen on the flagstone earlier in the afternoon. She accepted the explanation, but said she would call Hellen to ask her to look at it.

Tracy arrived home and sensed something was wrong. I didn't know what to do, or say so I said nothing.

A short time later, Hellen picked me and Tracy up and we went to the apartment. The little girl sat on her mother's lap as Hellen examined the child's face, and then she hopped over onto my lap. Hellen said that as a nurse, she was convinced the bruising was from the fall on our large flagstone entry. The mother said she was fine with it as long as Hellen was sure the little girl was okay. Hellen said she was, as the bruising was so slight it was hardly visible on the child's pale skin. We left with the understanding that I would babysit the next morning. The little girl gave me a big hug goodbye.

It was the last time I would ever see the child and her mother again.

When we arrived at the car, Hellen insisted I sit in the front seat. Tracy sat in the back. Hellen drove up the street, put the car in park, and severely beat me in the face for several minutes. I thought my neck would break as she pounded my face. "How do you like it? Huh? Huh?" I didn't try to protect myself because I figured I had it coming. Hellen never once asked me what happened. Tracy seemed upset after Hellen beat me in the car.

I was so ashamed. I never slapped a child again "to get their attention." I felt awful and thought about the little girl every day. I don't know if the mother changed her mind, or if Hellen called her and told her I wasn't allowed to babysit anymore. I figure Hellen made the call, but I will never know.

~

That first babysitting job is one of the most shameful stories of my childhood. When I saw that I had the capacity to inflict bruises on someone weaker than myself, I was afraid. I couldn't trust myself. As a young girl, I knew I would never be like Hellen, and yet, here I saw that I had the potential to be like her. I had to pray and get help to make the necessary changes or I would go down the same road Hellen had gone.

It is an understatement to say, I was terrified. My biggest fear could come true if I didn't change. But how?

Revisiting this period of my life has been difficult. First, I feel compassion for the child, then for the young teenager that I was. The child was left with an inexperienced, traumatized teenager. She was powerless in an extremely vulnerable environment. The last place she needed to be babysat was in Hellen's house.

In my memory, the child and her mother have no names. I did not write their names in my journals. I have no idea why. Yet, I know where they lived, and have driven by that apartment complex many times. If I could find them, I would apologize. Even after all these years, it just seems the right thing to do. I am truly sorry.

~

Although I had calls to babysit for other children, I didn't allow myself to take any jobs for the rest of the summer. I just couldn't do it. I was angry, shocked, and disappointed with myself. I was afraid that inside, I was developing into a horrible brute like Hellen.

It didn't help that Hellen reminded me (sometimes several times a day), about the marks on the little girl's face, and often as she beat me in the hallway. Many times, she used it as a reason to beat me.

It seems as if life itself confirms what Hellen has always said. I was

1978: 14 Years Old

handed an ideal opportunity and I blew it again. Right in front of God and everybody. My siblings have never done that. Maybe Hellen is right and God can't trust me with anything, not even an innocent child. I ruin everything. I am a loser, nothing but trouble. I am just a burden to everyone.

Deep down, I felt dirty, cowardly, and worthless. I was what Hellen said I was.

I was God's garbage.

~

Only later, much later, did I realize that while I may have had some responsibility for the light bruising on her left cheek, I couldn't have placed *any* of the bruising on the child's right cheek. She was cradled in my arms up against my chest, when I lightly slapped her left cheek. The slight bruising that developed had to have been from the fall on the flagstone…and although I had no justification whatsoever to slap the child –none– I had taken all the blame and Hellen had been only too happy to lay all the blame on me, and beat me for months afterward for it.

~

Too often we think sharing our weaknesses
will cause us to lose respect… I no longer believe that is true…
What I do believe is the more you tell the truth about yourself…
the more effective your leadership will become,
the more you will develop a true leading character.
The more you tell of your own failure of character,
the more God will use that for His purpose.
~ Dan B. Allender, Ph.D.

~

In the middle of all the despondency, life took an exciting turn for me one bright Sunday, in July, 1978. A man at our church brought his brother Duane, and Duane's friend Greg, to the Sunday morning service.

1978: 14 Years Old

After Tracy and I were introduced to them, I talked with Greg. I found him interesting, kind, and funny; he was older than me by several years.

Greg said he was a welder, and I was embarrassed that I didn't know what the word meant. There was some wrought iron railing nearby, and he showed me where it was welded together. Before he showed me, I'd never given any thought as to how metal was held together.

I enjoyed talking with Greg and hoped to see him again. I left the conversation thinking that he was different from the other guys I knew from school and church.

This was a new experience for me. I was drawn to him. When I got home, I cried. I liked him, but I knew I could never date someone 10 years older than me.

That August, Tracy turned 18, and she began to date Duane. After a short courtship, they were engaged and set their wedding date for late spring in 1979.

Phoenix, Arizona – 1978

Tracy curled my hair and picked out the outfit.

She purchased this professional portrait of me as a gift for mom.

Hellen set the 11x14 portrait on the floor until it got wet and moldy.

1978: 14 Years Old

~

Hellen had two main occupations throughout her life; as housekeeping supervisor in seedy motels, and a nursing aide in state-funded nursing homes. The jobs offered her freedom from close supervision. She used to say, "I can't stand a boss breathing down my neck."

I used to wonder why anyone would want to breathe down her neck. That visual puzzled me.

She changed jobs several times a year; sometimes she stayed at one place for as long as six months. We knew this was a strange pattern, but it was Danny who joked about it. "Most people get a gold watch after working at a company for 20 years," he said, "but Mom gets one if she works there for 20 months!"

He made a lot of jokes when she had several W-2 forms arrive in the mail at income tax time. He asked her, "Mom, is this all you got for last year?"

We didn't know why Hellen went through so many jobs, but she blamed it on the men in management. She said it wasn't her fault she got fired so often.

The motel jobs were her favorites. She loved having the title, Housekeeping Supervisor. She chose motels on freeway frontage roads, in low-income parts of town–the ones that rented rooms by the hour, half-day, or full day/night. She was given a master key that opened all the rooms. It allowed her to close off a room for cleaning–and then she'd use the room to take a nap. For years, she used the motel laundry soap and machines to wash her own clothes and uniforms. I thought all families had bath towels, washcloths, and sheets with motel names stamped on them because that's what our family used. The linen department in department stores puzzled me. I wondered who was dumb enough to waste money when they could

1978: 14 Years Old

go to a motel and get the linens for free.

Hellen told us how stupid motel guests were, especially the men. She'd watch them leave their rooms and walk to the pool with a towel and a book. When they were settled poolside, she'd stack extra towels in her hands, use the master key, go into their room, and steal their cash and anything else she could get away with. If the guest walked in, she apologized by saying, "Weren't you the one who called for extra towels?" She made me go with her so she could show me how easy it was. I saw her put stolen items inside the stacked towels. She called the cash "tips."

If the guest noticed the theft, Hellen herself wrote up a report. I watched as she consoled the guests by saying, "I'm so sorry this happened. We just hired a new maid and I don't know…there's something odd about that girl. I checked my schedule, and she definitely was the one who cleaned your room."

Hellen could put on an act. I watched in amazement at how genuine she seemed. As the guest left, she'd say, "Sir, I'm so sorry. I'll get this report to my general manager immediately. I just can't believe people do this sort of thing. What is this world coming to? Hardworking people like you and I who pay our bills, salute the flag, and give God His tithe will never understand stuff like this. The front desk will make an accommodation on your bill."

I was stunned by her manner towards them, when they were hurting so much. Their vacations ruined, she was the epitome of reassurance, gentleness, and generosity. Often, she gave them free meals in the greasy spoon restaurant in the lobby of the motel, and a free night's stay at the motel. Of course, she said that "all thefts are reported to the Phoenix Police," but I don't know of any time that she did.

Sometimes the guest wrote a note to the motel about the kindness of the housekeeping supervisor and her thoroughness when writing their theft report. I was puzzled by the ways she dealt with people. I

1978: 14 Years Old

didn't realize then, that she was just a master manipulator.

~

The nursing home jobs were always on the night shift and she'd arrange to trade with another opportunistic employee to cover for each another, so they could take naps, or so Hellen could leave work while on shift. Several nights a week, she would drive to the house to check on me, off and on, all through the night. It made it hard for me to steal a shower. I never knew when she might show up. She was purposefully unpredictable.

The nursing home jobs gave her a way to steal Valium and other drugs in addition to the residents' candy, jewelry, and cash.

~

High school started on a good note for me. During the first week of freshman year, I met a sweet, feisty girl named Kristi. She was kind to me. We had a class together and afterwards she walked with me to my locker that was in the middle, bottom row of a large section of lockers, out in the weather, sun, wind, or rain.

In the high school setting, most students didn't know about my history with locker-related pranks and fights at the elementary school. The few who did, happened to show up the day Kristi was with me. Their old game started right away and I remember thinking, *NO. Not today. I have a friend with me.* Though I pretended I didn't care, I was embarrassed by what they did to me.

Kristi was outraged and voiced her opinion. "Wilma! How can you let them treat you like that?"

"They won't leave me alone."

"Have you tried kicking them back? I would."

Kristi was very thin and petite, with a giant heart, and even bigger opinions. She would have never been someone the bullies would have messed with–at least not a second time.

"Well, Wilma," she said, "re-open your locker. Right now. Empty

1978: 14 Years Old

it out. Right now."

"Why?"

"Just do it. You can share with me. I'm not going to let anyone treat my friend like that."

I couldn't believe what I'd heard her say, "my friend." We had just met. During registration, they told us not to give our locker combination out to anyone.

"But the rules," I said. "How will I get my stuff? How will I know when you'll be at your locker?"

Would she really trust someone like me with her combination?

"I'll give you the combination, silly!" And then she laughed.

Kristi's locker was in a covered corridor. It was eye level and easy to use. If there was a perfect locker on campus, Kristi had it. She gave me the combination. She trusted me. Kristi told me half of the locker was mine. Throughout our high school years, we shared that same locker, and decorated it for each other's birthdays.

~

When I entered high school, Hellen ramped up all my punishments in a big way, but food was a critical issue.

Despite the free lunch at school, I spent most days drowning hunger pangs with giant drinks of water. I realized that if I had a part time job, I could use the money to buy food. I signed up with Call-A-Teen for babysitting jobs–the only jobs available–and the stress of my past babysitting experience factored in to my reluctance as well as my need to eat.

I worked for 50 cents an hour and stayed busy, but I was working for strangers. The phone rang often, and I didn't turn down any job on weekend nights. It was uncomfortable since I didn't get to meet the people until they came to my house to pick me up and take me to their home. I'd get into the vehicle not knowing if they lived one minute or one hour away. Most of the jobs were at filthy apartments, with roaches and mice, in the low-rent section of town. I'd get a few instructions, be introduced to the kids, and then the person would leave. The whole system puzzled me because I didn't know them, and they didn't know me, but they left me to watch their children.

The kids were usually fine, but it was during this time of babysitting, I was introduced to pornography. Most of those filthy apartments had pornographic magazines strewn all over. Often, the small children looked at them and laughed. I thought it was revolting. I saw things I wish I'd never seen, and some of the situations were scary.

1978: 14 Years Old

~ Counseling Notes ~

*How much more grievous are the consequences
of anger than the causes of it.*
~ Marcus Aurelius

I talked about the early morning of hopscotch with Tracy and how special of a memory it is for me.

The counselors said, "No doubt it would be. Tracy was good to you every opportunity she had. It's part of the survival/resilience in you to look for the bright side; to look for the fun thing, if there is one. Even through this counseling, at times you have said some of the funniest things, during the most difficult conversations. It doesn't surprise me that you found a way to have fun with Tracy during a hot and horrible summer morning in Hellen's house."

~

I still felt bad about the night my brothers got kicked out. I had hauled their belongings to the front yard.

They said, "Hellen had been snooping in their apartment without anyone's knowledge. Her lifetime obsession with snooping was nothing new, but kicking her children out was a shock to all of you. That she made you do all the heavy lifting is notable and punitive, but you have no blame here. I can see where you would feel safer with your brothers living there, but Hellen lived by her own agenda. She did not love her children by the Bible's standard of motherly love. And she proved that fact many times over to you and your siblings. It had to be terrible for your brothers that night as well. It is interesting that you remember very little of what Tracy was doing, though she was home. Hellen was angry and had your attention. It's understandable."

~

Later that night, I was beaten severely. I didn't know then, but the beatings caused serious injuries–a torn rotator cuff, a torn bicep and broken bones–and later required surgeries to repair the damage caused at the time.

The counselors said, "The beatings had nothing whatsoever to do with discipline. They were all about brutality, violence, and mind control. The beatings were more than a physical assault. They crossed over into physical, mental, and emotional torture. Abusers commonly enforce repetitive physical abuse to wear down the victim's physical, mental, and emotional defenses. It works. Hellen did whatever suited her perversions, whenever, wherever and as often as she desired. There was no excuse, no justification for what she did. None."

~

I asked about the most shameful event of my teen years–the bruising of little girl I babysat.

"Very often, children living in abusive environments hurt other children. You had a lot of anger you were trying to conceal. It is a blessing you were able to control that anger. What's remarkable is that you stopped that anger. With the volume of anger you had, it is amazing you did not give in to it and kill the child. You did what you had seen your mother do in those types of situations, as most young girls would do."

~

In counseling I discussed my response to meeting Greg.

"Your response is predictable. You meet a young man, who is kind to you. He has a career, he is mature and stable and what do you do? You go home and cry because you do not deserve someone that 'good.' But you'd sure love to marry someone like that. Conflict is ever present when you're dealing with all the false beliefs that you were facing. Greg offered everything that you wanted and didn't have. Of course, you liked him the day you met him. What's wonderful is that he liked you, too."

1979: 15 Years Old

The powerlessness we feel leads to the despair, deadness, loneliness, and hopelessness of an orphan, a child alone in a world that preys on the weak and unprotected. Despair and apathy grow. We begin to believe that it doesn't matter what we do because, we've concluded, nothing will change anyway.
~ Dan B. Allender, Ph.D.

The Times

The year 1979 brought news of Three Mile Island, the worst nuclear disaster in U.S. history. The U.S. embassy in Tehran, Iran was seized by terrorists with 52 hostages, and I had a nervous breakdown just before my 15th birthday.

If 1979 didn't start out cold, dark, and rainy, it should have. I began the New Year discouraged and went downhill…and it turned out to be the longest, darkest, most devastating year of my life.

~

Hellen worked to control everything and everybody, and she did not want Tracy to get married. Tracy was attending Arizona State University to study accounting. It was Hellen's dream, not Tracy's, and I heard Hellen talk about how proud she would feel, watching her daughter receive a college degree, knowing that she alone had raised her, without the help of any man.

1979: 15 Years Old

Though Tracy did not want to go to ASU, or become an accountant, she complied with Hellen's plans for her until Duane came into her life.

I liked Duane and he was good to Tracy. He seemed to be a nice guy, but what did I know? I was just a teenager. I knew Tracy was happy, and that was all that mattered to me. I didn't understand why Hellen had to act crazy and pitch fits. She was talking about Tracy, after all. Tracy wanted to get married. What was wrong with that?

Despite all the tension in the house, Tracy was wonderful. She wanted a simple church wedding and I did what I could to help her with the plans and preparations when I tagged along on her errands. We had fun working together, but Hellen made the weeks preceding Tracy's wedding very difficult, at best.

Tracy and I arrived at the house one day to find a handwritten letter from Hellen. She'd left it on the kitchen table for us to see:

> *Dear Tracy and Wilma,*
>
> *Due to your total lack of regard for the loving, Christian mother God bestowed, honored and blessed you with, I, Hellen J. Proietti, must hereby resign this day, as your mother. You will miss me, now that I've gone, but never forget, you will answer to God Almighty for the way you mistreated me. Don't say I didn't warn you. You both are gonna bust hell wide open for your unthankful, rebellious ways.*
>
> *Your former mother,*
Hellen J. Proietti

We both cried. I wondered, *how will we live without a mother? I've never been disowned before.* Hours later, our 'former mother' came back to the house to beat me.

Hellen's resignation letter was the first one of many, and a new pattern was established. If there was something Hellen couldn't control about Duane, the wedding, or an imagined irritation, of which there were many, she'd write another letter similar to the first one. Then, she'd leave for several hours, return to the house and order me into the hall for a beating. The resignation letters and beatings were just part of Hellen's control and new pattern.

Tracy cried each time we found a letter, and I grew tired of Hellen upsetting her. I learned to rush into the house ahead of my sister, check, and if a letter was on the table, I'd grab it, hide it, and later, tear it to bits and flush it down a toilet.

By the time the wedding day arrived, several of Hellen's letters were swirling in the city sewer. Hiding the letters from Tracy did nothing to protect me from the beatings.

My small intervention seemed to help Tracy through that difficult time. We found humor in joking with each other: "Well, if you're going to act like that, I hereby resign as your former sister and you'll miss me, now that I've gone. You'll answer to God, you will…"

There was only one time when Hellen walked in when we were reading the letter. Tracy and I had arrived hours later than planned, because the shopping had just taken that long. Hellen thought Tracy had to work that day but she had the day off. Tracy and I were standing at the kitchen table, having just finished reading about our "former mother, Hellen J. Proietti." I looked up and saw her standing there and popped off, "Well, Hellen, what are you doing here?" Hellen hit me so hard in the face that I landed several feet away. I do not know if she backhanded me; I did not see the blow coming, it came so fast. The house had a huge kitchen and I flew across the floor. Tracy and I laughed about it later, but it sure wasn't funny then.

~

My own turmoil continued to grow and like a storm rolling in, my life was getting darker each day. It was a difficult time because I was experiencing a freedom I had never been allowed before. Getting out of the house often and helping Tracy with the wedding was a memorable time for both of us.

Meanwhile, Hellen was angry, irritable, and cranky. She knew she was losing control of her favorite daughter. Tracy, set to be the college graduate with top honors of Hellen's dreams, was now threatened because of all things…a man.

Hellen hated men. Tracy was in love with a man. Hellen was not amused.

I paid the price.

~

On a Sunday evening, about three weeks before Tracy's wedding, I realized I had a distressing gynecological problem. I had to tell Hellen about it because I knew I needed to see a doctor right away. She told me to take a bleach bath (her recipe was three parts bleach, one part water) and I would be fine. I refused to take the bleach bath and was surprised that she didn't force me to do it.

The next day she took me to a gynecologist that she knew.

I was scared to visit a gynecologist for the first time. Hellen made the whole experience much more difficult than it should have been. She refused to leave me alone with the doctor or nurse for even a moment. The doctor ushered me into his office, telling Hellen he wanted to ask me some questions in private.

Hellen refused to allow that, pushed past him and sat down in the chair next to me. "She's a minor, by God," she said. "I'm her mother and you can ask whatever you need to right in front of me."

The doctor said, "Okay, then."

After some initial questions, he asked, "Are you a virgin?"

"Yes."

Hellen rolled her eyes, shook her head, and the sound of "Hrrrrumph!" came out of her mouth.

The doctor frowned.

"Look," Hellen responded. "You might as well know something about her right now. This girl is filthy. She stinks because she will not take a shower for weeks at a time. I've tried everything, and I can't get her to do it! Have you ever heard of such a thing?"

The doctor looked at me, frowned, and said, "Uh, no."

I looked at the floor. I knew that in a few minutes, he would know I didn't take showers. Though I had begged her, Hellen refused to allow me to shower before the visit, because I had refused the bleach bath.

True to form, Hellen had to make every passage, every transition in life painful, and my first visit to the gynecologist was no exception.

The concerned doctor discussed the diagnosis with us saying, "I'm not exactly sure what caused this problem. I'm going to give you a prescription that I want you to fill at the pharmacy right away. Even with these medications, I'm concerned she might still need further medical treatment. Make an appointment to see me again in a few days. At that time, I'll see if she needs additional medication, or maybe a different medication, depending on how the condition responds to treatment."

Hellen drove to the pharmacy and purchased the medicines even though she said, "I can't afford all that medicine. That doctor has a lot of money, but not me. I'm working, trying to support you kids, and I can't be throwing money away on a bunch of medicines, just because you want attention. You're not going back to that doctor, so don't be thinking that you are. He is just a money grabbing creep...all men are. And oh, by the way, I saw how you enjoyed his attention. You can't hide anything from me."

"Mom! I didn't...!"

Smack! She backhanded my face with such force that I felt blood run inside my mouth.

"Shut your fat mouth! You've caused enough trouble for me! If you weren't such a dirty, filthy, sorry excuse for a human being, much less a

1979: 15 Years Old

daughter...*dear God*...how am I supposed to raise this...this, **THING?** I'm gonna tell you something right now, so listen up. You've got three years 'til you're 18. You better figure out how to provide for yourself, because the day you turn 18, I resign as your mother. RE-SIGN! Can't come soon enough. I'm so fed up with you. Let welfare take over and feed you the rest of your sorry life, because you'll never amount to nothing anyway. You're so stupid someone's always gonna have to make every decision for you, feed you, make sure Wilma's taken care of, like the retard that you are. I wish to God I knew what I did to deserve having you for a child. I should have stopped after Tracy."

She dropped me off at the house where I spent hours crying. I wondered, *did the doctor see the bruises and burns on my body? How could he not?*

~

My stress levels escalated with Tracy's wedding just three weeks away. Deep down, I still hoped and prayed that when it came right down to it, *Tracy won't really leave me alone with Hellen, will she? I hope Tracy backs out of the wedding to stay with me. I'm terrified to be left alone with Hellen.*

~

Two weeks after I visited the gynecologist, I broke out with a severe case of shingles on my head, neck, face, and shoulder. Hellen insisted that Tracy take me to the doctor because she said I, "only wanted attention anyway." She said she, "couldn't be missing work all the time" to run me "to the doctor's office and all over town for medicine."

The doctor looked at the shingles. He asked a few questions and said, "Honey, you have shingles. You have the worst case of shingles I have ever seen in my career. Is everything okay at home?"

I opened my mouth to lie, like I had done so many times before, and surprised myself when a great, broken sob came out instead. I attempted to nod my head.

He looked down. Paused. Looked back up at me and said, "No. This is a nervous breakdown. This is a physical nervous breakdown. Instead of your mind having a nervous breakdown, your body is having one. Are you sure everything is okay at home?"

I nodded 'yes' as I sobbed. I didn't know what had come over me. The man was so kind. I wanted to talk to the kind man and I couldn't seem to talk. I wanted help so much, and I just couldn't find the words.

Tracy had a concerned expression as she watched me. She had never seen me cry like that.

The doctor was quiet for several moments; the only sounds in the room were my sobs. The doctor turned to Tracy said, "I want to see her again in three or four days. My nurse is going to give her two penicillin shots, and that should help her. I will give her a topical spray to help with the pain. Unfortunately, there's not much else we can do. I am very concerned about her though, and I'd like you to make another appointment for her. I really need to recheck the large blisters to make sure infection doesn't set in. Any questions?"

We had none.

Still crying, I walked down the hall and out of the doctor's office. Tracy took care of the bill and the next appointment.

When Hellen found out that the doctor had diagnosed me with having a nervous breakdown, she refused to allow me to see him for the follow-up visit.

After that, she never allowed me to see any medical provider for any reason, as long as I lived in her house. Hellen was angry, and I had no idea then how much worse my life was going to get.

~

Tracy married as planned on a sunny afternoon in the spring of 1979. The wedding went well, and she was a beautiful bride. I was proud of her and happy as I stood by her side and heard the wedding vows.

As her maid of honor, I wore my long hair hanging down and

1979: 15 Years Old

pulled forward, to hide the big shingles on my neck and ear. The photographer arranged my hair so that the shingles didn't show in the wedding pictures.

Tracy's wedding day. I was happy for Tracy.

I had a lot of sadness that day that I pushed away from my thoughts. I had to make the day as happy as possible for Tracy. My inner turmoil centered on two facts: Tracy had left me behind with Hellen and I wouldn't even be able to see my sister at church any more. She would be attending Duane's church.

I was devastated.

~

In the 17 months after Tracy's wedding, I went into depths of despair. Life became a nightmare that got worse every single day.

If only I could have known then, that within 17 months, I would be rescued. If I could have known, I could have had the luxury of hope.

But I had no idea.

The unrelenting emotional and physical pain wearied me and blinded my reason.

~

Hellen changed immediately after Tracy's wedding.

One afternoon, a couple of days after Tracy's wedding, I was putting away things from the reception, when Hellen called me into her room. I walked with dread down the hall, only to find her there wanting to show off her three new sex toys.

"Here, hold this." She said, smiling.

The thing looked gross. I looked away in disgust and refused to touch it. She laughed and told me I was "stupid and immature."

Hellen's new sex toys frightened me. I didn't understand why she would want to own such things, much less display them on top of her dresser.

Her twisted sexual appetite suddenly became more perverted, brazen, and aggressive. She knew there was no chance of my three siblings coming by, and she enjoyed the freedom it gave her to do what she wanted to me without fear of interruption or discovery. She kept the toys out in the open, on top of her dresser.

The brazenness of her perversions made my head spin, and I knew of no one to turn to for help. The word fear doesn't begin to describe the terror I felt.

~

Two other notable things happened during that first week. I moved into Tracy's old bedroom. It was directly across the hallway from Hellen's, but at the back of the house and very nice. Tracy had fixed it up while she lived there, and she had left her heated waterbed for me. I loved sleeping in her bed because it felt safe to me, and it was warm all winter long. Hellen always refused to turn on the heater in the house, even when the weather was cold.

One day I came in from school, sorely missing Tracy. On my new bedroom door frame was a swing latch with a hasp attached. There was a heavy-duty padlock hanging on the hasp.

It frightened me.

What? Was Hellen going to start locking me inside?

Another new punishment?

It turned out to be just that.

1979: 15 Years Old

A relative dropped by our house months later, during a rare visit to Arizona. She saw the hasp and padlock on my bedroom door and she was troubled. She regrets not reporting it to the police.

I wish she would have.

~

The changes inside the house were new, but my interactions with the outside world remained depressingly the same. I returned to school after a three-week absence after suffering from shingles and the nervous breakdown. Physically, I was pale and weak, and most of my teachers asked me why I had come back so soon. I told them that I didn't want to fail my freshman year of high school, and I didn't. The real truth was I felt safer at school than at Hellen's house.

On my first day back, another student tripped me as I arrived late to my General Business class. I fell hard, with my arms full of books. The spine on the typing book was broken by the fall. The teacher and the class roared with laughter.

~

I rarely spoke at school, just the bare minimum to get by. Then, occasionally, I would completely lose all composure and have an angry outburst or break down sobbing. The outbursts seemed to come out of nowhere, and I didn't know what to do to stop them. I felt like such a failure when I blew a gasket. I was weary with the constant hunger, the beatings, sexual abuse and strip searches. It was all too much to bear at times.

~

Hygiene was an even bigger source of humiliation for me in high school than it was during grade school. I was only allowed to own three skirts, three blouses, one light jacket, and one set of underclothes–the set I wore each day–for the final two and a half years I lived in Hellen's house. It didn't matter if I was going to church, or cleaning the alley behind Hellen's house, I had to wear the same clothes. It

1979: 15 Years Old

didn't matter if it was 115 degrees that day, or 40 degrees, I had to wear the same clothes. And every single day, the same underclothes, with the same rules. I was not allowed to wash them out by hand, but I snuck washings as often as I could.

My closet didn't even have extra hangers.

Since we didn't own a washer or dryer, it was important for me to find just the right moment to sneak washing my clothes in the bathroom sink. When I did, I had to use the little bars of stolen hotel soap and hang them on a hanger in my closet with the hope they'd be dry enough to wear to school the next day. Dry or not, I wore them. I was always afraid that Hellen would come in and catch me washing my clothes without permission. I wasn't brave enough to do it more than every six weeks or so.

Hellen only allowed me to take a shower every four to six weeks. I had to wash my hair on the same schedule. There was no shampoo, so I had to use little bars of soap Hellen stole from the motel, which left my long hair, a tangled mess. It took me hours to comb it out, depending on how sore my head was from the last beating. If my scalp was still swollen, it would take three hours. When I bought deodorant with babysitting money, Hellen found it when she ransacked my room. Hellen used my roll-on deodorant on her unwashed, unshaved armpits. As much as I hated smelling bad, once she used it, I never touched that deodorant again.

My clothes smelled horrible and so did I, but almost worse was Hellen didn't allow me to have a toothbrush. I heard the kids at school talking about brushing their teeth every day, and I wondered, *what would it be like to do that?* I wanted one, but what little money I earned babysitting, I had to save for the days when I had no food.

I also wanted pajama pants, but Hellen didn't allow me to wear them. I was not allowed to have my own nightgown–the only ones I was allowed were what Hellen stole from the motel guests, and they were inappropriate. She insisted I wear them without them washing them first. Wearing them with another person's body smells sickened me, but I had no choice.

After I started working a regular job, twice I spent my food money to buy a long, high-collared nightgown. It was a tough decision, but I hated wearing stolen nightgowns. Each time I bought a new one, it disappeared after a couple of days.

I was so disappointed.

Hellen continued to ransack my room two or three times a week. She dumped every dresser drawer out, flung my books against the walls, ripped the sheets off the bed, threw my eight-track tapes all over the room. After I got off work, I was required to hurry up and clean my "pigpen."

~

Hellen left me without food for days at a time. She didn't buy food for the house because she ate in restaurants. I stayed hungry most of the time. Though it had been going on for years, it really ramped up big time after Tracy left. Food was one of her main ways to control me, and it worked.

Every few months, Hellen would be 'generous' and buy a flat of canned peas or a sack of potatoes. I learned that I could make it on one can of peas, or one baked potato a day. I was hungry and didn't have much energy, but I could keep going.

Often, the potatoes rotted, and I didn't like them because there was nothing in the refrigerator to put on the potato except mustard.

I preferred canned peas and lived on them exclusively for weeks at a time.

In September as I started my sophomore year of high school, hunger drove me to apply for a job through the Comprehensive Employment and Training Act (CETA), a government program for low-income students. The program allowed me to work in the school's

1979: 15 Years Old

attendance office 30 minutes before school, during lunchtime, and two and a half hours after school. It also meant, I missed out on the free breakfast and lunch program.

Once I had a regular paycheck, Hellen refused to support me in any way other than the roof over my head. The CETA job provided money for food and necessities I needed until I was able to leave Hellen's house. Twice a month, when I got my check, Hellen required me to buy her the all-you-can-eat fish fry dinner at a nearby diner.

She said, "I've been buying your garbage all your life. It's high time, you start doing something for *me*. Start showing your good mother appreciation for once. Every two weeks, I want a decent meal. The whole works. Dinner. No cheap special either–an iced tea, and a dessert. And you can pay the tip, too. I've shelled out for you your whole stupid life. It's about time you learn to think about dear old mom. This is the best idea God's given me in a while."

I didn't think it was a good idea...or God's idea.

Subtracting my tithe and the cost of the restaurant tab, I didn't have enough money to buy food until the next payday. With the money I had left over, I bought canned tuna or a bag of potato chips. The salt in the chips, along with large glasses of water made me feel full. I had to eat whatever I bought right away because I wasn't allowed to bring food into the house. Hellen insisted on complete control over what, how much, and how often I was allowed to eat. If she found hidden food when raiding my room, she'd beat me and then eat it all in front of me to teach me a lesson. The few times that happened, it was hard to watch.

I often stopped at the day-old bakery after school. The lady knew me and was kind. Most days she'd ask me to haul big, black bags of stale doughnuts to the dumpster. I happily did, asking if I could have one or two for myself. She usually allowed me to take one, but rarely two. I hated putting those bags in the dumpster, seeing good food going to waste. It was hard not to take more than one donut, but I never did. Sometimes, the nice lady just chatted with me until I finally left empty-handed. Each time I stopped to visit, I was hungry and hoped for something to eat.

With my first paycheck, I bought a toothbrush and some deodorant. Hellen used the toothbrush to bleach her false teeth. I was too grossed out to use it after what she'd done with it. She laughed, telling me how stupid and wasteful I was.

No matter how many toothbrushes I purchased, Hellen took them. There were no safe places to hide them; Hellen found everything during her raids. Once, when I was angry that she had taken my brand-new toothbrush again (and I had only a little money left for food) I felt so desperate to brush my teeth that I tried to wash out my toothbrush with a stolen motel bar soap. I rinsed the brush with hot water, but I didn't get all the soap out like I had thought. I ended up with the taste of that nasty soap all over the inside of my mouth.

I gagged.

It grossed me out so much that Hellen's germs might have *still* been on the toothbrush that, I never attempted to sanitize it that way again. The germs and the soap were more disgusting than not brushing my teeth. I quit wasting my money on new toothbrushes and taught myself to brush my teeth with a bath towel. And that's how I 'brushed' my teeth, the rest of the time I lived in her house. It was better than nothing.

~

The intense isolation I felt in 1979 with my brothers and sister out of the house was immeasurable.

Hugh was going to college, working full time, and was dating. The university was 30 miles from our house; he lived in the dormitory and I rarely heard from him.

Danny left town to join a circus. After a while, he caught a bus back to Phoenix, but Hellen drove him crazy, so he didn't come by the

1979: 15 Years Old

house and he never called.

Tracy worked full time and I only saw her a couple of times a month. When we visited, I noticed she was happier than ever before. Tracy called often, but if Hellen was home I couldn't talk. She understood. Hellen would not let me go to her church, but I wished I could. I liked their church better, but I had to stay where I was.

~

Two days before my 15th birthday Hellen got angry and beat me bloody. She cussed and quoted scriptures, hollering, "I cannot bear one more-lousy minute in the same house with you. I'd sure like to know what God judged me for by sticking you in my life. I'm leaving, and I may not **ever** come back. You don't deserve a mother…not a good one like me. You don't deserve anything but the HELL you're heading for."

I had no idea what I had done to upset her, or why she thought she should beat me.

She left the house and I thought she would come back to get ready for work. There was no food. No potatoes, no canned peas, nothing. There hadn't been for days. I was so hungry.

I was surprised and worried when she didn't come home the next day. Though I was in pain from the beating, I tried to rush around making sure the floors were swept, the trash hauled to the alley, and the furniture dusted.

I went to bed that night with a heightened fear. Hellen had broken her pattern. She had never left me alone that long. I slept fitfully, waking often and walking through the house afraid of what I might find.

The sun came up in the morning and I was 15. I had gnawing hunger pains, but there was nothing in the house. Just in case I missed something, I checked the refrigerator. All it had was an old bottle of mustard, a jar of dried-up mayonnaise, and some packets of ketchup from McDonald's.

1979: 15 Years Old

I was sore and in pain as I pedaled my bicycle to school. I cried wondering how I would survive three more years until I could leave Hellen's house. Hugh, Danny, and Tracy had all been at least 18 years old before they got out.

Throughout the school day, I worried about Hellen. In a way, I hoped she had died somewhere. All day I expected to be called to the office to get the news. When that didn't happen, I became more frightened. I didn't know what she would do to me when and if she finally came home.

I stopped by the bakery after school, hoping for a donut, but the nice lady was busy. Her customers came in nonstop, so after a while I left. I wanted to tell her it was my 15th birthday.

I got on my bicycle and headed home. As I rode, I thought, *I've never had a birthday party before.* To get my mind off the hunger pains, I thought about how it would feel to have a party and people celebrating with me. I pictured streamers, balloons, pizza, cake, friends, and presents.

As I turned my bicycle down our street, the party vision faded away. Hellen's car was not in the driveway and I wondered, *is there another resignation letter on the kitchen table?*

I went inside and walked through the house; nothing looked different. No letter on the table, no food, no sounds. The house seemed empty, but I was scared that Hellen had committed suicide in her bedroom and I certainly didn't want to be the one to find her.

Then, I wondered, did Hellen forget it was my birthday? I knew she wouldn't buy me a gift; she didn't bother herself with that kind of thing. Still, I was so hungry I was hoping she'd let me eat.

Scared though I was, I gathered some courage and tiptoed to the end of the hall to peek into her room. I held my breath. "Mom?"

Her bed was messy, but empty. Thank God.

I walked through her bedroom to make sure I was alone in the

1979: 15 Years Old

house, and I was. I checked to see if there were any signs that she had stopped by, and I couldn't tell if she had or not.

A few hours later, I knelt by the couch to pray, thinking I would hear her car if she pulled into the driveway. I prayed, *God I don't need gifts or a party; I just don't want to be alone and hungry. Please let someone remember my birthday.*

After I prayed, the phone rang. Tracy and Duane were calling to wish me a happy birthday.

"Thanks."

Tracy asked, "So, where's Mom?"

"I haven't seen her for a couple of days."

"She hasn't called either?"

"No."

Tracy and Duane came over with my favorite German chocolate cake and the gift of a new Bible, and I was happy. My Bible had been falling apart and I was hoping for a new one. I cut the cake for them and a very thin sliver for myself. Eating sweets after so long without food always sickened me. I didn't have the courage to tell them I needed real food.

I know God heard my prayer when I knelt by the couch, then Tracy called and came over. Duane was always kind and generous. I could have told them I needed food and they would have fed me. I was just too afraid of Hellen to tell them.

A few minutes after they left, Hellen came in. She was in a pleasant mood. I was surprised and thought, *maybe she'll buy me dinner for my birthday.* She walked into the kitchen and asked, "So what did Tracy get you?"

"Oh, it's a Bible. It's so nice, and look how pretty. They had my name engraved on it." I held it up for her to see while admiring it myself.

Hellen barely gave it a glance, then eyed the cake and sat down at the table. I watched, stunned, as she ate the *entire* birthday cake. I didn't know how it would affect her diabetes, but she didn't seem to care. She gave herself an insulin shot, went to sleep, and later went to work.

She never said, "happy birthday" and she didn't notice the extra clean house. I went to bed still feeling hungry, but thankful for my present. I read the new Bible until I fell asleep.

~

Hellen continued to take me to church with her. While there, I thought a lot about the church that Tracy and Duane were attending and wished I could be with them. Hellen's church had lots of problems. Elderly folks were a majority there. When the pastor didn't bring the sermon to a close quick enough, several old women would shake their car keys (and arm fat) to signal it was 9 p.m.

Every few weeks, Hellen went on a crying jag. Her sobs would crescendo, and it caused everyone to be distracted from what the pastor was preaching. He'd cut the sermon short so folks could gather around Hellen to find out what was wrong and to comfort her. It was real soap opera drama.

I hated those services. Hellen wept to the church members that I was a rebellious teenage liar and they couldn't believe anything that came out of my mouth. Between sobs, she said I wasn't nice to her, and that I didn't love her. Then, the well-meaning church members would parade past me while scolding me and telling me to appreciate the wonderful mother God had given me.

I listened to what they said and kept quiet. I never once tried to defend myself, but simply thought, *if you only knew…* Yet, her outbursts, crying jags, cussing fits, fainting spells, and whatever else she could manipulate and manufacture, were *always* my fault.

Hellen's crying jags at church were embarrassing to say the least. I figured if Hellen could convince the church folk as easily as she did, I would *never* be able to tell them how bad things truly were.

1979: 15 Years Old

Public smiles.   *Private tears.*

The pastor had his hands full with all kinds of other problems, and one of them was the multiple times Hellen threatened to commit suicide.

Hellen's suicide attempts were similar to the days early in her marriage, when my dad was called home from the factory. The suicide threats were a tool for attention she'd used throughout her life, and she used it until she finally died–not by suicide–years later.

During my sophomore and junior year of high school, I was called out of class often because Hellen was threatening to commit suicide.

The suicide attempts were, for me, some of her most embarrassing public dramas.

One time, I was taken across town to an upscale hotel where Hellen was in a standoff with the police. Hellen loved a good standoff.

I arrived at the hotel and was escorted to the third-floor corner balcony. I remember thinking, *when she goes out, she'll go out in style.* Hellen had barricaded herself inside a room with the shades and curtains drawn shut. Outside, police officers hunched down on the balcony with bullhorns, asking her to come out of the room before she "committed the final act."

1979: 15 Years Old

The police negotiators enlisted me to help them talk her out of killing herself.

For once, I truly wanted to be back at school in Earth Science class. *And, I really hate Earth Science...*

The officers had me crouch down, with two officers on each side of me. One of them gave me the bullhorn. The big guy in charge instructed me, "Speak slowly, but loud. Understand?"

I nodded. I felt ridiculous.

"Hold it up like this and press this button. We need your help because we want to help your mommy."

I never called Hellen "mommy."

I held the bullhorn up. I pressed the button.

No words came. I had nothing to say. I looked at him. I looked at the others. My legs hurt. They were bruised and sore from the previous night's beating. I wasn't used to crouching down.

"Honey," said the big officer, "look, we need your help. Okay?"

"Okay."

"Say, 'Mom, I love you.' Say it real loud into the speaker."

My voice was a dull, quiet monotone: "Mom...I love you."

The officers glanced at each other.

The big guy tried again. "Okay. It's okay. That was your first try, and it can sound kind of funny hearing your voice through these things, but we are very concerned about your mommy. Do you understand suicide?"

"Yes."

"She's threatening to kill herself. Do you understand that?"

"Yes, I know. She does this all the time."

The officers frowned. The big officer sighed. "Okay. Let's give it another go. This time, real loud."

"Okay." My legs were cramping. I hesitated.

Big officer, "Say, 'Mommy, I want you to come home. C'mon Mommy, I love you. Come out of there. Please?'"

1979: 15 Years Old

In one breath, one sentence, I spoke just as I'd been instructed. But I couldn't hide my dull, half-heartedness, or my resigned monotone. I could follow instructions, but I couldn't hide the truth.

"Mom…I, want, you, to, come, home, c'mon, Mom, I, love, you, come, out, of, there, please."

None of the officers spoke. They looked at each other with concern.

I looked at each of the four officers, and then at the black hole of the hotel room. I took it all in. Without a word, I handed the big guy the bullhorn, stood up, and walked away with tears streaming down my face.

Walking down that stunning, third floor balcony sobbing, I wished Hellen would just do something. Anything. But whatever she chose, I wished above all else, she'd leave me alone. Forever. Whatever that entailed. I wished she'd just do it. Whatever it turned out to be.

~

An officer followed me down the walkway, then down the stairs. It was a humiliating, ugly situation in a beautiful, upscale hotel. He didn't say a word. I appreciated his thoughtfulness. There were no words to say.

The officer drove me back to school in the police car in silence. He was so kind.

The principal met us in front of the school and the officer thanked me, saying our efforts paid off. Hellen had come out of the hotel room and was receiving "appropriate medical treatment."

Whatever that meant.

Hellen arrived at the house late that night, acting as if nothing out of the ordinary had happened that day. She talked about the fantastic meal she had for dinner…and I had been out of peas for a couple of days.

Good thing my "efforts had paid off."

~

After other standoffs and suicidal dramas, the school's assistant principal, Mr. Wong, told the Phoenix Police that I couldn't leave school unless they thought the situation was truly critical. From then on, when the police called the school when Hellen threatened to kill herself, I was called out of class and notified of the standoff, and how long it had been going on. Mr. Wong said that the safest place for me was at school. He said it was the job of the police to do everything they could to save my mother.

Mr. Wong always asked me the information the officers requested. I was terrified of Hellen and I lied to Mr. Wong each time, saying everything was okay. I wanted to tell him and the police the truth, but I didn't think they would believe me. Hellen said they would put me in juvenile hall if I ever told about what I 'caused her to do' to me.

After I answered the questions, Mr. Wong would send me to the empty cafeteria to wait. Alone.

I'd sit at a table and wait with my head down on my folded arms. The cafeteria ladies always brought me a sandwich and a carton of milk. I'd eat the food, then put my head back down and cry. Those sweet ladies always came back, put a box of tissues on the table, and patted me on the back. Then they'd leave me alone.

While crying, I'd pray, *God, please let mom go through with the suicide and get it over with.* Then, I'd feel guilty and wonder, *if she killed herself, where would I go?*

Finally, Mr. Wong would walk to the cafeteria, tap my shoulder, and let me know that the police had notified them that the incident was over.

I'd go back to class.

I don't want to go 'back to class.' I don't want to lie to the principal. I don't want to go to juvenile hall. I want simple things. I want to go to school. I want to go to a good church. I want to be good enough so my mom will love me and let me eat. I want a mom and a dad. I want a toothbrush, and another pair of underwear. I want to take showers and have clean clothes. I want to live without bruises. I want pretty clothes. I want someone, anyone, to love me. I want hugs that don't make me scared.

Simple things, but they were not to be.

1979: 15 Years Old

*Phoenix, Arizona
Spring – 1979
Hellen Proietti
48 years old
at
Duane and Tracy's
Wedding.*

*No one knows
where she found
the blue, sequined dress.
She never wore anything
like that before or
after the wedding.*

*Tracy was horrified
and embarrassed
by both her
oatmeal-box-style hair
and the dress.*

We all were.

1979: 15 Years Old

~ Counseling Notes ~

The counselors said, "It's understandable that you developed a severe case a shingles right before Tracy's wedding. The abandonment and dread you must have felt to be left to live alone with Hellen literally made you sick.

It's notable that after the gynecologist and then the shingles diagnosis, Hellen never allowed you to see a medical professional for any reason as long as you lived in her house.

When Hellen introduced the new sex toys so soon after the wedding, it shows that she planned and purchased them prior to the wedding. She clearly waited until Tracy was out of the house to introduce them to you.

Regarding the swing latch and padlock on your bedroom door, that is simply criminal. It's too bad that your relative didn't call the police. Maybe you could've been rescued then. Hellen had no justification whatsoever for placing that on your bedroom door. None. And of course, it was criminal to even threaten to use it."

~

I briefly mentioned my 15th birthday because I was so afraid.

They said, "It's no surprise that your fears ran wild when Hellen broke her pattern. The mental and emotional torture she deliberately inflicted was criminal. To purposely abandon you for a couple of days after all her suicide attempts was awful. For a 15-year-old to have to search the home to see if her mother is dead inside, by suicide, is abusive on Hellen's part. She still had parental responsibilities to watch out for you even though the others had moved on. She had no right to leave for a couple of days with no contact whatsoever. That was abandonment. After all her suicide threats, your fear that she might be dead in her room, was justified. Later when she ate the whole birthday cake Duane and Tracy brought you, that was appalling. She couldn't let you enjoy anything, even your own birthday cake."

~

I questioned my indifference regarding Hellen's suicide attempts.

"Hellen's suicide attempts were more of her attention getting games that she had used since she was young. She was a master manipulator and she knew just how far to work the system to her advantage. She also knew that she was manipulating your emotions at the same time."

1980: 16 Years Old
January, February, March

I have been driven many times upon my knees by the overwhelming conviction that I had nowhere else to go.
~ Abraham Lincoln

The Times

In March of 1980, small earthquakes near Mount St. Helens in Washington signaled volcanic activity. By May, the volcano's eruption caused damage and loss of life and the New Year brought a suicidal despair that engulfed me.

I was just a sophomore in high school in January 1980 and felt beaten down and alone. Fear was constant. I was scared and didn't know what to do. I tried my best to keep going but I often wondered why.

Why keep going? I'm not allowed to do anything. I'm not allowed to have friends, or even a toothbrush. I'm not allowed to eat or have a change of underwear. I felt as though I was living in a dark, scary whirlwind, and it was hurling me down into a black bottomless hole. It's what I imagined hell to be like, and I figured, *that is where someone like me is headed.*

I believed, *whatever is wrong inside of me has caused me to have the life I have. I don't know how the badness got into me, and I don't know how to get it out, though I've tried everything. Whatever it is, I am* different. I cause Hellen to do things to me that she says she didn't have to do to Hugh, Danny, or Tracy.

When I looked at my three siblings–now all adults–I realize that I've never been like them and weep when I realize I can never be. No wonder Hellen wants to commit suicide...she has three good kids and one bad.

Me.

~

Now as an adult, I am stunned by the perfect storm of manipulation, domination, and control Hellen had achieved in my mind. She had methodically twisted my thinking into believing she and my siblings were good, and I was innately and permanently bad.

~

Hellen was never clean regarding her personal hygiene. She seldom brushed her false teeth or washed her hair, and she took a bleach bath every four to six weeks. She didn't just smell bad–she absolutely reeked. I used to play a memory game tracking when Hellen took a bath, and then try to predict when her next bath might occur. It was usually six weeks later.

Hellen had very little bladder control. I mopped the floor between her bed and the bathroom every other day because she couldn't make it in time. Her clothing and bed reeked of body odor and urine. Hellen's bed had large, brown roaches and she complained about them crawling on her while she slept. I hated when I was required to lie in her bed–the roaches and Hellen grossed me out. They were both big, fat, and repulsive.

Yet, I rarely saw a roach in my bedroom.

One of Hellen's weird fascinations was her insistence to be watched while she dressed, undressed, took the rare bath, and went to the bathroom. I was forced to stand in the bathroom and watch her. I hated it. I couldn't understand why someone would want that.

I wanted privacy.

1980: 16 Years Old: January, February, March

Adding to my distress, Hellen insisted on watching me when I'd dress, undress, and when I went to the bathroom. I would wait for hours to go to the bathroom, trying to wait until after she went to work. I wasn't allowed to shut the bathroom door. I hated that I silently complied. I was very afraid of her. I hated how weak I was. I hated her, and I hated myself.

I was weary with the pain, the bruises, the headaches, the strip searches, the sexual abuse, the hunger, shower restrictions and the beatings…just weary. The lack of hygiene was disgusting and remains difficult to describe. My body felt as if it were 90 years old. If I moved my arm or my foot while asleep, I'd jolt awake in pain.

My body truly hurt, but my mind was dying. The unrelenting emotional and physical pain wearied me and blinded my reason. I cried for hours every day. I wasn't living–I was barely surviving.

I prayed for help to be good enough that my mother could love me.

I know God preserved my sanity through that difficult time.

~

One day while I was working the CETA job in the school attendance office, my supervisor told me to go to my guidance counselor, Mrs. Hagg. She was a large, older woman, and I didn't like her. When she talked to me, she used a singsong voice like she was talking to a small child about a very, special surprise.

When I arrived at her office, she was waiting. I wanted to make the visit quick, since I was on the clock for my job. I asked her why she'd requested the visit. She smiled and explained that there had been complaints about my "odor from the office personnel." I swallowed hard, feeling as though someone had just punched me in the gut. Really hard. I sat quietly determined not to volunteer any information.

She asked, "Do you shower every day?"

"Yes."

"Do you use deodorant every day?"

1980: 16 Years Old: January, February, March

"Yes."

"Is everything okay at home?"

"Yes."

"Would you like me to call your mother about anything that might be bothering you?"

I jumped. "No."

I didn't mean to jump. I hoped she hadn't noticed.

"Well, I'm sure her and I could talk, you know, woman to woman." She smiled again.

"No. She's um…my mom is busy at work. She can't have calls. I'm fine. Anything else? I need to get back to work. I'm on the clock."

"Ummm. Well, no. That'll be all today. Thank you, Wilma."

I felt bad for lying to her.

As I walked away from her office, I prayed, *I'm sorry for lying to her. Please forgive me, God. It's just that, well, I'm more afraid of mom than I am of You. I believe You'll understand. I'm sorry I had to lie to her.*

From then on, I snuck showers more often. I'd wait until Hellen was gone at night, and then I'd take a super-fast shower. She had disabled the lock on the bathroom door, so I was terrified she would come home and hear the water, then barge in and beat me while I was naked. I was absolutely terrified of that.

So…I devised a system. I broke two of Hellen's rules; taking a shower and shutting the bathroom door. The moment the door closed, the clock started. When I opened the door 20 seconds later, I had showered, dried the tub, the shower curtain, and had my nightgown on. I had no time to dry my body with a towel. That was a luxury I couldn't afford. Washing my hair or dirty clothes was out of the question, but at least I didn't have to stink. The 20-second showers were a terror-filled act of desperation. I needed and wanted to be clean, yet I feared Hellen's wrath more than I feared my own stench or the taunting of the kids at school. Each time I opened the door, I was

1980: 16 Years Old: January, February, March

scared she would be standing there, ready to beat me for disobeying her rules.

I was never caught sneaking a shower, but even after the humiliating meeting with Mrs. Hagg, it still took me 10-12 days to work up the nerve to try it again.

Afraid.

Always, every living second, I was afraid.

~

Other than my friend Kristi, high school was not the relief that I had hoped it would be. The kids taunted me as I walked through the corridors each day. The movie "10" starring Bo Derek, came out during that time. I didn't see the movie, but I heard the kids talking about how Bo was so beautiful, she was rated a '10.'

I heard things like, "Negative seven" when I walked by groups of boys.

The kids couldn't have known that their words only sped up the dark whirlwind that surrounded me. There was nowhere I could go in life that did not include pain. Everywhere I turned, just brought pain.

Praying was my only place of refuge.

~

In my sophomore year, the manager of the school bookstore stopped me every few days trying to collect the $12.00 I owed for the previous year's broken typing book. I was working my job, but I needed every dime I earned to buy food and personal items. She might as well have been asking for $1,200.00. I just didn't have it. I offered to do some work for her to pay the bill, but she said that the district required cash, check or money order. If I'd had any inclination that the broken typing book would become an issue, I'd have gladly given the bookstore lady a dollar a payday until it was paid. I didn't think of it at the time because I still went most days with no food at all.

I was frightened when she called Hellen at work to tell her payment was due for the broken book. The phone call turned into a huge

1980: 16 Years Old: January, February, March

argument. Hellen hung up on the bookstore manager, left work, and drove to the school for an in-person screaming match. It was ugly. I saw it happening and walked to class, crying. Hellen was humiliating, and I didn't want to be around her.

A short time later, one of the secretaries summoned me out of the class to come the front office. I walked in and saw Hellen sitting in the assistant principal's office, the same man who regularly fielded calls from the Phoenix Police during Hellen's suicide standoffs–Mr. Wong. He was also my boss's supervisor.

I was scared by the look on Hellen's face and could tell this was not going to have a good outcome. She looked ready for war.

Mr. Wong asked me to explain how the typing book had gotten damaged and I told him the truth.

Mr. Wong looked at Hellen and asked in a calm way, "So, why haven't you just paid the money? It's only $12.00 dollars."

I thought, *Ugh. You're off to a bad start, Mr. Wong.*

Hellen cussed and through clenched teeth said, "Look, mister. I am a poor, single, divorced mother, working two jobs to support all my children, and if you want that book paid for, make the kid who tripped her pay for it, or pay for it your own idiotic self. Are you so stupid to think that I don't know that my taxes provide your paycheck?"

"Oh, please," he said, "your daughter was responsible for the book and she returned it broken. Simple enough. Are you really implying that in the last eight months, you haven't had an extra $12.00 to take care of this bill?"

I thought, *Oh, my. Wrong move, Mr. Wong.*

Hellen yelled, cussed some more, and pounded her fists on his desk. Her face was beet red, as she leaned her big bosom over his desk, putting her face directly in front of his. I was sure he could smell her from that close up, too.

Mr. Wong bolted up from his chair and walked around the desk.

Hellen grabbed his tie and shirt collar, twisted them into a knot, and slammed him hard up against the wall. She pinned him there... the toes of his highly polished shoes were barely touching the floor. Hellen's five feet, six inches, towered over him and surpassed his own slim build by well over 150 pounds.

The school secretary watched the scene play out from behind her desk. I listened as she reported the assault, blow-by-blow to the police dispatcher. I pleaded with Hellen to stop–but then I stopped because I was afraid she'd turn on me.

I watched as office personnel rushed around the office to watch from a distance, but no one stepped in to help Mr. Wong, or me.

I hurried to the opposite corner of the office, buried my face in my hands, and cried.

The office staff and my co-workers witnessed the scene. I was sure I would be fired after the police hauled Hellen away.

About that time, the principal, Mr. Carlile, came running in to the office. When I heard his voice, I turned around to watch.

"Now Mrs. Proietti, I promise we can work everything out. Yes ma'am. Just let Mr. Wong down...uh huh...yes, just like that...uh, let go of his tie, ma'am, uh huh, very good, very good. Here, why don't you come over here, and let me pull this chair out for you."

He turned to the onlookers and said, "We got it all under control everyone, you can return to your offices. Thank you."

With Hellen sitting down, Mr. Wong was trying to regain his composure, but his ego was not retrievable. Mr. Carlile quietly said to the school secretary, "Everything will be fine. Let the police know we can work it out from here. The incident is under control." God heard my prayers in the corner of that office and sent Mr. Carlile to help.

Then he seemed to notice me. Startled at my hiccupping from crying, he called me over and put his arm around me. "Now don't worry about a thing. We will work it out. Why don't you sit with my secretary? I think she has some caramels at her desk. I'm pretty sure she would take a break and share some with you. There, there, take a big, deep breath, that's better."

As I stepped out of the office, his secretary was just arriving with the glass of water. Hellen and Mr. Wong were eyeing each other as though they were ready to kill. I thought, *it's a good thing they don't have guns. Especially Mr. Wong. He has been humiliated in front of his boss and most of the office staff by a big, fat angry woman in a dirty, too tight dress, hanging lower in the front than in the back, with her slip showing. Poor guy. He didn't stand a chance.*

The school decided not to file assault charges. They forgave the $12.00 for the broken typing book and I was excused from classes the rest of the day.

I would rather stay at school, thank you.

When we left the school, Hellen bragged, "Well, I'll tell you one thing. I'm downright proud, you hear me, I said, I'm downright proud of myself for standing up to that idiot man. I won. Clear and simple. I won. Yup, I had to show those men a thing or two about not pushing around a single, divorced woman, just because they are men–with body parts I don't have–but I won, by cracky, and they won't be pulling their shenanigans on me again. I showed them who's boss. Did you see how that old coward, Mr. Wong, withered when I reminded him that my taxes paid his paycheck? Why, I could fire him if I wanted."

I didn't understand how all that worked. I just wished I'd had $12.00. Yesterday.

The end result, was that I was able to keep my job and the staff was kind to me.

Hellen went on for weeks, bragging about her victory over the stupid men at the high school.

~

After that incident, a few teachers came to my aid. The first time it happened, I was sitting in class during attendance. A teacher stepped into the classroom and talked with my teacher. Then, I was dismissed to leave with the visiting teacher.

Out in the corridor, the teacher explained that he was on a prep break and thought he'd spend some time with me. He walked me through the cafeteria, and the sweet cafeteria ladies had food for me: a sandwich, apple, and a carton of milk. I ate while we strolled around campus and talked together. Then, just before the class period ended, he walked me back to class.

At first, I didn't understand. I worried about missing my schoolwork and having to make it up, but the teachers had worked it out, so I was excused from the assignments I missed.

The male teachers walked with me more than the female teachers. I didn't realize how much the staff was watching out for me, but I was grateful. I appreciated the food. I didn't know what I did to deserve their special kindness and I was afraid I would blow it somehow. Those walks meant a lot to me. I appreciated the efforts they made to reach out to me.

Unfortunately, the gap was too wide, and I was too afraid to reach toward them for help. The teachers treated me as though I was important and gave me many opportunities to talk about what was happening, but I never said a word to them about my life, my mother, my terror; not one single time.

Ever.

~

I continued to have a crush on Greg, but I knew he was too old for me. I was sad that I was too young to be someone he would consider. Besides, I knew he deserved a good girl, not someone like me. I didn't know why Greg dropped by the house occasionally to see me. I invited him into the house only if Hellen was there; otherwise, we'd stand outside and talk. He always gave me some cash in case I needed something. When he was gone, I'd wish I was old enough to marry him. I thought he was just stopping by to be nice.

After we were engaged, he told me he had prayed, "God, I'll wait for her but will You hurry up?"

I lived for his visits. I realized he would eventually marry and thought, *God bless the lucky girl.*

I kept these thoughts to myself. If I had shared them with Hellen, I would have been in trouble. A typical conversation with her about men was all about their forced slavery of women; she thought men were pigs and brutes. "Men just wanna keep their woman barefoot and pregnant. You want that? Huh? Huh?"

"Actually, no," I'd reply.

Later, when I was alone, I'd consider those conversations and think, *it's like she wants me to hate men just like she does.* I'd look at married women and wonder if Hellen was right about all that stuff.

~

One night after a church service, Pastor Murphy walked up to me and pointed his finger in my face. "I keep feeling a need to tell you this, Wilma. If your mother ever starts hitting you, you need to run. I'm afraid that all the venom and bitterness she has for your dad and Danny will come out and she could easily hurt you."

It was the only time he'd said anything to me like that in all the years I had known him. And he was one of the gentlest men I'd ever met. I stood there listening with a swollen ankle and bruises under my clothes from a recent hallway beating.

"Okay."

Inside I thought, *if she ever hits me? If? What do you mean if?* It was incredible to me that he didn't know and couldn't see that I was regularly being beaten. I found no words to explain to him.

1980: 16 Years Old: January, February, March

I figured, *God has not shown him what a rotten person I am or he wouldn't have warned me.* I thanked God for not telling him that I was so bad. It was bad enough that God, Hellen, and I knew.

~

Two days after his warning, Hellen beat me in an especially violent way. It seemed she was deliberately trying to break a bone. She grunted as she swung my head through the hall, yanking my hair, her fists and kicks striking at full force. I pleaded for her to stop, when suddenly I remembered the pastor's advice. In that moment, the only hold she had on me was fistfuls of my hair and somehow, I managed to break loose.

I ran.

I ran, leaving whatever hair she held onto behind. I heard it ripping out of my head. I ran to the front door and planned to run to a nearby restaurant to call the police.

At the front door, I put my hand on the knob, and froze.

I heard loud sobbing. Screaming sobbing. It was coming from the other end of the house. Though I was frightened, and my heart was pounding, I tiptoed down the hallway.

At the end of the hall, I looked in Hellen's room. She was lying on her bed, in hysterics. Unsure of what to do next, I walked down the hall. I went into the living room. I turned on the television. I turned up the volume to drown out the sound of her crying. She continued to scream-cry. It was a weird hysterical sound.

I sat in a chair and tried to calm down.

I was trembling and wanted a drink, and when I realized I was too afraid to get one, I cried.

It was the first and only time I had ever managed to get away from her.

Later that night, Hellen got ready and left for work like nothing had happened.

It took me a few weeks to recover from the injuries. She beat me again within a few days, before I recovered.

1980: 16 Years Old: January, February, March

~

The greater the power, the more dangerous the abuse.
~ Edmund Burke

~

A few times a month, Hellen ordered me to the living room to sit in a particular chair. I referred to those times as The Lectures.

Hellen would sit in her recliner and begin talking in a calm tone. "You see, Wilma, I love you and I'm genuinely concerned about your future. It is my job, as the godly mother that I am, to properly fulfill my duties and sit you down and have a frank talk with you."

I'd get an instant stomachache. Then, she would begin a two- to five-hour lecture.

Contorting her face, she railed, "You're a rotten, dirty, hopeless, scumbag. Do you even realize what a disgusting, fat, stupid, and ugly girl you have grown to be? Can you even fathom what a disappointing burden you've been to me? I never wanted to give birth to you in the first place. You're such a no-good, rotten loser, if I didn't love you so much, I'd disown you. After all, most mothers would if they were stuck with you. You need to thank God that I'm not like other women. I've worked hard, provided for you and you don't appreciate how good you've got it."

I believe you that I'm worthless.

Yet, there were moments that I wondered, *why do you waste your time on me? And, what happened that you never wanted to give birth to me? And, if you didn't want me before I was even born, how is that my fault?*

"And you can forget ever finding a man, because no man in his right mind would ever want a lazy pig like you. If you do manage to dupe one, it would be my moral duty to save him from you."

I'd think, *so, let me get this straight. If I'm a pig and you're my mother, what does that make you?*

Then she'd question, "Why did I get stuck with such a sorry excuse for a daughter like you? What did I ever do to God? Huh? Huh?"

"I don't know." *You tell me, I'd truly like to know.*

"I don't know either. Look, I might as well be the one to tell you, there is no heaven for someone like you. You can forget ever hoping to glimpse that beautiful city."

That's awful news and I believe you're probably right.

But I might as well be the one to tell you to stop spitting when you talk and to use more Fix-O-Dent on your false teeth.

I'm tired, hungry, I have to go to the bathroom and I'm sick of all your pompous, how-great-thou-art's.

"It's not for unappreciative, selfish brats like you that can't even show proper respect to the wonderful, godly mother you've been given. You may have the Church people fooled, but I know what you really are."

At this point, I decided I'd better listen or maybe she'd tell the church folks. I didn't want that. She used scripture and Bible examples to prove to me how truly awful I was. Her voice was growing louder, her face was turning red. I knew she was just warming up.

"Evidently, you are a judgment in my life for some reason that I just can't fathom."

Later the family secret was revealed. It proved that Hellen could in fact 'fathom' the reason. Yet, another one of her countless lies.

"It will be the most blessed day when I can finally unload the burden of having to raise you."

Why am I a burden? I thought children were a blessing?

"Then I'll be able to understand what the children of Israel felt like when they were freed from Egypt. I guess everyone has a cross to bear. Life's road has been hard, and it's your fault. You need to be honest for a change, Wilma, and face the facts. That's what I'm trying to help you do today: Face the facts. If only you could act like the Christian you claim to be, if only you were appreciative and less mouthy, you wouldn't make my life the constant hell that you do."

On my really angry days, I'd think; *who is making who's life a constant hell, Hellen? Are you taking 20-second showers? Hey, Hellen are you being beaten in the hallway? Are you starving Hellen? How about your hair? Is it laying in clumps in the hallway? Are you afraid every second of your life Hellen? How many lectures are you sitting through with your butt stuck to a chair for hours Hellen? Let's talk about 'constant hell', Hellen. Ya, let's talk. I've actually got a lot to say.*

"And stop with all the crying like you've got a hard life. You don't know what a hard life is. You're so spoiled you can't even think straight. I mean, you've got it downright made. You can read the Bible all you want, but even that book agrees with me. And by the way, knock off the Pharisee nonsense."

Pause. She'd wait, sighing and rolling her eyes until I'd reply.

"Pharisee nonsense?" I knew she'd mimic the question.

"Pharisee nonsense? Pharisee nonsense?" She was yelling and slamming her fist on the arms of the chair. "There you go again! Playing stupid! You're gonna split hell wide open for that!"

No response.

She settled down a bit, then talked in a slow, deliberate way as if I were a small child: "Let me spell it out for you. Pha-ri-see? They were people in the Bible that had a holier-than-thou attitude. And that's you, smarty-pants. You think you're so much better than me and all you are is worthless dog poop. You want scripture for that? I'll give it to you. Revelations 21:8. It says that even God doesn't want you because you are going to burn in hell for being such a dirty liar. You claim to love God, don't you?"

"Yes."

"Then you just proved what I just said. You're a liar and you're going to split hell wide open. It's my responsibility as a mother to warn you."

1980: 16 Years Old: January, February, March

"How am I lying about loving God?"

The only time I was stupid enough to ask that question, she screamed, "The old innocence trick. Gotta spell it out for you, do I? As stupid as you are, I don't know why I'm surprised. You say you love God whom you haven't seen but you don't love me who you have seen! That makes you a liar. Find the scripture that tells you it's okay to be a stupid, ugly Pharisee who is ungrateful for the wonderful mother you have been blessed with. Here! Find it, oh Sister Christian."

She threw a huge Bible at me. I caught it, set it on my lap, and didn't open it.

"OH, no! You're not getting out of this. Find it, I said!"

Making a feeble attempt to look through the Bible, I said, "I don't know of a scripture that says that."

"THEN WHY DON'T YOU CHANGE?"

"I don't know."

She mimicked what I'd said, "I don't knowwwww. Well, I'll tell you why you don't know...because you're an idiot and you don't have one functioning brain cell."

Oh, sure, now I recognize your caring Christian attempt to help me. Took my one functioning brain cell a moment, but I've got it.

"What God did give you, you've wasted dreaming up rhymes with your head in the clouds, but don't fool yourself–I've noticed you haven't written any of your stupid poetry about me! I'm the reason you're even alive, yet you have the gall to dream up stupid rhymes, leaving me out. Why?"

I have no interest in writing a poem about you. I couldn't write what a wonderful godly mother you claim to be because you aren't. And I wouldn't EVER write that I love you, because I'm pretty sure I hate you and I'm afraid God is not pleased with me for it.

I was appalled, so I said the first thing that came to my mind, "I don't know."

"Oh, there you go again. I dddon't knnnow. Well, I do know. You don't appreciate me. You're useless. Hugh, Danny, and Tracy can go out and take care of themselves, but what are you gonna do when I'm dead and gone? Sleep around town for your keep? Probably. You're nothing but a whore anyway. As your mother, I'm telling you, you better wise up, and make it snappy."

I didn't know what "sleep around town" meant or how it would "keep" me, but she said it often. I didn't know what a whore was, but I figured I must be one. She said it all the time. I figured it couldn't be a good thing, since I wasn't any good.

Hellen moved the conversation fast; almost like the auctioneer I'd seen on TV, I couldn't keep up with her, and no matter what I said, I was always wrong.

Hellen required me to look her straight in the eye during the entire lecture and it was hard to do. It made it impossible to shutdown my mind. I hated when she asked me questions. She'd begin in a conversational tone, and then switch to sharp and cruel. It caught me off-guard the first few times.

"So, let me ask you something. Why can't you be clean like Tracy? Did you ever open your idiotic eyes and see that she is thin, smart, and pretty? Why can't you use that brain you waste writing worthless poetry, and apply yourself to something smart like Hugh? By the way, how is it you can never write nothing poetic about your wonderful mother, huh? Huh?"

I said nothing. *What can I say to something like that?*

"I asked you a question and I expect an answer."

"I don't know."

"Of course, you never know! It's because you're not grateful! Produce something that looks like decent writing for once, and maybe I'd see some value in all that time you waste. Have you taken a look at Danny lately? He's earning his own way, not sitting around rhyming stupid words that no one will ever read. Wilma, did you ever notice that Hugh, Danny, and Tracy don't even want to be around you? They come here to the house to see me. Did you notice? Huh? Huh? I want an answer."

"Yes. I noticed they come to visit you." There was an unspoken rule that I must give the answer she wanted. I felt like a machine. I wanted to tell her, *I am hungry, I need the bathroom without you watching me, and I need clean clothes.* But I didn't dare say it.

If I gave the wrong answer, there was "hell to pay." I had "paid" in the past.

If I cried, she'd smile, and the lecture lasted longer.

The one time a lecture lasted for five hours was torture, both physically and emotionally. I remember thinking, *I'd rather clean a yard full of weeds than sit and listen to you ramble on and on.* I sat there hoping for a phone call to interrupt her onslaught of 'help.' Often Hellen got up to get food, or to go to the bathroom, but I wasn't allowed to move until she was finished with the lecture. It wasn't so bad if I had just gone to the bathroom when the lecture started, but if I was on my way there when I was told to sit, I was going to be miserable for a long time. I never had an accident, but I had several close calls. She threatened me that if I did have an accident, she'd teach me a lesson I'd never forget. *Would it be as bad as my bottom molded to this chair for five hours? I'm already covered in bruises…*

The afternoon of the five-hour lecture Hellen seemed determined to 'help' me no matter how long it took.

~

Noise proves nothing. Often a hen who has merely laid an egg cackles as if she laid an asteroid.
~ Mark Twain

~

Sitting forward on the edge of her chair, creating less space between our eyes, she glared at me and calmly said, "I gave birth to you and as your mother there are things I am required by God to tell you. Do you hear me?"

I nodded and thought, *hours more than I want to.*

Then, I tried tuning her out.

For a moment, all I heard was, "Now, Wilma, *blah blah blah blah*...."

Continuing in a slow, deliberate voice, she twisted up her face, "You, no one else, I'm talking about You! You are nothing but a filthy, dirty pig. You are a worthless piece of trash."

And, you claim to be my birth mother. What does that make you?

"If we could, we'd all scrape you off the bottom of our shoes, like dog poop."

Then do it and let me go.

"You don't seem to get it, but everyone else sees what I see. We all watch as you ruin every solitary thing you touch. Tracy sees it. Hugh sees it. Danny sees it. So, what in God's name is your flimsy excuse?'

Crying, I hung my head.

I am horrified and embarrassed. I didn't realize that everyone knew I was worthless. I thought I was covering my flaws better than that.

Then she'd require eye contact again.

"Cry all you want, you fat crybaby, but somebody's got to tell you the truth. You may not believe it now, but I'm doing this because I love you. You've been raised in the same house, with the same loving mother as Hugh, Danny, and Tracy, yet you turned out to be the biggest disappointment on God's green earth. Don't you see that Tracy is good, and you are bad? Tracy is clean, and you are dirty? Tracy is smart, and you are stupid. Tracy is pretty, and you are ugly. Tracy is fun, and you are a burden? Tracy has friends and you don't? Tracy takes good care of her things, and you trash everything you're given. Tell me something, what are you going to do if you end up getting stuck with a bad daughter someday, like I did? What are you gonna do?"

I don't know, but I'm not going to lecture her or call her 'fat crybaby, loser', or any of the other stupid, mean names you call me under the banner of love. It's true, Hellen, I am afraid of you. You do horrible, frightening things to me. But, no matter how much you beat me, drug me or brainwash me, I will <u>never</u> be like you. All your efforts are working to propel me 180 degrees different from you. One thing you need to know, Hellen, if I'm blessed with a husband and children, I will never, ever be like you. I will love my husband and children. Truly love them. Not sickly 'love' them. But I will love them in the true meaning of the word. They will be the JOY of my life. And here and now while you ramble on in your self-righteous, arrogance, I commit to loving the husband I do not know and I commit to cherishing the children I dream for the chance to be honored to raise.

I'm sorry you're stuck with me, but did you ever think that maybe I am stuck with you? Because I am stuck. Trapped actually. So much so that I pray for rescue or death, if death is the only rescue God permits. I will gladly accept whatever rescue He allows. As long as rescue comes.

And hey, Hellen, I can see that Hugh, Danny, and Tracy are good and I am bad. I just didn't know that other people could see. That's devastating.

But I still have a dream or two left. So I keep praying. Keep hoping. You, Hellen, are not in my future, if I have one. Just so you know.

~

I called her Hellen as often as I could in my mind, after she slapped me across the kitchen floor for saying it to her face. It just felt good to do it. Later, I'd feel bad and repent. But, in the moment...it just felt really good.

~

Over the course of countless lectures, I took Hellen's words to heart and I based my self-worth on her opinion. I figured, *my dad must have realized he couldn't stand me, and that is why he never bothers to contact me.* I wondered, *where is he, what is he like, and is he still alive?* I felt so alone in the world, and I believed it was better for everyone if I stayed by myself. I wanted to die.

Hours after each lecture, I wept praying, *God, I don't know how to do better. No matter what I do, it's wrong.* I continued to call the days I wasn't allowed to eat a fast, yet, all the praying, fasting, and seeking God didn't seem to make me smart, pretty, or good.

The Lectures messed with my mind a great deal. Hellen's words darkened my hopes, dreams, and beliefs in myself and the future. I'd mouth off to her in my mind, and then figure God viewed that as disrespectful. I'd repent just in case He thought that way. The Lectures remain one of the worst memories I have of surviving Hellen's house. They were nothing short of brainwashing, and the repetition proved extremely powerful, warping my reasoning, clouding my vision. Instead of helping me, Hellen exploited my vulnerability.

It took years of hard work and patience to achieve healing. I think of this scripture daily: Proverbs 18:21 (KJV) "Death and life are in the power of the tongue…"

~

I felt bad for God because I pestered Him so much. I thought He must be relieved when I was sleeping. At least He could have a break from me then.

In an effort to soothe myself, I tried to write about the anguish I was experiencing in my mind, body, and emotions. Perhaps it helped the most, by allowing me to share with the pen and paper the nightmare that consumed my world. After writing, I tore the pages up and either burned them on the gas stove or flushed them down the toilet. I couldn't chance Hellen discovering them.

I endured multiple lectures and concluded that I should *at least try* to write a poem for Hellen to see if it could bring some peace. I felt forced to write it after Hellen's lecture about 'writing worthless poetry.' I hoped maybe it could even lessen the frequency of the lectures. I was so tired of them. Regardless of what she thought or said, I refused to include that I loved her, or that she was a 'godly mother.' This is the poem.

To My Mother

My mom has been good to me.
I think she even spoiled me.
She works more than anyone I know.
I appreciate that....and she knows.
Sometimes she yells at me and,
I get mad and think she's mean.
I'm pretty stupid to think like I do.
'Cause I know it's really not true.
So, this is for my mother.
'Cause there's no one like her
no not another.

Wilma Proietti

~

I was dying for Hellen's love and approval, and Hellen died not granting me either one. I was never good enough, or smart enough in her eyes, to merit her love. Yet, Hellen carried the poem with her to show off my 'love' for her (that I'd actually refused to write about) at work, church, and at my school. The fact sickened me, and it didn't change The Lectures at all. It didn't even lessen a Lecture by a minute.

I was sorely disappointed. I was also angry that I had given in to her intimidation and wrote something for her to haul around in her purse. No matter what I did, I failed.

~

1980: 16 Years Old: January, February, March

The Lectures showed another cruel side of Hellen who unbelievably–dressed up as Santa Claus during Christmas time. She was so obese that she didn't need pillows to fill out her Santa suit. I was required to dress up as an elf and attend her company parties and watch as she entertained her drunken supervisors and fellow employees. I was uncomfortable when the drunks grabbed me and pulled me onto their laps. It was weird seeing Hellen hugging her co-workers.

After leaving the parties, we dropped by the children's ward of the local hospital. In the 1970s, security was lax regarding visits from Santa Claus. She was always welcome, and it puzzled me how she could bring so many smiles to other children's faces, and so many tears to mine. When I'd walk through the hospital corridors with her and see all the happy faces of the staff, parents and children, it confirmed to me that I was genuinely rotten inside. Often, it seemed as though there were confirmations to my badness wherever I looked. I assumed that God was trying to show me that Hellen was good, the sick little children were good, but I was dirty, disgusting, unacceptable and therefore worthless. They could smile and appreciate Hellen and I couldn't.

Hellen used those events to emphasize how others appreciated her, and to prove what a stupid idiot I was. I could see her point, but I didn't know what to do.

I repented often for any unknown sins. Yet, in spite of all my repenting, I didn't become good. That puzzled me, and I tried harder, repenting daily.

1980: 16 Years Old: January, February, March

~ Counseling Notes ~

*'Twant me, 'twas the Lord. I always told Him,
"I trust you. I don't know where to go or what to do,
but I expect you to lead me," and He always did.*
~ Harriet Tubman

The hygiene restrictions were humiliating for me and I asked about the risks I took regarding them.

The counselors said, "The 20-second showers were an act of total desperation. They also show your resolve and resilience in the face of unspeakable abuse as you continued to try to care for yourself, attend high school and work your part time job, all the while dealing with Hellen's relentless cruelty.

You have a lion within you that kept fighting, even when you thought you couldn't go on, you held on. You washed your hair with bar soap. You washed your clothes out in the sink and wore them wet to school on cold mornings. You did what you could with what you had. You did not give up. That alone is amazing. You did not give up."

~

The typing book fiasco was one I didn't understand because it made Hellen look bad. I asked about it in counseling.

"Well, Hellen probably didn't intend for it to get that out of hand. When it did, she had to calm herself

1980: 16 Years Old: January, February, March

down and appear completely reasonable with the principal and put the blame on the assistant principal. It may have worked, since the assistant principal's ego was wounded. Either way, she was bound to have left a mark in their minds that they didn't want to deal with her for minor reasons. They probably already knew that, from your elementary school history, but she took a risk that day. If the police had arrived, Hellen would've faked a diabetic episode, like you saw her do through the years."

Pastor Sawyer added, "Hellen was a master manipulator, and she knew just how far to work the system to her advantage."

~

I asked about the lectures because I would feel bad about the 'back talking' I had in my thoughts.

"The Lectures were nothing short of old-fashioned brainwashing. They were mentally, physically, and emotionally abusive each and every time. Hellen requiring you to maintain eye contact would have made it hard for anyone to drift off or shutdown.

Your resilience shows in your private thoughts. Your thoughts and feelings were normal and anyone going through what you were, would've had similar thoughts and feelings. You were not rebellious or disrespectful as you feared. You were normal."

~

I felt awful that I wrote the poem for her. I didn't want to and I only did it to try to ease the pressure while living in her house. I was proud of myself for refusing to give in and write the things she was hoping for.

1980: 16 Years Old: January, February, March

They said, "The poem you felt pressured to write for Hellen again shows your resilience and independence. Your refusal to include that she was a good mother, a godly mother, or that you loved her, was obvious. Yet, Hellen failed to recognize your blatant omission of what most mothers would hope for from a child, that they are a good mom and the child's expression of 'I love you.'

Hellen apparently believed she had 'won' by manipulating you into writing something special for her. In fact, you wrote something just to get by, deliberately withholding the treasured phrases because they weren't true. That took courage and guts. She could have made things difficult for you if she had picked up on what you were thinking. Like I said before, you have a lion within you that kept fighting when you thought you couldn't anymore."

1980: 16 Years Old
April, May, June

Courage is not having strength to go on;
it is going on when you don't have the strength.
~ Theodore Roosevelt

The Times

The springtime of 1980 brought news of tragedy for Operation Eagle Claw when eight U.S. soldiers were killed attempting to free hostages in Iran. 3M began the sales of its latest product: Post-it Notes, and new technology introduced the first fax machines. And, I missed most of life around me as I focused on one solitary thing: survival.

Along with the growing verbal and physical abuse, the sexual abuse had worsened to epic proportions.

When Hellen was home, my life was absolute hell.

Hellen became increasingly violent as my body developed and entered puberty. Hellen crudely expressed her excitement about the changes she saw in me. I loathed the changes, and I was very uncomfortable. I didn't know how to handle Hellen's rules about my personal hygiene, or what I could do about it. I wanted to ask, *what brought this on?* but fear always stopped me. Asking any question

1980: 16 Years Old: April, May, June

meant loose front teeth and busted, bleeding lips. Asking would turn into a strip search.

Asking just wasn't worth it.

I buckled under the crushing load of Hellen's perverted, cruel punishments.

The agony overwhelmed me.

I began trying to live for just a few minutes at a time.

Sometimes that was too much.

I focused on one solitary thing; survival.

~

Hellen's sexual appetite was information that I should have never known. I was horrified by the things she did. Horrified to the extent that at times I was mute with shock and terror.

Countless times in the middle of the night, I'd be asleep in my bed and awaken to find Hellen saying and doing the most perverted things to my body. The first time I awoke and realized, within seconds, that she was standing by my bed and sexually abusing me, she was very involved in her fantasy, so I just faked being asleep. My heart pounded hard and I was afraid if I breathed wrong, Hellen would know I was awake. I was terrified of what she would require me to do if she knew I wasn't sleeping.

The next day, she smiled and said, "I went in your room last night to check on you. You weren't covered up." Then, she would graphically describe the dirty fantasies she had while watching me sleep. I didn't understand why she talked to me that way. I found her descriptions disgusting. She watched me closely as she spoke, calculating to see if I had been aware of her touching me.

After that, her middle of the night visits were a regular event, disturbing though they were.

~

Sometimes, after a night of sexual abuse, Hellen would take

me to McDonald's the next day for dinner. She demanded that I behave overwhelmingly grateful that she was allowing me to eat, or I'd get in serious trouble. I had to put on a phony happy face and be overly pleasant and chatty, or she would become enraged at my ungratefulness. I found it hard to smile and laugh at her vulgar jokes that I didn't understand. My jaw ached for days after a beating and I had difficulty chewing with my teeth knocked loose.

It seemed hypocritical when she bowed her head to pray over dinner at McDonald's, though I did thank God for my food. I didn't get a hot meal often, and I was grateful.

Ironically, Hellen offered a hot meal when I could least enjoy one. The pain I was in literally sickened me. I did eat when she bought me food, but it was difficult to chew, swallow, smile, and pretend that I was happy to be having dinner with my mother.

The times when Hellen didn't allow me to eat after the abuse were especially difficult. Often, she'd continue the abuse with no reprieve. It was bad enough without gnawing hunger pangs at the same time. She seemed especially angry during those times.

I don't know what made Hellen decide to take me to McDonald's for dinner after a night of sexual abuse, and starve me on other days. The only thing predictable about Hellen was her unpredictability. I never figured out that part of her system, if in fact she had one. The times she decided to let me starve, she appeared angrier than normal; vicious, actually.

The whole McDonald's thing caused great conflict for me. I wanted, even felt as though I needed to go because I was so hungry, but it deeply troubled me. I wondered if it was Hellen's way of 'paying' or making it up to me somehow, for sexual abuse or the beatings? If that is what Hellen thought, then, *was I for sale to my mother? For food? For anything?* I had no one to ask, but it distressed me a great deal. After several months, I finally concluded that I was not, since I had no choice in either matter and I despised what was happening.

So, I worked frantically to learn each new set of rules Hellen made and tried diligently to follow them. I lived in so much fear I didn't have time to examine the reasoning behind things. If, in fact, there was any reasoning.

I could rarely calculate what was going to upset her next, or when she would allow me to eat again, or when I'd be allowed to use the bathroom, take a shower, or even sleep alone, unbothered all through the night. It was scary trying to navigate her weird behavior.

~

Then, there were the unspeakable nights…

Hellen's bedroom was dark and cold. Its filth matched her perverted mind and the unspeakable horrors I experienced in that room. She had been a smoker since she was a teenager. She claimed to be above such sinful behavior, unbecoming to a godly woman like her. Yet, my siblings and I knew about her habit.

The cigarette burns on her clothes and bed were difficult for even Hellen to lie about. She was careless, and I was afraid she would catch her bed on fire.

Although Hellen ate breath mints often, nothing counteracted the effects of her smoking and not brushing her false teeth for several weeks at a time.

Her room reeked of smoke, urine, dirty clothes, and putrid body odor. I dreaded seeing the large, brown roaches scurrying around in there.

But that wasn't her only revolting habit. Almost daily, she'd call for me to come into her bedroom where she'd be laying on her bed naked, exposing herself.

"Did you need something?" I'd ask.

"Get me glass of water. Hurry up. I'm thirsty."

I'd return with a glass of water and be disgusted by her foul smell. I'd try to completely empty my lungs when leaving her room. The foul smell lingered, and I hated it.

1980: 16 Years Old: April, May, June

~

Hellen's basic pattern for the sexual abuse began with a brutal hallway beating for an unknown reason. After each beating, I had little physical or emotional energy and I suffered severe headaches and dizziness from the blows to my head. My body ached in pain and emotionally, I felt depleted and defeated.

A short time after the beating, Hellen would call me in at my physically weakest and emotionally despondent moment. Hearing her voice, I'd feel the rise of fear in my gut.

She'd order me to her bed by saying, "Come in here to my room."

It was a command, not a suggestion.

"No mom, I'm really tired."

Pleading exhaustion was a delay tactic that never worked. Yet, I tried something every time. When she called me, I was required to go to her.

"Ah, come on in here now, you know I love you."

I hated hearing her say, 'I love you,' because she permitted no more delay at that point. She had zero tolerance for any procrastination. Terrified, I'd reluctantly get out of my bed and walk into her room.

Each time I walked in, I'd find her in bed, naked and exposed, all 300 pounds of her. I was disgusted at the sight. Then Hellen would pat her filthy bed, saying, "Come. Lay by me."

Trembling, I'd lay down on my side, with my back to her. As she moved her obese body towards me, I felt shock by her intense body odor. Hellen reeked of sweat, garlic, and onions.

As the nightmarish touching began, I became mute. Physically, I choked. My throat tightened, I found it hard to breathe, and was unable to cry. I shutdown my mind, as fear overwhelmed me. I squeezed my eyes shut so I could not witness the nightmare of what was happening to my body. Lying in her bed, my heart pounding in my chest, I felt as though I were drowning in a sea of revulsion.

I'd hear her say, "You're my baby girl and you know I love you." Then, in silence she'd play out her perversions on me.

I shutdown my mind, hid in my hiding place. I was a trapped teenager, standing at the edge of hell.

The abuse was painful; yet, I found that submitting made it get over with faster. Lying in Hellen's roach-infested bed, every time I prayed the same silent prayer, "Jesus, Jesus, Jesus," repeatedly while she did what she wanted, as long as she wanted.

Then, with her hands, and her feet, she'd shove me out of her bed. I'd stumble, confused and hurt back to my room, and collapse into my bed.

I felt as if part of me had died in her bed.

~

The nights of sexual torture were a separate class by themselves. They included the stolen drugs and Hellen's signature brutal beating in the hall.

Afterwards, she would call me into her room. In pain, I'd ease my body out of bed, and obediently walk into her room. Once in a while, she'd give me a small pill, and I swallowed it without question. I have no idea what kind of drug she gave me. I knew what was going to happen, and after a beating, the pill helped block the pain. It left me barely aware of what she was doing to me, but dopey enough to be cooperative. Often, I felt dizzy and sick to my stomach, but I didn't know if it was caused by the pill or the beating.

Dizzy with a headache, my body beaten, swollen and bruised, I'd lay on her bed wishing I could just die. My throat tightened, and I felt mute. I found it hard to breathe and I couldn't have called out for help if I tried.

Until the day I die, I will remember her sickening touch, her vulgar fantasies, and the smell of my own skin burning when she held her lit cigarettes against my skin.

She played out her perversions until she tired of me, and then

1980: 16 Years Old: April, May, June

used her feet to shove me out of her bed. As I stumbled in silence, sobbing towards my room, my throat would open, and I'd vomit into my mouth.

I'd swallow the vomit, too afraid to go to the bathroom without permission, as I gently eased myself down on my bed. I didn't know a person could throw up, then swallow it, but fear taught me it's not only possible around Hellen, it was the wise choice. I couldn't take a chance in drawing Hellen's attention that I was vomiting. I was in so much pain I wanted to die.

After each of the drugged nights of sexual abuse, Hellen left me as if I was garbage in the street. Every part of my body hurt, from head to toe, inside and out. I suffered killer headaches and earaches, my teeth were loosened, my jaw hurt, my neck sore and stiff, and my shoulders were swollen from being kicked. I had chest pain and my ribs hurt when I took a breath. My back was bruised and my insides ached. My body was burnt from her cigarettes, and I had no chance to heal between beatings.

Pain and bleeding were a normal result of those nights. Whether from the intense beatings or violent sexual abuse, I do not know. There was no one I trusted to ask.

So much pain. No Tylenol.

In the morning, I'd make my way to the bathroom. I felt desperate for a shower, but was too afraid to take one. I didn't think I could raise my foot high enough to put it over the edge of the tub, if I were able to attempt a shower. I knew that with the extreme pain I was in, I couldn't shower in twenty seconds, and I didn't believe I could survive another beating.

~

With tears flooding my face, I'd slowly pedal my bicycle to school. Physically, it hurt to breathe, and doing anything more seemed unbearable. Emotionally, I was in agony. I thought my lowest point had been when I'd had the nervous breakdown.

I couldn't have been more wrong. I didn't know that the human spirit could break, but mine was broken.

I had difficulty concentrating on my school work, and I felt drowsy from the drugs the night before. I went through the school day, silent, dazed, and unfocused. Alone and afraid.

Always, always afraid.

~

The feelings of self-hate, self-disgust, and the self-loathing that followed each night in Hellen's bed were devastating. I despised myself for not being smarter, stronger, or physically fighting her. I despised the coward I was. I felt like a total failure.

She said I caused her to do those things to me.

How did I cause her?

Could I make her to stop?

How could I tell anyone what I caused her to do?

Why would I tell on myself?

~

The complete, silent submission Hellen required during the sexual abuse was part of the dehumanizing and identity crushing she was working in my mind. She destroyed me and convinced me it was my fault. The shame that results from submitting to the things in her bed is incomprehensible and difficult to describe. Words are hard to come by, though I've searched for them.

Until I got help, I blamed myself, and shame overwhelmed me.

~

After my rescue, my medical records clearly document that Hellen's beatings and sexual abuse included internal injuries that later required surgeries. After a major surgery to repair some of the damage Hellen caused, the surgeon told Greg and I, "I've never seen such severe internal damage in all my years of practice." Shaking his head, he looked directly at me and said, "Inside, you were mutilated."

~

It took God, a dedicated pastor and his wife, a loving husband, and skilled counselors to help me heal past the damage she inflicted, and to have the beautiful life I have today.

Without help, I wouldn't be where I am.

~

But then, at 15 years old, I lived in agony. I couldn't see the bigger picture. I was blinded by pain and I was unable to reason properly.

I had one focus: Surviving.

~

I shall allow no man to belittle my soul
by making me hate him.
~ Booker T. Washington

~

1980: 16 Years Old: April, May, June

~ Counseling Notes ~

The most difficult and emotional topic to talk about was the sexual abuse and torture. The counselors were kind and helped me immensely.

They said, "You were Hellen's personal sex slave. (That was one of the hardest things to hear in counseling.) It is common for abusers like Hellen to focus in on one particular child, even if they abuse the other children to some degree. There was no way any child could have been good enough to stop an abuser like Hellen.

Predators will hurt someone; it just depends who they can get access to. Predators like Hellen, manipulate normal childlike love, trust, and the child's innate physical and emotional needs to gratify their wicked perversions.

Abusers who torture their victims often want the victims to be 'just like them.' There are two types of abusers. Both dehumanize the child in their own mind, and in the child's mind.

The first type doesn't care at all what happens to the child after the abuse is finished. The child is to them just something to find their perverted sexual release in. The second type of abuser first dehumanizes the child, and then diligently works to imprint themselves into the mind of the child.

Hellen stunk, she made sure you stunk, she was

1980: 16 Years Old: April, May, June

sexually perverted, and she controlled you into cooperating in her sexual perversion. Specifically, Hellen used starvation to control you. It is a very effective tool. Hellen combined spiritual, emotional, physical, and sexual torture. It is called, Systematic Ritual Abuse–on many levels. It is intended to strip the victim of their identity for life, completely dehumanizing them. This type of abuser deserves the death penalty."

Dr. Laine said, "It has enormously negative impact when the only parent breaches trust, and abuses the child. In your case, you had absolutely no one to turn to. The only parent you knew, was emotionally traumatizing you, physically beating you and sexually torturing you. It has an extremely negative impact. The years of gynecological and other health problems, and surgeries, are a direct result of the violent sexual torture.

You are an exception. God has been good to you. You shouldn't be able to function on any level after what you've been through. You shouldn't be able to speak. When we listen to you speak, and when we see you, the striking thing that comes to our minds is that God has done an amazing work in your life. You being able to function is clearly the grace of God in your life. You shouldn't be able to function on any level at all. To be sitting here talking to us is a miracle. You have a relatively normal life, with a few issues. You do have issues, but miraculously few given the extreme extent of the abuse you suffered."

Pastor Sawyer asked, "When did the abuse begin?"

Crying, I answered, "I don't know. It just always was."

Dr. Laine said, "In my professional view, with the PTSD and trauma you have, I feel confident the abuse started when you were preverbal."

"I will never truly know."

"You are a miracle. You are a survivor."

1980: 16 Years Old
July, August, September

The most important thing in communication is to hear what isn't being said.
~ Peter Drucker

The Times

Former actor and California Governor, Ronald Reagan, became a nominee for president. A gallon of gas cost $1.19. And, due to record high sugar prices, Coca Cola began substituting high-fructose corn syrup for half of the sucrose used in the recipe. The world seemed to spin on just fine every day, with no one noticing my anguish.

Succumbing to the agony I lived in every day, I devised a perfect suicide plan.

I simply had to get out.

~

The hot, scorching summer temperatures arrived. I was beyond despair. I didn't know it then, but I was in the final weeks of living with Hellen. My rescue was just around the corner. But I didn't have a clue.

~

I worked through the summer for the CETA program. Though I earned more money working full time, Hellen made sure I stayed broke. When I'd get a paycheck, Hellen gave me a sob story about how the other kids chipped in and helped her, and 'by God,' it was my 'turn' now. I didn't have a choice. She took most of my two-week earnings, requiring me to be a 'cheerful giver.' I paid my tithes and tried to hide a few dollars away for food. Only once, did I dare complain, and the four-hour lecture and beating weren't worth it.

Most days, I continued to go hungry. Sometimes people brought food into the office and shared it. I was thankful for everything that came my way.

~

As the abuse continued, I lost focus and the ability to see beyond the black cloud swirling around me. I did my best to cope with the daily nightmare. The sexual abuse was physically sickening. I was afraid that I was losing my mind.

Hellen's unrelenting cycle of punishments wore me down until my reason numbed and I felt as though I were stumbling around in a dark storm. She terrorized me, controlled my mind, stripped me of all privacy, dignity, and dehumanized me. There was no part of my life, my hopes, my dreams, my future, or even my bodily functions that Hellen did not manipulate, dominate, or control. She had no boundaries. I didn't believe I had a right to fight. I didn't know how to change the rotten person that I had always been.

Every failure to predict Hellen's mood just proved to me that *I am a very, very, stupid girl.* I thought, *if I pray more, maybe I can better predict her moods.* I worried that *God isn't helping me because He is disappointed in me.*

Hellen constantly reminded me, "You will never succeed in life because you are such an incredible idiot. A real loser. And that's all you are. This is not a matter of you simply making a mistake here or there. It's who you are–a god-forsaken loser. Get it?"

I got it.

1980: 16 Years Old: July, August, September

~

Greg wasn't afraid of Hellen. He clearly didn't like Hellen, but he liked me. One afternoon when he stopped by, Hellen invited him to sit at our kitchen table. After some small talk, Hellen said, "I'll tell ya Greg. This one here (pointing at me) is not what she looks like. She sits here all pious and Christian-like, but I'm the one that has to live with her. You'll never know the trouble she's caused me. I cannot wait, I mean to tell ya, I cannot wait, until that girl turns 18. Finally, my job will be done. I don't see any way to be free from the burden of that child until then. Lord, help me. I just don't know how much more I can take of her constant lying and rebellion."

When she finished, Greg turned to me, smiled and asked, "Want to get married?"

Smiling, and meeting his eyes–without hesitation–I said, "Yes."

Then, we laughed.

Hellen smirked. "That'll be the day," she said. "I doubt you or any man for that matter could or would want to put up with this one."

My head and my heart were swirling, and I don't remember the rest of her rant. Greg left shortly afterwards.

I thought he was brave to not be afraid of her.

I was afraid.

~

Except for an occasional trip to Tracy and Duane's house, Hellen kept me isolated from socializing most of the time. I was allowed to go to church, school, and babysit. I ended up spending most of my time with Hellen or alone. I wasn't allowed to have friends in the house. Hellen constantly accused me of bringing boys home while she was at work, but I never did. I didn't bring anyone to our house.

~

I continued to write, and with the encouragement of my English teacher, I entered writing contests. My writing won a place in the high school literary arts competition. I was shocked because I was a nobody on campus. I was also surprised and honored when two of my poems were published in a national *Poetry Anthology*. I couldn't afford to buy a copy of the published book and Hellen wouldn't. I was so disappointed.

Later, when Greg found out, he purchased four copies.

~

The year before, someone gave me a small toy organ with no legs. I would set it on my lap for hours and play songs. I wrote verses for the songs I knew. I could only play the melody, but it helped to pass the long hours I spent by myself.

The little tidbits of my life that summer were visits from Duane and Tracy, Greg stopping by to say hello, the toy organ, and writing. Tidbits. Little things, that meant a great deal, but they kept me going and eased the loneliness.

~

One evening, I was home alone. At about 7:30 p.m., a man came to the front door and he was yelling while pounding on it. The man watched me as he peered through the glass in the door. Then he went to the backyard and beat on the patio door.

I was scared, so I called the police. The police dispatcher heard the man yelling and pounding. I wanted to leave the house, but she told me to stay put; she said the police were en route, as well as a helicopter.

While I waited for help, the man grew more belligerent. It sounded like the patio door would break. The dispatcher pleaded with me to stay on the phone while the front yard lit up from the helicopter's spotlight.

The police arrested the drunken man. He said he worked for Hellen at the motel.

The officers asked me to call Hellen and have her come home to identify the man. I did, and she said, she would "be right there." While we waited for her, two officers asked if they could walk through the house, and I told them yes. They asked me to stay with the officers in the living room.

I could hear the officer's voices and their boots on the linoleum as they walked through each room. I heard them opening the linen closet, the heating unit closet, and dresser drawers and other closets.

I had no problem with their search because I had nothing to hide.

I knew that when they opened my dresser drawers, they wouldn't see any underclothes and that was a relief. I was wearing the only set Hellen allowed me to own. It was the only time I felt relief that Hellen had not allowed me to own any others.

While the officers walked through our house, I worried about getting in trouble from Hellen. After I'd thought about it, I didn't think she would want them to see the house, but I didn't know why. Her room was dirty but everything else was clean.

After they walked through the house, they asked me a lot of questions.

The questions scared me. My stomach hurt. I only gave them the answers I knew Hellen would allow.

"Do both your parents live here?"

"No."

"Does your dad ever visit?"

"I've never met him."

"Do you have a stepdad?"

"No."

"Does your mother have a boyfriend?"

"No."

"Do you have siblings?"

"Yes. Two older brothers, and a sister."

"Do they live here?"

"No. My sister is married. My brothers are away at college and working."

"Do your brothers ever spend nights here?"

"Never."

"Are there any men in this house?"

"No."

"Do you have any boyfriends?"

"No."

"Who else regularly stays here?"

"Just my mother and I."

The questions kept going. I thought they were just passing the time waiting for Hellen to show up. They kept asking me how long it took her to drive home from work. I told them it was less than 10 minutes. They asked me where she worked, and I told them the name of the motel.

They said, "Well, that's not far at all, is it?"

"No, it's not far, but she drives really slow." They laughed.

Some of the officers took the drunken man away, even though Hellen never arrived to identify him. I couldn't imagine what was taking her so long.

Next, a sergeant arrived, and the same two officers asked if they could walk through the house with him. I said it was fine, as I had nothing to hide. Again, they asked me to wait in the living room with the other officers.

The officers and the sergeant spent several minutes down the hall and when they returned, the sergeant asked me all the same questions. I gave him the same answers I had given earlier. I was even more nervous this time. I hoped I was handling things right. I knew I'd get a beating if I messed up. The longer the officers stayed, the longer it took for Hellen to arrive, and the more scared I got. I was biting my nails. I didn't want to cry. I was determined I wouldn't cry.

But I felt like crying.

Then the sergeant asked, "Are you safe?"

I froze. Looking at the floor, I lied, "Yes."

1980: 16 Years Old: July, August, September

Frowning, he asked, "Is anyone hurting you?"

Unable to look at anyone, I shook my head and quietly said, "No."

They waited for Hellen until 10 p.m., and then left. Afterwards, I was scared. I paced the house and was embarrassed when I realized the officers had surely noticed Hellen's sex toys on the top of her dresser and the padlock and swing latch on my bedroom door.

Hellen came in 20 minutes later and began questioning me. "Why did you call the police? What did you tell the police and why in God's name did they stay here so long, for a stupid brat like you?"

I began to explain about the man pounding on the door, but she interrupted.

"I cannot fathom why you had to call the police because one of my employees simply knocked on our door. When, pray tell me, will the big, fat crybaby ever grow up? Look at all the trouble you caused just by wanting some attention. Dear God, what will the neighbors think?"

I thought I had done the right thing by calling the police. I had messed up again. When was I ever going to stop being an idiot?

Later, I realized the officers had offered me an open door to talk about Hellen and I just couldn't tell them. They had been so nice to me, but if they found out all the trouble I caused, I figured they probably would have taken me to jail, like that man.

~

It was only after my rescue that I realized the police had tried to help me the night they searched Hellen's house. I understood too late that my intense fear blinded my ability to recognize their offers to help.

I now know that I could have been rescued that night. It was right there. I could have been safe that night. I just didn't realize it when the officers were there. My rescue was so close.

I've kicked myself a thousand times over.

~

1980: 16 Years Old: July, August, September

My world continued to grow darker by the day.

I was wearing down, and I remember the moment when I decided that either Hellen or I was going to have to die. I simply could not handle living in constant pain any longer. I spent a month trying to figure out how I could kill Hellen. Her obesity was a real problem. After considering all my options, I realized if I did come up with a plan, I'd be too cowardly to carry it through. I just couldn't kill her. She was my mom, after all.

So, I decided I had to die.

I was to blame for the trouble anyway. I started praying God would let me be run over by a truck on the way to school. I pictured a white moving truck, with no writing on it. I hoped for a hit-and-run, because I didn't want Hellen to get a settlement check.

I wrote Tracy a letter telling her that I had been praying to die. I told her I loved her, and I wished her a good life. I pulled my waterbed mattress way back and hid the letter. I figured if I died, Tracy would help Hellen clean out my room. I didn't think Hellen pulled the mattress back when she ransacked my room each week. That was too much work.

The more I thought about dying the more I was sure it was the answer to everything in life. I would never have to go to Hellen's bed again, there would be no more strip searches, no more gnawing hunger pains, no more beatings, body aches, no more ripped out hair, no more lectures. Dying was the answer.

Hellen's questions, beatings, the strip searches, the hunger pangs, the agony of daily life, fueled my need to die. I couldn't focus on anything except shutting my eyes forever. I lived in shutdown mode, detached from life. I read some stories about people giving up and dying and so I tried giving up. Day and night, I begged God to let me die. It seemed like such a simple request. I even quoted the scripture, "If you ask anything in my name, I will do it."

When I failed to die, I was mad. I couldn't even 'will' myself to die right.

~

When school started in August, I was the first to arrive in the bike racks at 7 a.m. each morning for my CETA job. As I locked my bicycle, I would angrily shake my fist towards God and ask, *Why God, why? What's another day? Why couldn't you have let me die this morning? Oh God! WHY another day?* Tears running down my face, I'd lock up my bike, and walk to my job in the attendance office.

I'd walk through the day, not paying attention to my classes or assignments, thinking, *it doesn't matter...I'm going to die today anyway.* I looked at teachers and students thinking, *this is the last time I will see them.* I lived to die. I was resigned. I had found the answer to my problems.

I'll be dead before sundown. I have found a way out of Hellen's house.

Bicycling home, I took the busiest streets I could find. When turning on our neighborhood street, I'd burst into tears, angry with God.

Why God, why? Why another night? Oh God NO! Not another night!

When I didn't die, I thought, *I am such a loser even God won't answer a prayer from me.*

I felt so lost in life.

~

I had reasoned this out in my mind,
there was one of two things I had a right to,
liberty or death; if I could not have one,
I would have the other.
~ Harriet Tubman

~

I put my energy into trying to make it through each day, and there was nothing left for dreams. I couldn't consider a future with what I was facing. Survival required me to be hyper vigilant, trying to predict her next move to avoid as much pain as possible. At the same time,

1980: 16 Years Old: July, August, September

I felt dead inside, living in shutdown mode, abandoned. As awful as I believed myself to be, I figured, *I am abandoned for a reason. Who wants a piece of God's garbage? Hellen doesn't. I don't. No one else appears to either.*

Every so often, I entertained dramatic moments in my mind about shooting Hellen through the temple while she slept naked in her bed. I wondered, *will I kill any roaches at the same time?* I thought about calling the police, the officers arriving and seeing her disgusting, filthy room, and her naked body. *Then what?*

Oh well, I knew I wouldn't be able to do it even if I could get my hands on a gun. I'd seen too many police movies.

~

Suicide appeared to be my only option. My plan had only one absolute requirement–it had to work the first time. I thought, *suicide attempts are Hellen's game, not mine. No one is going to find me holed up in a motel room with the police talking through a bullhorn to get me to come out. That is just plain humiliating.*

After much consideration, I came up with the perfect suicide plan. I would take all of Hellen's stolen pills, about 30 bottles in all, mix them and take them on an empty stomach. They were Valium or sleeping pills. I figured, *I can get most of them down quickly with a large glass of water. I will take all the pills and die on the kitchen floor. Right where she tried to kick me to death all those times.*

This time, I'll die without one kick. Same place, pain free. My choice. No kicks.

I had watched Hellen take one or two pills and they knocked her out for four or five hours. I didn't understand the weight ratio in regards to dosages, but I understood if two pills did that to her, 30 bottles worth of pills would probably kill me.

After I developed my plan, I had to decide when to do it. Never knowing when Hellen might stop by the house, day or night, posed a problem. Also, since Hellen had disabled all the locks on the bedroom and bathroom doors in the house, I would not be able to lock myself in any room. That was a problem. I did not want her to find me in time to save me. I couldn't imagine what she would do to me if I survived. I was afraid she'd kill me, making it look like I killed myself.

But I had my plan. I felt good to finally have a plan.

In my worst moments I knew, *I just have to get to those pills, and then it will be all over for me. I have the perfect plan. I just have to find the perfect time.*

~

At a particularly low point one afternoon, Greg dropped by. Hellen wasn't there, so we stood in the doorway talking.

"I just wanted to come by and see how you are doing."

"I'm okay. How have you been?"

"Fine, but I've had you on my mind a lot lately. I brought you some money. I thought you might need it."

"Oh. Thanks, but I'm okay."

"No. I brought it for you. I want you to take it and buy whatever you need."

Taking the money, I replied, "Thanks. That's so kind of you. I appreciate it."

I was thankful for each of his visits. I just wished I could marry him. I knew it would never happen, though. Hellen would never allow it.

~

The summer nights in 1980 were especially difficult. Hellen was working for a motel and she'd steal a room several nights each week. We had an evaporative cooler at our house but Hellen preferred the air conditioning in the motel better. She'd close off a room for 'maintenance,' turn down the air conditioning, and require me to stay overnight with her. Even though the rooms had two queen beds, she made me sleep with her. Drugs and sexual abuse happened in those motel rooms and I hated every moment of those nights.

Lying in those motel beds, I'd think about the pills at home. While enduring her nasty perversions, I'd escape in my mind to the medicine cabinet full of drugs that would free me forever. I'd promise myself, *the moment I get back to the house, I'll get the pills and take them.*

I wanted to die.

I was convinced that I was the epitome of shame after experiencing the demoralizing, dehumanizing things Hellen did to my body. Death seemed to be the only cleanser. I thought about, hoped for, and planned to die every single day.

In the morning, nauseous, tired, and dizzy from a night of drugged sexual abuse, I had to sterilize the motel room, and make it ready for paying guests. While I cleaned, Hellen went to the restaurant for breakfast. I wasn't allowed to eat.

Later, Hellen mocked my Christian convictions. "Well, did the little thief sleep well last night?" she asked.

The first time she did this, I asked, "Thief? What are you talking about?"

"Oh, you play the innocent role so well! It seems to me that Sister Christian's convictions and all your Bible reading didn't prevent you from sleeping last night. Did you pay for that room?"

Obviously, I hadn't. "No."

"Well, I stole it, and you slept in it, so you're a thief, too. You took part in my sin."

I repented. I prayed to God to be forgiven. I desperately hoped He understood I'd felt awful. I hadn't meant to steal.

~

After my experience at Bible camp, I spent a lot of time praying in my room. Occasionally, prayer time turned into a beating.

I'd think I was alone in the house when Hellen was working the night shift at the nursing home. Kneeling by my bed, I'd pour my heart out to God about everything troubling me. I had no friends, no one to talk to, so I talked to God since He was my best friend. Most of the time, I had no words for my pain; just great, heaving sobs, as soon as my knees touched the cold, hard floor.

I'd pray until my chest hurt from weeping, then I'd painfully rise from the floor and crawl into bed. So weary. My body was bruised, my spirit broken. I didn't worry as much about the physical injuries, but it was how I hurt inside that troubled me.

I didn't know if God was happy to hear from me or disgusted. I just knew I felt better after talking to Him. Unloading the pain in my mind seemed to help me feel better.

Yet, there were nights when Hellen slipped into the house, unbeknownst to me, and heard my anguished cries. As I knelt on the floor, telling God all about my troubles, I wouldn't hear Hellen come into the house. She'd quietly slip my door open, and then *suddenly* yank me off the floor by my hair, ripping out chunks in the process. Then, she'd drag me into the hall for a beating.

She'd holler, cuss, quote scriptures and scold me for praying.

"You've got it made in life but you're just too stupid to know it. Stop all your idiotic bawling, squalling and slinging snot."

After the beating, she'd leave me lying on the kitchen floor, calmly straighten her nurse's uniform and go back to work. It was usually one or two in the morning.

On her nights off, I didn't attempt to pray. I was too afraid and hoped God would understand. Either way, I sobbed each morning as I bicycled to school. Sometimes it was hard to see through the blur of tears. I'd arrive at school with a swollen face, and red eyes.

Nobody seemed to notice.

~

Life was a vicious cycle, but my conclusion stayed the same. *If only God would let me die, everyone would be happy…especially me.* That's all I wanted. It seemed like such a small request. Yet, I couldn't seem to get that prayer answered. So, I kept quiet and waited for death to come. That's all I could think to do.

I'm sorry I am still breathing. I don't want to be.

Often, I stood weeping in front of the cabinet with all the bottles of pills. I'd try to get the courage to just take them and get it all over with. I'd stand there looking at the stolen pills and cry and cry and cry. Wanting to live, and yet wanting so much to die. Conflict was ever present in my troubled mind.

Each time I told myself, *if I can just make it through one more day, maybe I'll be good enough that Hellen will start loving me tomorrow… or maybe God will let me die tomorrow…*but that tomorrow never came.

~

My lowest point in the summer of 1980 came one Tuesday evening around 9 p.m.

I arrived home from work around 5:40 p.m. in the afternoon feeling exhausted and very hungry. The last food I'd eaten was a can of peas the prior Saturday night. I felt weak, shaky, and lightheaded. I'd been drinking gallons of water in an effort to feel full. It hadn't worked.

As soon as I walked in the house, Hellen yelled for me to come to her bedroom. I needed to use the bathroom, but I hated her watching me so I skipped it and went into her bedroom. She got up off her bed, barking orders. "Stand at the foot of my bed and take off all your clothes. Now. Hurry up. I ain't got all day."

I looked at her, stunned. I had just gotten off work. I had to go to the bathroom. I was tired, and starving. *Could she ever be kind to me? Ever?*

"Helllooooo?" she said. "Do I have to beat some sense into you, or are you gonna take off your clothes, Miss Modest One? Oh, Sister Righteous, are you gonna obey your mother? Still believe the Bible? Huh? Huh?" Her cruel words, military style of speaking, and now, a sing-song were disturbing.

I couldn't believe it was happening again, but I undressed. I wept as she petted, fondled, yanked, and pulled at various parts of my body. She'd pretend she was reaching out to gently touch me, then suddenly viciously pinch and twist my skin. When I cried, she cussed at me and spit in my face.

When she finished with me, she said, "Out in the hallway. Now."

I realized she was going to beat me, and that freaked me out. I was naked. One of my greatest fears was that Hellen would beat me when I was naked. I was afraid it could become yet another 'new punishment.'

Quickly, I scrambled into my clothes. She chuckled. I got most of them on, when she yelled, "I said, Get out in the hallway, you whore!"

Partially dressed, I stepped into the hall.

She ordered me to stand with my hips and calves touching the end of the hallway.

It was similar to all the other beatings. Shoving my head down to my knees, she beat me, slamming my head into the walls, door jambs, and door knobs all the way to the end of that long hallway. This time I didn't cry. Just mute resignation. Then, she hurled me onto the kitchen floor.

Exhausted and weakened with hunger, I laid on the floor while she kicked me repeatedly. I thought she'd tire of it, but she didn't. I thought, *maybe she'll just kill me now, and get it over with.*

Finally, I pushed myself up onto my hands and knees, only to have her lay a vicious kick into my left hip. I collapsed onto my right side, while she kicked me in my chest, stomach, and pelvis. The pain was severe, and I drew on what little strength I had left, to rise to my feet.

Breathing hard, my hair matted in my nose and eyes, I automatically reached for the broom and dustpan, and swept up the piles of my hair in the hallway. I searched for my glasses pushing my hair out of my face.

Hellen watched and smirked.

After I threw the dustpan of hair away, she left early for work. It was 6:20 p.m. in the evening and she said, "I'm meeting friends for dinner before work. Don't let any boys in the house and keep the doors locked. Clean up this place and show some appreciation for your mother. It won't hurt you none."

The beating had lasted for over 30 minutes.

I wept after she left, because I had no food. The evening dragged by and I developed dry heaves from the intense pain and hunger. I doubled over in front of the toilet, vomiting bile throughout the long evening. I began to worry, *did Hellen hurt something inside when she had kicked me?*

I was at rock bottom.

With every beat of my heart, I was desperate to die.

I feel like the biggest coward on the planet.

I can't fight her because I am a coward.

I can't ask for help because I am a coward.

I can't take the pills because I am a coward.

I hate living.

God isn't answering my prayers to die.

He's quit listening to a troublemaker like me.

I can't even die right.

What a loser I am on Life's road.

At 9 p.m., I walked to the medicine cabinet and opened the door. I had a 32-ounce cup to hold all the pills from the bottles. I had another 32-ounce cup full of water. I couldn't take another day.

I want out. It was time to die.

My last strip search can be at the county morgue. I am done.

Hellen has been right all along. I am a quitter. I am quitting life.

The medicine bottles blurred through my tears as I wished it could've been different. I knew that whatever it was in me that caused

1980: 16 Years Old: July, August, September

Hellen to do bad things, it was the reason I needed to die.

No more delays, but now.

I reached for the first bottle and opened it. It was so full, the cap barely snapped onto the bottle. I poured the bottle into my empty cup. The small pills barely covered the bottom. I still had 29 bottles to empty.

I turned and vomited bile again.

I was so hungry I was trembling. I stepped back to the medicine cabinet, determined to go through with it this time.

Crying as I emptied the bottles, one thought pierced through the darkness in my mind. *I've got to tell Tracy goodbye. I should try one time to reach her, just once, and if I can't reach her, at least I tried.*

Doubled over with stomach cramps from hunger and nausea, I walked to the phone knowing that they didn't have a phone and I would have to call Duane's brother. When I dialed, I thought, if I can reach her, maybe, just maybe, I can hang on for one more day.

It was 9:30 p.m.

Duane's brother answered and I asked if he could get a message to Tracy. He said they were at his home and he asked Tracy to take the call.

"Wilma?"

When I heard her voice, I broke with sobs.

"Wilma! Please, please, just tell me what's wrong. I will help you."

I couldn't stop sobbing.

"Wilma, please, if you'll tell me what's wrong, I'll help you."

"I'mdkm humkgng."

"Wilma, I can't understand you. Say it one more time for me, and I promise, I'll help you."

"I'm......." The dam burst. Heaving, uncontrolled sobs, I felt at once surprised and relieved.

"Wilma, please. Please, listen. Whatever it is. I'll help you. Talk to me." Tracy's voice broke on her last words. She was crying. "Please say something. Just please talk to me, whatever it is."

1980: 16 Years Old: July, August, September

"I'm...hungry." I was hiccupping now, like a small child.

"Where's mom?" I heard anger in her voice.

"At work."

"We're on our way."

~

Tracy and Duane came over with a slice of angel food cake and two cans of soup.

My body hurt from the kicks to my chest, stomach, and pelvis, making each breath painful. I had a severe headache. It was impossible to pretend things were okay.

I didn't talk much but sat down to eat the soup cautiously sipping it, afraid of another round of vomiting. I kept down the small amount of soup I was able to sip, but I couldn't touch the cake.

Duane sat and watched me, and Tracy's concern surprised me. I realized she would have been sad if I had taken the pills instead of calling her.

Knowing that Duane and Tracy cared, and would help me if I called, changed me. Somebody in the world actually cared about me. I didn't feel so alone.

They saved my life that night.

I hid the rest of the food and made it last for several days. I put it in a bag on a hanger in my closet and covered it with my jacket. Then, I zipped up my jacket. Hellen wouldn't think of looking for food on a clothes hanger.

When a teenager commits suicide for no reason, probably someone, somewhere knows why.

Hellen, would have known. And only Hellen.

Tracy and Duane saved my life that night.

They gave me the one thing I had run out of.

Not food. I had lived without food.

They gave me what I couldn't live without for one more day.

Hope.

1980: 16 Years Old: July, August, September

~
Many of life's failures are experienced by people who did not realize how close they were to success when they gave up.
~ Thomas A. Edison
~

1980: 16 Years Old: July, August, September

~ Counseling Notes ~

I asked about the night I called the police when the drunk was pounding on the door.

The counselors said, "In 1980, you would have had a difficult time convincing the police that Hellen was sexually abusing you. It would have been a huge risk, and the chances that she could have talked them out of believing you are high. She was a master manipulator. She had many professionals fooled, and if you had failed, I believe she would have killed you, or made you wished she'd kill you.

The fact is though, that she had you so afraid of her, that you wouldn't have been able to tell the police. When the abuse goes on for a long time, the child is completely powerless to speak about it until it is over. They simply cannot do it."

~

I asked about Hellen pulling me off the floor by my hair when I was praying.

They said, "Hellen knew you found peace and relief from praying, and she couldn't let anything relieve the pressure she was trying to build in you. She couldn't let anything get in the way, even God, of what she was working in you. Also, as sick as it sounds, when you were on your bedroom floor praying, you were not available for her sexually. That alone is enough, in a sick mind like hers, to

1980: 16 Years Old: July, August, September

justify a rage to jerk you up off the floor by your hair."

~

I talked about reaching my lowest point on that Tuesday night.

The counselors said, "The feeling of powerlessness is a poison that doesn't come from the Bible. Hellen worked to poison or convince you that you were powerless from the time you were a little girl. God helped you by showing you that you weren't powerless. You could get help and you did. You hid some food and kept going. Although you didn't know it then, your rescue was just weeks away. He gave you strength at your weakest moment."

1980: 16 Years Old
Autumn Begins

Heroes rarely look the way we draw them in our minds: attractive, imposing figures with rippling muscles and strong chins. More times than not they are humble beings, small and flawed. It is only their spirits that are beautiful and strong.
~ Richard Paul Evans

The Times

Cordless phones, the Sony Walkman, Pac-Man, and the Rubik's cube were new and on the minds of Americans in the summer of 1980. My prayers were answered, and my life completely changed in about 17 minutes.

I was surprised when Hellen made a sudden decision to move out of the house she had purchased from the Layton's. She put the house up for sale and it sold in two weeks. Her plan was to move the two of us to Casa Grande, 90 miles south of Phoenix. She'd joined a church there in anticipation of the move and decided the pastor's 19-year-old son was the man I should marry.

Horace and I had met at Bible camp. He looked like an identical twin to the kid on the cover of *MAD magazine*. At camp, I'd watched and heard him say nasty things about girls as they passed by. I decided then and there, *he is ugly both, inside and out.*

Hellen told me, "When we get to Casa Grande, you'll see he's the one for you. He'll never amount to much, but it's the best shot you've got. I figure you'll live paycheck to paycheck for the rest of your life. But hey, why should you have it easier than me? You need to take this boy and run, or you won't get another chance."

"I don't like him. I saw how he acted at camp when girls walked by. That's not the kind of guy I want."

"They're all like that!" she said. "That's how men are. He'll at least pay your bills the rest of your life. I'm sure as hell not gonna do it. And as stupid as you are, you're sure gonna need someone to do everything for you. Mark my words, your mother's right about this one. You'll be so happy for attention from a boy, you'll rope him in. I know what's best for you."

I prayed and fasted for God to kill me. I had to get away from her. I had to.

The thought of moving away from Tracy scared me. It would be long-distance charges to call her. I didn't know how I could manage with Tracy so far away.

~

The money Hellen received from the sale of the house provided an opportunity for her to buy Duane and Tracy's mobile home, and then take what she called "a much-deserved vacation."

Before the move to Casa Grande, her vacation was all she talked about, but refused to say where she planned to go, or with whom. She said, "I've done my time raising kids so I'm gonna finally do something for myself. I'm gonna take a vacation, and I'm not telling anyone where I'm going. I won't answer to anybody, and I'll not be telling anyone how long I'll be gone, by cracky. I'm not even going to answer to God about what I'm gonna do while I'm away."

I thought, *wow, you're tough. You're not even going to answer to God about what you're going to do. What would you be doing that you wouldn't want to answer to God about? I thought you were a 'godly mother' who was going to be 'clean' when you 'stand before the Lord.' Where's all your scriptures now?*

She was not going to take me on her vacation, so in preparation for me to stay with Tracy and Duane while she was gone, Hellen signed a medical power of attorney and put them in charge.

~

Since I would be attending Tracy's church while Hellen was on vacation, she decided to have a sit-down talk with Pastor Sawyer and his wife. I was scared, as I knew she didn't like the young preacher and his wife. She arranged a time for us to meet at a restaurant for breakfast.

I was beyond nervous. Hellen was too pleasant, and I knew something was up. I couldn't imagine what she would have to say to Pastor Sawyer and his wife, but she claimed she had important information they would 'need.'

September 6, 1980 was a bright, sunny Saturday morning that did not match the dark anxiety I was feeling before the planned breakfast meeting. I liked the pastor and his wife, but I was terrified of what Hellen might say or do.

After we ordered breakfast, Pastor Sawyer asked, "How can we be of help to you?"

Hellen smiled and took a deep breath. She seemed pleased to have their full attention and explained that I would be attending their church with Tracy and Duane while she went on an extended vacation. A vacation that she, by the way, grandly deserved.

I knew they were already aware of that information, so I wondered why she was dragging out the conversation.

When our food arrived, she told them what they 'needed to know' about me. Then, speaking in hushed, confidential tones, she warned, "Look. There is just no reason to pretend here. Some things you just need to know if you're gonna allow her to mingle with the folks at your church."

1980: 16 Years Old: Autumn Begins

"Oh?"

"You see, Wilma here puts on a pretty good show that she's a Christian, or shall we say *trying* to be, but I know how she *really* is."

Pastor Sawyer looked at me but asked her, "What do you mean?"

I thought, *oh my, she is so embarrassing. Where is she going with this conversation?*

"Well," Hellen said, casting her eyes around making sure the conversation was indeed private, "Well," she said, clearing her throat, "I'll just be plain, okay? Wilma is a whore. Simple as that. She's been sleeping all over town. Personally, I've never met a bigger liar than this girl sitting next to me. You cannot believe one word that comes out of her mouth. She has a wild imagination and cannot be believed."

Though hungry, I could barely swallow a bite of pancake. Pastor Sawyer and his wife were frowning as they listened. I didn't know what 'whore' meant, and I was puzzled by the term 'sleeping all over town.' Even if I had been, (and I hadn't) how could sleeping be bad? Whatever it meant, I was sure Hellen wasn't complimenting me.

"Well, she sure seems like a nice girl to us." Pastor Sawyer answered.

"Oh, she can sure pull the wool over your eyes. This is why I needed to meet with you before my vacation. It would be in your best interest to consider the kind of trouble you'll be allowing to mingle with your flock."

I'm trouble? So much that he needs a warning before I temporarily attend his church?

I was sitting next to the pastor's baby who was in a high chair. I was relieved to have somewhere to look as he smeared syrup all over his plate, tray, and himself. He was blond-headed, bright-eyed, and cute. He was happy. At least somebody in our group was having fun.

I was humiliated. I couldn't tell if they believed her or not, until Pastor Sawyer said, "Thank you, but I'm sure we will be just fine."

"Okay, have it your way. Just so you can't say I didn't warn you."

"Well, okay, but I'm sure we will be fine."

1980: 16 Years Old: Autumn Begins

I was humiliated and all I said was, "Thank you for breakfast." I was thankful for a hot meal even if it was hard to swallow.

"You're welcome," said the pastor.

Hellen let them pay the bill, and we left.

The breakfast was embarrassing, and I later learned the Sawyers did not believe Hellen but they had been very troubled by the conversation.

~

Hellen appeared to be in a good mood, though she was quiet on the drive home. I sensed the change in her mood, so I stayed quiet and on high alert. I was still trying to figure out what she meant by 'sleeping all over town.'

~

Hellen turned the car onto our neighborhood street, still brooding. Then, just before she pulled into the driveway she said, "If Tracy will come and get you, you can pack your stuff and leave now."

What? I was stunned.

They were the sweetest words I'd ever heard.

I sprang into action.

I hurried into the house, picked up the phone, and dialed Tracy's number...praying so hard, pleading with God that she'd be home. She was rarely home on Saturday mornings.

She was.

"Tracy! Mom said I could leave right now, if you'll come get me."

"Leave? As in, move out?"

"Yes."

"I'm on my way."

Click. No goodbye. Nothing.

Only my siblings could have understood how monumental that was. Tracy made the 20-minute drive in nine minutes.

While I waited for her, I packed two paper grocery sacks. Since I wasn't allowed to own much (my closet and dresser were basically empty), I packed my coat, two blouses and two skirts in one paper sack. In the other bag, I put two spiral notebooks of poetry. In my rush to leave, I forgot to retrieve the letter I'd written to Tracy that was still hidden under the waterbed mattress. I've always wondered who found that letter to Tracy.

I walked into the living room just as Tracy opened the front door. She listened as Hellen told her she had given the young preacher a proper warning and if he wanted a whore to attend his church, then he would have it.

I could tell that Tracy was irritated.

Then Hellen went into her bedroom to lie down.

"Is there anything else you need to do before we leave?" Tracy asked.

"No."

"Let's get out of here."

Once outside, Tracy asked, "Do you want the stereo I left for you when I got married?"

"Yes, but I'm afraid to go back in."

"We'll go together."

We walked inside, picked up the stereo, mumbled a quick goodbye to Hellen, and walked out the door.

Once I walked down that hallway with the stereo–the hallway where I'd been beaten so many times–I never set foot inside that house again.

Ever.

It was Saturday, September 6, 1980, and I was free about 17 minutes after Hellen had spoken those liberating words.

Tracy still refers to that Saturday as, "The day we rescued Wilma."

1980: 16 Years Old: Autumn Begins

~ Counseling Notes ~

I had a lot of questions about why Hellen let me go the morning of the breakfast with Pastor and Mrs. Sawyer.

I wouldn't know the answer until 1998.

The counselors said, "Hellen's decision to move to Casa Grande was no doubt an answer to your prayers. Although you didn't find out why she made the move until 18 years later, God opened a door for your escape in September 1980. It doesn't matter what Hellen thought, what hopes she may or may not have been chasing, what matters is that you were freed from her control and you never had to go back. You prayed for God to rescue you, and He did."

~

Pastor Sawyer said, "The breakfast with you, and your mother Hellen was disturbing. My wife and I couldn't understand why any mother would talk about her daughter in such cruel and demeaning ways. It was awful to listen to and we did not believe the things she said about you. You just didn't carry yourself like the type of girl Hellen was describing. We could only think that maybe she was afraid you had something important you might need to confide and perhaps she wouldn't want some things told. Maybe she would want us to look at you as the liar she said you were. We did not believe her and we left the restaurant worried about you."

1980: 16 Years Old
October, November, December

You may be deceived if you trust too much, but you will live in torment if you don't trust enough.
~ Frank Crane

The Times

Former actor Ronald Reagan, was elected as the 40th President of the United States, and my year that began with suicide plans, ended with wedding plans.

Duane and Tracy had only been only married for 18 months when they took me into their home. It must have been a real adjustment for them to have a teenager living with them. I am grateful that they made me feel welcome and safe. After staying with them for a few days, Tracy took me to Sears and bought me brand new underwear for the first time in my life. I thought she and Duane were rich.

At first, I found it awkward adjusting to all the new rules and privileges that were part of living with Duane and Tracy. It felt strange not to be afraid to take long hot showers, and I washed my hair anytime I wanted to. Tracy provided quality shampoo, so my hair didn't knot up like it did when I used the motel bar soap that Hellen had stolen.

Washing and ironing my clothes was a novelty to me. Tracy showed me how to adjust the heat temperatures on the washing machine, dryer, and iron for different colors and fabrics. I loved wearing clean, pressed clothes.

Tracy took me to a dentist. I had never visited a dentist before. My teeth hurt all the time, but I thought it was because Hellen had loosened them so often with her fists. (I didn't tell the dentist.) After the cleaning and x-rays, the dentist said I had 16 cavities–and I was sixteen years old.

I liked having my own toothbrush, but it seemed irresponsible to leave it in the medicine cabinet. Sometimes, I opened the cabinet door just to check on it. Of course, it was still there.

Tylenol was in the cabinet where I kept my toothbrush. I asked Tracy if I could have some. She showed me how to read the dosage label and handed me the bottle. It seemed to help. My body healed. I watched day after day as the bruises turned green, then yellow, and then faded away. I was feeling better than I had in a very long time.

~

Just after Hellen left for the vacation, Duane and Tracy moved into their new home. It had a lot more room and a fenced yard. I was happy to help with the move. The time I spent at their house was enjoyable because my sister and brother-in-law were always busy or having friends over. I didn't spend days or nights alone anymore. It was a completely different world.

True to her word, we never found out where Hellen went on her vacation or if she travelled with anyone. She simply disappeared for about a month and returned. She never talked about that time and died years later without revealing anything to us about it.

~

On Friday, October 3, 1980, Hellen called to say she would be back on Sunday and expected to spend time with me. I didn't know what that meant and immediately felt sick.

I asked Tracy if I could stay at the mobile home alone. It was empty, clean, and ready for the transport truck to move it to Casa Grande.

Tracy didn't want me to stay there alone on Friday night. I kept asking, so she reluctantly dropped me off on Saturday afternoon. She left me with a dinner she had packed for me.

I didn't need food. I couldn't eat anyway. I paced all night long with such despair, such anguish, for a while I couldn't even cry. I felt so weighted down and so devastated I didn't know what to do. As I paced, my life rolled through my mind like a horror movie. The beatings, the kicks, her fists, my hair in the dustpan, her lectures, the strip searches, the roaches, my mind in shutdown while my body endured unspeakable sexual abuse, the cigarette burns, the 20-second showers, the hunger, the purple bruises, and on and on my thoughts went. Somewhere during all of it, the dam burst and I couldn't *stop* crying.

I begged God to save me from that nightmare. I literally begged. I was in agony.

I pleaded with God. *Please God, dear God, I promise everything, anything, but please, please don't make me go back to Hellen's house. Please God, I'm begging. Anything You want, God, I'll do it, just please, please don't make me go back. Oh, God, I'm so afraid to go back.*

I paced the floor for several hours in agony at the thought of living with Hellen again. I made innumerable promises to God. I begged, pleaded and bargained with Him. *Anything You want, just please don't make me go back. Please.*

At Bible camp, I'd heard preachers talk about a closet of prayer. I had no idea what that meant, but in the early hours of the morning, I felt so desperate I thought, *if that's what God wants, that's what I'll do.* I climbed into a little closet, shut the door, and tried to pray. It didn't seem any different than praying while pacing the floor, except it was hot in there. I decided to pace outside the closet. I hoped God would understand.

1980: 16 Years Old: October, November, December

I drank water and continued pacing. Around 4 a.m., I fell asleep on the floor with my jacket rolled up for a pillow.

Tracy picked me up Sunday morning for church. I was desperate to get back to the trailer as soon as the service dismissed. I was afraid of a beating if I wasn't there when Hellen arrived.

I spent the day at the trailer alone. Unable to eat, still pacing, I again promised God anything and everything, pleading with Him not to make me go back. I begged, pleaded, and begged some more. I don't know how many promises I made Him, but I was desperate.

The afternoon was another round of terror-filled memories playing in my mind like a bad horror show. With each memory, I begged God more earnestly and made even more promises. I'd had a taste of freedom, a taste of real life, thanks to Tracy and Duane. The thought of going back to live with Hellen was unimaginable.

I wept and wept and wept. I was inconsolable.

~

Hellen arrived at the mobile home at 4:30 p.m. in the afternoon. In the month since I'd seen her, we both had changed in dramatic ways.

While living with her, I hadn't realized just how filthy she was. Now I wondered how she could stand her own stench. I realized I hated her with a powerful venom.

I had grown accustomed to regular showers, using shampoo, and a toothbrush. I had new clothes and I was happy. I knew I couldn't go back to living that hellish life with Hellen.

I decided, no matter what, I would never go back to living with Hellen.

She told me to get in her car to run some errands. I did, and she talked nonstop. "When we move to Casa Grande, life will be so much better. I can't wait to get out of this Egypt. I never should've moved back to this hellhole in the first place. Mark my words, Horace will marry you. When we settle in Casa Grande, you'll thank me that I found some boy that'll want you. Don't doubt me on this. I know

1980: 16 Years Old: October, November, December

what I'm talking about."

The fear in the pit of my stomach grew.

After the last of her errands, she drove towards Duane and Tracy's new house.

"Now, listen to me. When we move to Casa Grande, you need to start showing Horace some sweet attention, from day one, you hear me? Face the facts, you're nothing to look at, with no brains besides, and you've gotta grab the first boy that…"

She was mid-sentence when I couldn't listen to her anymore. Right then, a strength came over me, and I spoke. "I don't want to move to Casa Grande. I want to stay here with Tracy. I'm doing well in school, I have a job, and I don't want to leave Phoenix."

I braced myself for her fists. I'd known for days she would start pounding me. I'd dreaded the pain of her fists.

But…all was quiet. No fists, no slaps, no cussing or yelling. Nothing. I was shocked.

Then she said, "I knew they'd brainwash you."

Brainwash me? Call it what you will. I don't care what you think they are doing to me, as long as I don't have to live with <u>you</u>. I didn't say one word.

My thoughts were whirling. Something was off. Hellen had broken her lifelong pattern.

God had intervened. He had heard my prayers.

Now driving slower than the speed limit, Hellen was reduced to a half-hearted rant. "You're gonna regret this. I'm telling you. I've picked out a decent boy for you. But…nooo. You're so stupid you're gonna shun your mother and her wise choices for your life. Well, missy, we'll see. I doubt Duane and Tracy even want you. They're probably chomping at the bit to get you out of their hair. I sure know the feeling."

When we got back to Tracy's new house, Tracy met us at the door and said to me, "Wilma, take a shower while we talk to mom."

I took an extra-long shower. I was afraid it would be my last one for a long time.

When I walked into their living room, Tracy said, "Mom has agreed to let you live with us."

I looked at Hellen in disbelief. "Yup. That's right. They think they wanna take on a 16-year-old? Well, let'em help themselves. They'll be ringing my phone as soon as I arrive in Casa Grande wanting me to come back for you. You're way more trouble than they realize. Well, have it your way. I'm going home."

I was speechless…for a moment, and then I said a simple, "Bye."

I was overcome with relief.

In the time it had taken for my shower, their conversation changed my life forever. The place I would live and the church I would attend, and they were exactly the places I wanted to be.

~

I appreciated Tracy leaving me at the trailer alone on that Saturday afternoon and night. There was immense turmoil inside me and I needed time alone. I agonized about going back to live in Hellen's house and made up my mind, I just would not do it. Period.

Yet, there was one small peculiar feeling I couldn't deny.

Hellen had let me go…without any argument, a cussing fit, or a fight.

She truly didn't want me. She didn't fight or argue to keep me.

My own mother didn't want me.

I was surprised by how much that hurt.

She had used me, abused me, and thrown me away.

I was her unwanted trash.

Hellen left the house. I didn't even watch her drive away.

~

Later that night, I awoke several times with tears on my face and pillow, remembering that I was staying with Duane and Tracy, and

1980: 16 Years Old: October, November, December

God had answered my prayers. In that hazy, half-asleep state, I'd cry with profound gratitude, falling back to sleep in awe of what God had done for me.

Me. The sorry excuse for a daughter, me. The worthless nobody. Wow. You answered my prayers. Thanks, God.

It was such a radical change from what I had believed was the only possible outcome: I didn't die. I didn't have to die, and now I was safe with Duane and Tracy. I was happy that I had lived.

Truly, You have worked a miracle for me.

~

Soon, we settled into a daily routine. Tracy drove me to school each day; we lived too far to ride my bicycle. With regular showers, clean hair, clean clothes, and having brushed my teeth, I felt like a new person. Eating regular meals boosted my energy and outlook. The kids noticed and started talking to me. I performed well in school. School was a completely different experience.

In the evenings, Tracy taught me basic cooking skills, insisted I complete my homework, and I helped with the housework. Greg and several other friends from their church visited often. I enjoyed seeing how friends hosted one another in their homes. The more I spent time around Greg, the more I wished I was old enough to marry him. I often wondered about the lucky girl he'd marry. I wished I were older, so it could be me.

~

Late one evening, after dinner and Bible study, Tracy and Duane went to bed. After a shower, I went to bed. A few minutes later, there was a soft knock on my door and then it opened. Tracy, less than five feet tall, stood there in her robe. She flipped on the light and said, "Get up. We don't live like pigs here. Clean up this room before you go to sleep. Goodnight."

Shutting the door, I heard her go back to her bedroom.

1980: 16 Years Old: October, November, December

I got up and put my dirty clothes in the hamper, then put the ironing board and iron away. In less than three minutes, my room was clean. I shut the light out and lay down on the bed.

A tear trickled down my face. Soon, I was crying. I put the pillow over my head, so Duane and Tracy wouldn't hear me. *I know it sounds corny God, but I feel loved.* Before that night, no one had ever cared if my surroundings were clean and well cared for. It didn't matter because I didn't matter.

Tonight, I mattered.

~

Although it was probably hard for Tracy and Duane to have me, I have to admit that it was also a major adjustment for me to live in their home. Sometimes I felt as though I were living in a dream world. Other times, I was afraid Hellen would show up and order me to leave with her. I had nightmares that she was taking me away from Tracy.

~

Being away from Hellen's constant abuse, no longer having to focus on daily survival, I began to think about other things. Specifically, I wondered about my dad. *Was Angelo alive? Did he care about me?* I had to find out. I wanted him to know who I was, so I wrote him a letter. He replied immediately and included $10.00 to spend on stamps.

We wrote on a regular basis, getting to know each other through letters. Through his writing, I discovered his love for his two hunting dogs, and his large one-acre garden. I longed to talk to him on the phone, to hear his voice, but he said that long distance phone bills were just too expensive. So, I waited and wondered what my dad's voice sounded like.

~

Duane had been a friend of Greg's for years, and Greg kept stopping by to visit. He often stayed for dinner. I thought he wanted to see Duane, but on Saturday, October 11, Greg asked me out on our first date. He was kind and funny and I enjoyed spending time with him.

My courtship with Greg was a special time. He was easy to talk to and he had a great sense of humor. We took long walks, talking for hours.

He proposed a few weeks later, on November 8, 1980.

I was that lucky girl I'd wondered about.

~

When Greg proposed, I made the decision, *Hellen is in my past, but Greg is my future.* He didn't need to hear about my past. What I didn't consider then was that I couldn't hide the physical or emotional scars.

Greg would eventually have to know.

~

What a change my life had taken. Life had been so empty, so lonely and hopeless. Now, I had friends, I was engaged and planning my wedding. After the long years of abuse and torture, the good things seemed to happen so fast.

I was happy, yet concerned, because I needed Hellen's signature for the marriage license. On November 16, we travelled to Casa Grande to get Hellen's permission to marry. Hellen agreed to sign for the marriage license. I was concerned about Hellen pulling rank and not signing if we waited too long, so we planned a short engagement and announced it the next day.

Over the next two weeks, Hellen threatened not to sign if she didn't get her way about the wedding details. She wanted to choose the colors, the attendants, the flowers…and anything else she could think of. She wanted the wedding her way, or we wouldn't be able to get the license.

After the invitations were mailed, Hellen grew more insistent that we orchestrate the wedding her way. Weary with her demands, we asked Pastor Sawyer if we could elope. He encouraged us to try to work through her demands as best we could. It was good advice.

We planned everything just like we wanted, then made some phone calls and discovered that we could purchase the marriage license 30 days prior to the wedding. We went to a justice of the peace court with Hellen on the 30th day before the wedding and got the license. After we had the license, we didn't worry about her demands. They were ridiculous anyway.

Hellen did not offer to help us in any way with our wedding, though she had been involved with Tracy's. I was embarrassed but not surprised. My father, Angelo didn't offer either.

Pastor Sawyer and his wife, Duane, Tracy and Greg's parents, helped us with the plans. Greg and I spent our evenings and weekends shopping for wedding items. Together we chose the flowers, the cake, and even my wedding dress. We put our money together and paid for everything.

~

Picking out the wedding dress created a distressing problem for me. I couldn't discuss it with anyone, not even Greg.

Two years before, I had been with Tracy when she tried on different dresses before she'd settled on the one that was right for her. I watched as the sales women casually slipped in and out of the dressing room as Tracy tried on the gowns. I was appalled watching the saleswomen zip the dresses and adjust the fabric while Tracy stood there and listened to their comments about style and fit. She appeared to be fine with it, but it freaked me out.

I knew then, at age 14, that I would never have that kind of an experience. The thought of other women watching me try on dresses horrified me. The thought of them seeing me undressed, touching my body, zipping the dress, looking at how it fit…well…I knew I couldn't handle it. The memories of Hellen watching me dress, undress and touching my body were too painful and recent.

When I was engaged, I wasn't able to go to a bridal shop to look around or try on anything. Feeling trapped in my fears, troubled, and sure I could tell no one, I had to find another way. One of my friends was

1980: 16 Years Old: October, November, December

an excellent seamstress, though she was just 14 years old. She agreed to make my wedding dress for $40.00 dollars. She did a beautiful job.

I was barely comfortable with the arrangement, but it was the best of my options. Greg and I picked out the pattern, the fabric and the lace. He drove me to her house for the fittings. When she took my measurements, I couldn't stand still when she wrapped the tape measure around me. I found myself shrinking away from her. Finally, she handed the measuring tape to me and picked up her pen and paper. She instructed me where to measure and I told her each of the measurements. Overall, our collaboration worked except my dress turned out to be a bit too big and we had to work together on the adjustments.

At the final fitting, I walked down the hall into the living room. Seeing the look on Greg's face, and hearing his conversation stop mid-sentence, was a special moment.

We both had tears in our eyes.

1980: 16 Years Old: October. November, December

~ Counseling Notes ~

My response to Hellen returning from her 'much deserved vacation' seemed extreme. I asked if the agony I experienced was normal.

The counselors said, "Of course, it was normal. Although Hellen had sold the house, she still retained the authority to require you to move with her to Casa Grande and you were well aware of that. Anyone in your shoes would have been terrified. It's understandable that you would have wanted to spend those hours alone. There is no way for you to have avoided those painful hours, after knowing the safety and freedom Duane and Tracy provided. You were so well cared for with them. The thoughts of going back into the hell of Hellen's house and the sexual torture, I don't know how you survived the night with the memories by yourself. God surely strengthened you. It's clear He gave you the right words the next day to stand up to her, and you did."

Pastor Sawyer said, "It would be normal to wonder why she just let you go. Your feelings that day at Duane and Tracy's that she just threw you away were normal, though you felt relieved at the same time. Conflict is a major component here. You had hoped for so long that Hellen would find you good enough to love. But that is all wrong. You don't have to be good enough to love. When you look at a newborn baby, what does that baby have to do to be good enough to love? Nothing. We love that baby just like she is. Hellen couldn't love you because she didn't have the heart of a mother. You don't earn love. God loves us, not 'because', He just loves us.

It was wonderful that Duane and Tracy took you into their home and treated you so kind. God truly provided a safe haven for you. What kindness and generosity they showed making sure to provide your clothing, transportation to school, proper training, dental work and finally, wedding planning. They were just what you needed at that time.

You followed a path many young abused girls follow. You married young, and you chose an older, mature man with a career. That is often very typical for a girl from your background. A man like Greg presents security and stability and that is something you never had. It is great that the two of you were able to plan and pay for your wedding together."

1980: 16 Years Old: October, November, December

Our Wedding
I tightly hugged Greg to get away from Hellen.
She reeked of body odor.
I couldn't bear her body touching mine.
I couldn't get away from her fast enough.

1981 to 1985

Anger repressed makes one deceptive.
~ Pastor Sawyer

The Times

In January 1981, the 52 U.S. citizens taken by militants in Tehran, Iran were freed after they'd been held hostage 444 days, and just after my 16th birthday, I married Greg MacLiver.

Our wedding was held on a beautiful winter day in 1981. It was the first wedding ceremony Pastor Sawyer performed.

Hellen arrived five minutes before it started, reeking of body odor, urine, and fake Chantilly perfume. Big surprise. Her hair was dirty and her attempt to comb over the large, unwashed knots failed miserably.

There were 75 guests in attendance to celebrate with us. After the reception, Greg and I left for a week-long honeymoon.

We found out later that Hellen took our remaining wedding cake home for herself.

~

I was beginning a new life. It was hard to believe that only a few months earlier, the only hope for my future was to die.

Before our wedding, I innocently thought I could shut the door on my old life and open the door to my new life without blending the two.

I was grossly mistaken.

The abuse I survived affected me more than I realized.

1981 to 1985

~

We returned from our honeymoon and settled into married life. Greg went back to work, and I went back to high school.

Within days of returning home, I began having nightmares about Hellen abusing me. Greg would wake up and try to comfort me, but I just couldn't wrap my mind around the fact that I was finally safe from Hellen.

Three weeks after the wedding, I developed a high fever. Within a day, I had another severe case of shingles.

Mid-way through my junior year, after semester finals, I dropped out of high school.

~

Early on, I confided in Greg bits and pieces of the physical and emotional abuse but told no one about the sexual abuse.

In an attempt to survive in Hellen's house, I had complied with shameful things that I believed were inexcusable. By keeping the secret, I believed I could hide what a despicable human being I was. I lived in panic that someone would discover what I had done to survive. Rather than expose my contemptible self, I stayed mum.

I didn't realize that keeping the secret poisoned every relationship I had. My thinking was not a healthy foundation for building a marriage.

A few months after our wedding, Greg and I purchased our first home. We were excited to move, but I was scared in that house. At times, I was too afraid to go into the dark kitchen for a drink of water. Greg was baffled by my fears. I didn't understand them either and was embarrassed by them. At night just as I fell asleep, I'd bolt upright, sure that someone was choking me. I'd sense that someone was in our bedroom and open my eyes to find no one there.

Nightmares and flashbacks were constant. They were often accompanied by physical pain, fear, and heart palpitations.

One day I saw a can of peas on the grocery store shelf. Immediately I was back in my dark days, hungry and left alone with only a can of peas. I stood in the grocery aisle overcome with tears. A woman walked towards me and asked me if I was okay.

I assured her I was.

~

Just after our first wedding anniversary in 1982, we found out we were expecting a baby. We were both excited.

As the pregnancy progressed, I began to reflect on the role of a mother, and I was afraid of what kind of mother I would be. My biggest fear was that I would be like Hellen.

I was afraid that if the baby cried a lot, I'd hurt it, as Hellen had hurt me.

It took me weeks, but I summoned all my courage and confided my fears to Greg.

His answer was kind, thoughtful and wise. I still remember his words.

"Well, if the baby makes you so upset that you think you might hurt him or her, then do nothing. It would be better than hurting the baby."

Though his words were helpful, I began having nightmares that Hellen was hurting my baby, in an effort to hurt me.

Greg didn't have much knowledge of the abuse I had survived. The better my life became, the more I was scared to tell him about my childhood. I thought that in telling, I'd risk the only good life I had.

So, I protected the secret.

~

Except for Tracy, I couldn't stand for any female to touch me. I couldn't tolerate a hug, or a pat on the shoulder. I would jump if a woman accidentally bumped into me.

Abuse in Hellen's house was the only reality I knew. I was without a normal, healthy point of reference, although I didn't realize it at the time.

The things I believed, the fears I had–none of them were reality based. They were all in my mind. I believed Hellen's lies and they had an enormous impact on every part of my life.

I awoke one morning to discover I was in labor. Greg was already at work. I called him and we went to the hospital.

Nothing prepared me for the experience of labor and delivery.

During the pregnancy, I had been monitored by a male doctor. After enduring years of sexual abuse from Hellen, I thought a male doctor was best for me. In my naiveté, I didn't consider what the hospital experience would be like.

I froze with fear when I realized female nurses would perform exams on me during labor. The labor and delivery nurse was large, like Hellen. She bragged about her own strength and said, "Ah, labor's nothing. Life will toughen you up. Look at me, I'm tougher than you think. I used to drive a New York taxi. A little labor pain never bothered me. You learn real fast how to toughen up when you drive a taxi."

I wasn't just scared; I was terrified. Labor did not progress. After 12 hours, the doctor said, "Since you've failed to progress in labor, I'm recommending a cesarean. Although you and the baby are both doing just fine, it's getting late and we might as well get this over with."

Greg and I were both disappointed with the decision. We had taken the labor and delivery classes the hospital offered, and we were looking forward to a natural birth.

I didn't tell anyone how devastated I felt inside. When the doctor said I 'failed to progress,' I thought, *he must know I'm a failure, like Hellen knew.*

I felt sorry for Greg that he had married a failure like me.

~

Just after midnight, we welcomed our beautiful, healthy baby boy. We named him Jeremy.

The next night, around two in the morning, I lay in the hospital bed holding my baby. I looked at his face, counted fingers and toes, then I'd wrap him up tight in the blanket and smile. Then, I'd unwrap the blanket and re-count his fingers and toes, marveling that my body could produce such a beautiful miracle.

After several times of wrapping and unwrapping his blanket, I held him close to me. I couldn't imagine loving anything more than I loved my beautiful son.

Moments later, I wept as memories of Hellen crashed in like a flash flood.

I couldn't imagine calling him names or beating his head against the wall.

I thought about Hellen a lot that night. *Surely*, I reasoned, *Hellen had felt the same love for me as a baby, as I have for my baby. I can't recall what I did to destroy her natural motherly love, but it must have been bad. No wonder she had to treat me the way she did.*

What if I never changed? For someone to turn a mother's heart like I did, I wasn't only a horrible child. I am a horrible person.

Crying, I looked into my baby's eyes and said, "I'm so sorry. I'm so sorry you got me for your mom. You deserve so much better. I'm so sorry. At least you have a good daddy."

~

When our son was two years old, Greg and I sold our first home and moved into a travel trailer. We began to build a three-bedroom home. Many times, throughout the design and building process, Greg asked me for design ideas. I told him some, but I kept most of my thoughts to myself. I had married 'up.' I didn't want him to know how stupid my thoughts and ideas were.

The home Greg built for our family was nice and comfortable.

We had three bedrooms, two bathrooms, and a fireplace. Greg built a workshop and fenced in the backyard. It was a good place for our family.

~

In early 1985, Duane and Tracy came to our house for dinner.

Duane looked at me and said, "Hey, Wilma, did you know your mother is living with a bull dyke?"

"What's a bull dyke?" I asked

He explained it was a masculine lesbian. It was Hellen's new, live-in girlfriend.

I was shocked. In 1985, it was not the acceptable thing to 'come out of the closet.'

The odd thing was, when I saw Hellen and her girlfriend together, Hellen was dressed as the feminine one. Hellen was a lot of things, but feminine was not one of them. Her girlfriend wore men's uniform work pants, with her work shirt tucked in, and she had a fat, man's wallet in her back pocket. Hellen and her girlfriend were both morbidly obese, but Hellen was the smaller of the two. They leased a house together in north Phoenix for a year.

Once again, Hellen viewed herself as a trailblazer, ahead of her time–doing what she wanted, when she wanted, with who she wanted. She didn't care who thought what, and whether or not what she was doing was acceptable in society. She answered to no one, not even God.

Phoenix, Arizona – 1985
Hellen 54 years old.

Her health was declining and she would not take care of herself.

1981 to 1985

~ Counseling Notes ~

I was irritated but not surprised by Hellen's behavior at my wedding. It seemed like her taking the wedding cake home, was a déjà vu to her eating the cake I got on my 15th birthday.

The counselors said, "It was not shocking that Hellen showed up at your wedding at the last minute. Making you wait was her pattern. By arriving moments before the ceremony began, she could add to your anxiety of whether she would or would not be there for you. It followed her pattern of always making you wait. It was just more of her manipulation and control. It was also shameful and low-class for her to take your remaining wedding cake home."

~

I questioned my logic regarding leaving my past in my old life and starting my new life.

The counselors said, "It's not surprising that you broke out with shingles after your wedding. The stress of needing to get past the wedding; of needing to secure that Hellen could never take you back, of needing that marriage license signed, that must have been overwhelming.

It is common for individuals to believe that they can just sweep their past under the rug and not deal with it. It wasn't so easy to forget your past and move on, like you thought. It affected you until you got help and faced it. Trauma and abuse have to be dealt with and faced or they affect every part of your life and the lives of those around you. You react even if you think you're hiding the pain."

∼

I asked why the birth of my first son stirred up such uneasiness.

The counselors said, "It is common for a major life event to stir up old or unresolved memories. I'm not at all surprised that Jeremy's birth brought back a flood of memories and nightmares."

1981 to 1985

Our Wedding Day 1981
I was the lucky girl.

1981 to 1985

*Phoenix, Arizona
1981*

1986 to 1995

The work of restoration cannot begin until a problem is fully faced.
~ Dan B. Allender, Ph.D.

The Times

In 1986, the cost of a postage stamp in the U.S. was 22 cents. On January 1, 1995, it cost 32 cents. Throughout my early years as a wife and mother, I continued to write, though I rarely shared my writing with others.

I was still writing letters to my dad. Then, out of the blue, there was a break in our letter writing. I didn't understand why, so I sent him a letter. I expressed how much I enjoyed his letters and getting to know him.

Weeks went by without a response.

~

A short time after we moved into our new home, Greg and I welcomed our second baby boy. This time I felt better about myself as a mother, but I still had a lot of fears.

A few hours after Ryan was born, Greg left the hospital to pick up our 3-year-old while I rested. Greg returned a short time later and handed me a letter from my father.

I opened the letter immediately.

My father wrote:

> *I was enjoying writing to you as well as receiving your letters. But then I realized that you are just spying on me for your mother. I don't need her nonsense in my life. Don't bother me anymore.*
>
> *Love, Dad*

It had only been three hours since our baby was born. I couldn't believe that after six years of writing, he'd quit for that reason.

Greg felt bad. He had been sure that a letter from my father would be welcoming news.

I said, "It's okay. I still need to call my mother and let her know the baby was born this morning."

I called Hellen. She listened with interest until I told her we named our baby, Ryan.

"Oh, you named that kid a sissy name! I'm not calling him that."

Stunned by her response, I said, "No, Ryan is not a sissy name."

Greg stared at me. He could hear Hellen through the phone.

"It is too a sissy name, and I will not call him that! Why, I'll just call him Garth. Now that's a man's name."

Garth was a drug addict and part of our extended family.

I said, "No, mom. You're not calling him Garth."

The conversation was escalating fast. Hellen was getting angry.

Greg and I were both stunned.

"I'll damn well call him whatever I want to call him! So, I'll call him Garth from now on. Garth it is."

With strength and calm I didn't know I possessed, I firmly said, "Mom. You will call him Ryan, or don't bother calling me. At all." I quietly hung up the phone.

Greg said, "I'm so sorry. In less than 10 minutes, both of your parents deserted you. I'm sorry."

"It's okay."

"It's got to hurt."

"It does, but I'm not surprised by Hellen, just surprised by the letter from dad."

~

A month after Ryan was born, I sent my father a birth announcement and expressed my thoughts in a letter. I told him I could understand why he would think Hellen was behind our six years of exchanging letters, but in fact, she was not. I expressed how much I had wondered about him throughout my childhood and hoped we could continue to correspond.

I was surprised and pleased a couple of weeks later, when dad resumed writing to me.

~

My concern for the safety of my children seemed to grow as the boys grew. I couldn't stand anyone tickling the kids, for example, and if someone started, I intervened.

My fears caused a lot of questions in Greg's mind, but I provided few answers. When Greg asked me about why I intervened when the kids were being tickled, I finally told him.

Greg was the first person I told about Doyle and the time he tickled and then molested me. I was surprised that I couldn't tell Greg without crying and feeling stupid. I still believed Doyle had been able to hurt me because of my own stupidity. As I spoke, I discovered how angry I still was about Hellen and Doyle. My anger surprised me.

Greg listened, outraged, and I thought, *he is disappointed in me for not being smarter at the time.*

When I realized Greg was angry at Hellen, Doyle, and Ilene, I was stunned.

Greg pointed out that no adult has the right to hurt a child, and all the adults were wrong.

Greg provided balance in our home, and he worked through the years to not allow my fears to dictate the way we raised our children. I learned to trust and appreciate Greg's balance, though my trust and appreciation didn't come easily or fast. Greg and I did not allow our children to be tickled, and we did not make them hug anyone they chose not to hug, even family members.

~

Find the courage to be authentic. Not everyone will like you, but no one can if they don't get a chance to know you.
~ Lori Deschene

~

Greg was an amazing dad. He loved the boys and enjoyed spending time with them. I knew, *they are good and I am not.* I feared, *if Greg discovers who I really am, he will send me away, to protect the kids.* Although he never implied that, I was just afraid.

Writing was important to me, and I continued to write throughout my early years as a mother. I wrote a lot of poetry and humor essays, and I kept a journal. I was writing one day when I realized I had a choice in life. *I can be bitter or grateful, but I cannot be both.* I recall wrestling with the decision for weeks–considering all the options between living in hate, in fear, or in love. In many ways, I believed I had a right to be bitter. I felt robbed. As I considered the bitterness of my childhood, I knew, *I do not want to become a bitter old woman.*

So, I chose gratefulness.

I still do.

~

I loved being a mom. On the outside, I was a housewife, a mother, and a friend. I was busy with birthday parties, trips to the library, shopping, and raising our sons. On the inside, I was defeated and scared that someday, someone would blow my cover and I would lose everything and every single person I treasured.

The longer I kept the secret the heavier it got. Whenever Greg and I had a disagreement, it was a full-blown disaster in my mind. I was sure that I had shown Greg how stupid and worthless I truly was.

I was failing and I couldn't blame anyone but myself. I remember thinking, *Hellen was right. I'm a loser. I ruin everything. I am so stupid and now I'm failing as a wife.*

I cried often when I was alone, especially in the shower.

~

As the kids passed certain age milestones, memories of the abuse I'd suffered clouded my mind like a dark storm. I'd experience several dark days in a row, speaking little and avoiding my friends. The dark clouds in my mind were troubling and caused nightmares when I slept.

Around Greg and the kids, I tried to act normal, but they noticed. At times, I was withdrawn or short-tempered with them, and I regret those times.

My unpredictable behavior caused questions in Greg's mind and he tried to help me through my dark thinking and irrational fears. I couldn't sleep without a nightlight. I panicked when I got hungry and I had nightmares of Hellen entrapping me in her dirty, roach infested bedroom. I often woke up crying. Greg comforted and held me until I fell back to sleep.

Greg grew frustrated with my dark days and silence, but I just couldn't talk about the memories that tormented me. I was afraid that leveling with him would ruin the good life I had. As a result, the memories tormented my mind and fear dictated every decision.

~

Over time the secret became a sickening ache inside. I felt as though I had seen and experienced too much. I genuinely felt ruined and I blamed myself. Guilt overwhelmed me. Living in my own solitary prison of fear, I was unable to free myself. I felt most comfortable when I was spending time alone. I needed someone to help me, but I didn't know who to ask.

Patience is a virtue for sure, and Greg was patient with me, so I began to tell him bits and pieces, and even, a few memories of the sexual abuse. Greg listened with tears and compassion.

Confiding in Greg changed things for me, but not in the way I'd feared. Greg didn't reject me; instead, he encouraged me to get counseling help.

~

The damage done through abuse is awful and heinous, but minor compared to the dynamics that distort the victim's relationship with God and rob her of the joy of loving and being loved by others.
~ Dan B. Allender, Ph.D.

~

I began counseling with Pastor Sawyer and his wife but it was slow going for a while. *If I trust them and if healing is possible, then I know I'll have to expose the secret in the process. That is inconceivable to me. Each time I tell the Sawyers a small part of Hellen's abuse, I die inside for days because I told.*

I felt so vulnerable and worried, *what if I trust the counseling process and Pastor Sawyer is wrong? What if I really can't get better?*

~

Pastor Sawyer was the first to teach me that speaking about the abuse breaks the power the secret held on me. It took a long time for me to push past my fears and expose the depravity of Hellen's abuse. I wish I could have unloaded it all in a few counseling sessions, but I didn't have the courage.

Once I started talking about the abuse, I expected to be done with it. I was so wrong.

It got worse before it got better. The fears, flashbacks and nightmares caused upheaval in my life. I wavered. At times, I trusted the process; other times I worried that I was beyond help. Maybe I could never be free from a lifetime of pain.

I felt as though to heal, I had to relive the hell I had been rescued from.

I did not think I could do it.

Trusting the counselors with the secret of my abuse seemed like the biggest gamble of my life. If they were right, that I needed to expose the depravity of it all in order to heal, then the payoff might actually be what they were saying it would be. If they were wrong, if I was placing my trust in them and they hated me afterwards, then the gamble was going to cost me everything and everybody I loved and valued. I was beyond scared.

In spite of my fears, I slowly made progress.

As I trusted and disclosed more details of the abuse, I began to feel some relief. They believed me after a lifetime of being convinced that no one would. My trust in them and the process grew.

~

Hellen's torture caused a lot of questions in my mind about God. My faith that God truly loved and cared about me, as an individual, was weak. I confided in Greg the disturbing questions the abuse caused to my faith. Greg encouraged me to ask Pastor Sawyer my questions, but I was afraid.

A few weeks later, I wrote my questions down and gave them to Pastor Sawyer. Some of my questions were:

Did God allow it to go on because I was bad?

Was God mad at me?

Why didn't God rescue me sooner?

Did He hear all those prayers I prayed?

Why did it happen to me?

Did I deserve it?

And, the hardest questions of all–

Do I have to forgive Hellen?

Why should I forgive her?

And, then the most important one–

How do I forgive myself?

Disclosing my faith questions was difficult because I thought it was disrespectful to God to even have those questions. The trepidation I had to overcome, just to ask the faith questions, caused me to realize how much Hellen's cruel indoctrinations continued to control me.

Pastor Sawyer said, "Thank you for this list. None of your questions surprised me, in fact, I think it's only normal to have them."

I relaxed a great deal.

Pastor Sawyer said, "There are evil people in the world and sometimes we cross paths with them. But God did hear your prayers and He did deliver you out of Hellen's house."

"Did I cause Hellen to do all that to me?"

Pastor Sawyer asked, "What would your children have to do to *cause* you to beat them in the hallway, like your mother did to you?"

"I've never done that to them."

"I believe that. But what would they have to do to *cause* you to beat them or sexually abuse them?"

"Nothing. There's nothing they could do to *cause* me to do that to them."

"Exactly. And there's nothing you did as a child or teenager that *caused* Hellen to do *any* of the evil things she did to you. Just because she said it, doesn't make it true. She had zero justification for what she did, so she had to blame you. Are your sure there's nothing your kids could do to cause you to hurt them like Hellen hurt you?"

"I'm positive."

"Well, then you need to apply the same judgment to the little girl Wilma, and the same judgment to the mother Hellen."

~

I went through highs and lows during counseling. I had times when I felt as though I could see through all of Hellen's lies, and the path to healing was well established. At other times, I'd look at the landfill of memories I still needed to sort through, and collapse under the strain.

During those times, I was convinced I didn't possess the strength to face it. Through it all, the nightmares and daily flashbacks continued.

I wondered if the pain was as permanent as the scars.

In my journal I wrote:

> *The memories are coming back and tormenting me. They are like a horror movie playing nonstop in my mind. How is sorting through this nightmare from decades ago, going to help my life now? The memories take me places in my mind that I do not want to go.*
>
> *Oh, what am I to do with this landfill of garbage in my mind? I have no choice but to die with this troubling me. I do not have the courage to ask the questions, because then I'd have to tell the stuff that I cannot speak about. If I tell anyone, the relationship I have with them will be forever ruined. Crying as I write this, I realize that no matter how wonderful people are, I am really, totally alone. I must live and die with this shame alone. I have no choice.*
>
> *Hellen ruined my childhood; to tell about that now would just taint and scar my adult life. Why would I give her that opportunity? Hasn't she done enough damage to my life? The abuse damaged the dark places of my soul, and I will die with this. Nobody can ever know the things I know...but oh, how I wish I could lay it all down.*
>
> *I've always known that the scars are part of me and that I will never be normal. Hellen's violence and perversion sickened my life and permanently crippled my thinking. My belief system (doctrines) formed with unnatural twists of distrust, fear, and anger. I cannot think of one thing left intact, as God designed. I know God is trying to heal me, yet I am afraid to hope. I'm afraid hope will*

only bring more disappointment. What would it be like to live a day without fear? I have no idea. I'm ashamed at the coward I was. I am different from other people, and if they really knew me, they would leave me. I am a dirty pig, so how can I ever love my scarred self that I hate?

Death seems like my only hope for peace. I am a failure, even at counseling. I fell asleep last night, and woke up crying in my sleep; that hasn't happened in a long time. I knew then, that it's unrealistic to even hope that counseling could help someone like me. Because of the things I saw and experienced, I am beyond help. How troubling that help arrived too late for me. I am so sad. I feel so alone.

Always, always alone.

~

Overwhelmed by the enormity of it all, I turned to the familiar comfort of writing. I wrote *The Choice* and gave it to Pastor Sawyer.

The Choice

Shame – the inner disgrace
That is haunting me.
The despondent voice
That wearies my soul.

It constantly swears
I will never be free,
From the dark secrets,
That only I know.

1986 to 1995

The scars of Shame
Grow daily it seems.
They make me
Different from you.

Shame dictates my thoughts,
Cripples my dreams-
Distorts the trust
That I have in you.

I can't remember living
A day without Shame.
A brutal oppressor,
That keeps me bowed low.

It's always insisting that
I am to blame,
For the dark secrets,
That only I know.

Shame was content to
Quietly control my life.
Until I considered
Your words of Truth.

Then Shame attacked
With a vicious fight,
And I was torn
Between Shame and you.

1986 to 1995

Now, daily Shame taunts
My memory to face,
The anguish
From so long ago.

Cruel images flash
-that if I could I'd erase-
From the dark secrets,
That only I know.

At night, Shame descends with
Its most perverted tirade.
As I sleep
In my bed unaware.

With vile pictures playing,
I awake so afraid,
From another dark round,
Of tormenting nightmares.

For hours, I wait
For the morning to come.
Afraid, in the dark
So alone.

Shame's taken my sleep
To remind me again,
Of the dark secrets,
That only I know.

1986 to 1995

Shame's blanket of contempt
Has shrouded my mind,
Filtering out,
All light of hope.

Though I search all around,
I'm unable to find,
A light in the
Dark rooms of my soul.

Oh, I know God is able
To make blinded eyes see.
He can deliver from
The hell in one's soul.

But Shame has me convinced
God won't do it for me.
Because of dark secrets,
That only I know.

Shame has always controlled
Every part of my life.
Constantly nagging
My thoughts each day.

Insisting that I,
Am dishonest to fight
The glaring truth, that I,
Deserve this blame.

1986 to 1995

Shame constricts my life
A little more each day.
The choices I make
Reflect its control.

Though disappointed, I must
Choose to side with Shame,
Because of dark secrets,
That only I know.

I thought the classes you offer,
Might be my chance,
To sever myself from
This life with Shame.

Instead, I discovered,
I lack the courage it takes.
I am too coward,
To confront the pain.

So, I must find a way
To convince you it's best,
For you to help others, and
Leave me alone.

Shame swears I will only
Find peace in Death.
Because of dark secrets,
That only I know.

1986 to 1995

I'm very sorry that I
Shut down in my mind,
When I begin to hear
The doctrines you teach.

Shame argues that they
Don't apply in my life.
Because of the secrets,
It's Shame, I believe.

There's no doubt that I
Am different from the rest.
They strive to reach
Life-changing goals.

I'm not looking for change,
I'm waiting for Death.
Because of dark secrets,
That only I know.

Shame is boldly arrogant,
As it negates your counsel.
Cynically chuckles about secrets,
I cannot explain.

Clearly, you're wasting
Your time trying to help me.
I'll die with this Shame,
That I so desperately hate.

1986 to 1995

With a heavy heart,
In spite of my need,
I must let
Your kind offer go.

The doctrines you teach,
I just don't believe.
Because of dark secrets,
That only I know.

W.M.

~

I realize *The Choice* expresses a defeated point of view. In places, it even has suicidal tones, although that was not my intent when writing it.

I wrote it from exactly where I was at that time and it helped me express thoughts, I couldn't verbalize any other way. I've since met other trauma survivors that this resonated with for many of the same reasons I felt when I wrote it: despair and hopelessness.

Pastor and Mrs. Sawyer were kind and gentle, but firmly refused to accept my defeated choice. I'm thankful they saw potential for healing that I did not see.

Confiding in Greg and seeking help through counseling was a life changing set of decisions. Throughout the ongoing healing process, I have had to *keep* making the decision to go forward.

Pastor Sawyer said, "Hiding is a killer. You can choose to stop hiding. Every step is a choice."

I realized I had to deal with the abuse, or die with it.

Pastor and Mrs. Sawyer continued to believe that God had brought me through the abuse, and that He would provide healing. Though skeptical, my trust in them grew. I continued to work through the memories, even when I got discouraged by my slow progress.

1986 to 1995

Through it all, Greg was my mainstay.

~

Tracy called me one afternoon in December 1988, and asked, "Guess who just showed up at my front door?"

"I don't know."

"Our dad. How soon can you get over here?"

Greg and I took our children to Tracy's house to meet my father. I had no memory of Angelo, and I was nervous about meeting him for the first time.

My father did not look like the picture I always had in my mind. I was 24, and he was 74 years old. Angelo was short, heavy set, emotional, and nervous to meet us. After a few intense minutes, we all seemed to relax a little.

We visited for less than a half hour, and then my father asked Tracy to take him back to the hotel. He was exhausted.

Angelo, just before coming to Phoenix to meet with us kids.

~

I didn't know what to think about my dad. I just knew that I kind of liked him. I also knew Hellen would not approve of our meeting. I rearranged my schedule so I could spend every minute possible with my dad during his week-long visit. Greg and I hosted a dinner for him and my siblings in our home, along with all the grandkids, even though my brothers and their families chose to decline the invitation.

At the end of the week, Greg and I arranged for a dinner at an upscale restaurant in Scottsdale. I called and spoke with the manager explaining that the family would all be together for the first time in 23 years. The manager offered a private dining room, with multiple servers.

My brothers agreed to attend that dinner with their wives. We left the grandchildren with babysitters.

The pictures of that evening show tension on all our faces when we first met in the restaurant. My father was seated at the head of the table, with Hugh and Danny on either side of him, then Tracy and me next to our brothers.

Hugh and Danny asked tough questions.

"Why didn't you ever look us up?"

"Why did you and mom fight so much?"

"Why do I still have the scar on my back when you hit me with a hammer?"

"Why did you wait until now to look us up?"

I choked back my tears throughout the questions, thankful that Greg was next to me. Afterwards, I had a lot of respect for my father, because he never once dodged a question, changed the subject, or became defensive. He looked each of us in the eye and gave straight answers. That took guts.

As the dinner progressed, we all relaxed.

I have no idea what we ate that night. I saw it all through tears, with my heart pounding.

Out in the large lobby of the restaurant, we took photos before saying goodbye. In the pictures, we are all laughing and relaxed.

It was the only dinner we ever had together as adults, with our father.

It was a dream come true to meet my father. I am thankful for all the time I got to spend with him.

As our children grew, Hellen's health steadily began to fail. In early 1990, after a lifetime of careless, junk food eating, obesity, and unmanaged diabetes, Hellen developed gangrene in her toe. She spent a couple of months in the hospital where she suffered multiple strokes and had both legs amputated.

After Hellen lost her legs, she cared even less about the repercussions of her eating. Bedridden, but with a microwave and mini refrigerator within reach, she ate constantly. Without her legs, she weighed over 200 pounds.

As the months passed, she continued having one stroke after another. We stopped counting at 17, though she had several more. Her doctor said, "I've never seen anyone survive as many strokes as your mother."

I wanted specific information. "Are they mini strokes, or how would you rate them?"

"She lost the use of her right arm with the last one. The one a week ago affected her speech. That's pretty big. The others…well, some have been small. Overall, I'd give them a medium grade." Shaking his head, he added, "I've never seen anything like this in my career."

~

If you were meant to fix or save or rescue them,
wouldn't they be fixed saved or rescued by now?
~ Courtney J. Burg

~

When Hellen had recovered enough to leave the hospital, she was transferred to a state funded nursing home, due to her declining health. She became a resident in the same type of facilities where she herself had been employed.

Hellen hated every moment she spent in the various nursing homes. As a resident, Hellen was consumed with terror. She knew what happened in nursing homes at night, with 'nurses' as she had claimed to be. She wept, screamed, cried, and tried to bite everyone who came near her. The staff took her false teeth away from her, but then she threw cups and anything she could get her hands on from her bedside table at the staff. The administration ordered her into restraints. She was evicted from one nursing home after another for violent, aggressive behavior. Often, she lasted in a home only 24 hours, before being transferred to another one.

Finally, she landed in one in Apache Junction, Arizona. There, the staff only permitted two big, burly young men to lift her, give her showers, and tend to her catheter and bowel needs.

Once, I drove over an hour to visit her there. I found her alone in her room. She was crying. "What's the matter, mom? Why are you crying?"

"Those dirty men wash me in the shower, and they look at me. It's a violation of my privacy. I hate it."

"Don't they have a lady who could help you?"

"They said I was too heavy to lift. The young men have to take me to the shower."

She put her head down and cried some more.

I didn't know what to say.

Did she remember the strip searches, and the violations of my privacy?

~

Hellen preferred to stay in the hospital. She'd beg to stay there, pleading with the doctors not to send her to the nursing home. She'd complain about minor aches and pains, so they'd order more tests–anything to delay returning to the nursing home.

~

As I watched her health decline and her fears escalate, I knew I had some things to say before she died. Throughout the years, I'd pondered, prayed, and asked God for the chance to confront Hellen.

I felt a strong desire to confront her as an adult, regarding the abuse and torture during my childhood and teen years.

I spent months considering my motives, and concluded I needed Hellen to know a few very important things.

When I became an adult, I realized Hellen was a felon because of what she'd done to me. *Nothing and no one ever gave her a right to do those horrific things.*

I wanted her to know that while she duped me as a child, I was not duped as an adult. I had been incapable of making her do any of those things. She had lied, manipulated and tortured me in every way possible, and I wanted her to know all her efforts to ruin me had failed.

The fight was over and she had lost.

Hoping for a confrontation that would bring closure, I set expectations, and boundaries. Hellen needed to be awake, alert, with no recent medication in her body. It was important that I speak confidently in a thorough manner. I had no intention to be cruel. I prayed I would leave with no regrets, no cowardice, and no hatefulness. I wanted to be kind, candid, and perfectly clear. I didn't want to forget anything or say something for which I'd have to apologize.

After years of praying, God nudged me at the perfect moment, gave me the words, and provided the courage to be candid.

It happened on February 11, 1994. Hellen lay resting comfortably in a hospital. The doctors wanted to discharge her, but no nursing home in the valley would accept her. The doctors were working with social services to find a new placement. For the first time in three years, her health was stable.

I drove to the hospital with no intention of confronting her. My plan was just to check on her, and then I planned to have lunch with a friend. The confrontation I had prayed about was the furthest thing from my mind.

At 10:14 a.m. that morning, I walked into Hellen's room. I don't know why I noted the time. After a few moments of small talk, I had a sudden, gut feeling that now was the time.

And I hesitated.

Still, the feeling was intense, *Now. Do it now.* So, trusting my gut, I stopped the small talk and confronted Hellen about the abuse.

Once I started speaking, there was no holding back. I had waited a long time for the opportunity and the words flowed like a dam had burst somewhere deep inside of me. I looked into her eyes and said, "Mom, I know and you know what you did to me."

Then I paused before I repeated, "I know. And you know."

She began crying. My voice sounded deeper than usual.

"Mom...." I paused for emphasis. "I know...and you know."

She refused to look at me. She called out, "Hugh. Hugh. I want Hugh. Hugh."

With unflinching determination, I spoke about how she had destroyed my childhood. Somehow, I was able to stay calm. No tears, no anger, no disgust. No drama.

"You stole my childhood."

She continued calling out for Hugh. He had helped her many times when she was in need, but not today. Hugh couldn't help her today.

This was a matter between Hellen and I.

I waited for her to quiet down. I had to know that she heard every word I said.

~

When she quieted down, I spoke.

"Mom, you stole my childhood, but you will not get my adult life. The things you said and did to me will not ruin my marriage. You will not get that."

Hellen refused to look at me and lay there unable to suppress big heaving sobs.

"Mom, you will not get my relationship with my children. You stole my childhood, but you will not get anything or any part of my adult life. Nothing, mom."

After a few more private words, I stopped, and waited.

She continued to sob.

I had my closure.

With a sigh, I said, "I love you, mom."

I waited.

Hellen grew quiet. She didn't apologize or say that she loved me. Either would have been hard to believe.

I waited a few more moments. Hellen didn't respond in any way. She refused to look at me.

As I stood at her bedside, I felt a huge weight lifted from me. I had done what I'd needed to do, with three gifts from God: courage, clarity, and kindness.

I turned and walked out of her room at 10:25 a.m. Eleven life-changing minutes had passed.

It was the last time I saw my mother alive.

~

Two weeks later, to the day and the minute, at 10:25 a.m. in the morning, Hellen took her last breath and died in that same room, in that same bed. She was 62 years old.

~

I'd been out that morning, and when I came home, I noticed the blinking light of the answering machine. I pressed the button. "Hello. I am Sonya Sordakowski, a social worker here at the hospital. I am calling to inform you that your mother, Hellen Proietti expired at 10:25 a.m. this morning. I'm very sorry. If you have any questions, please call the hospital. Thank you."

I was stunned and thankful I had followed my gut and confronted her when I did.

I paged Greg on a job site. He called me a short time later.

"The hospital just called. Mom's dead."

"I'm sorry. I can't imagine how you're feeling. Have you talked to Tracy or your brothers?"

"No. They're all at work."

"Do you want me to come home?"

"No. I'm okay. I just need some time to gather my thoughts."

"Okay. If you need me, page me and I'll come home. It's no problem."

"Thanks."

I walked around the house, crying as I absorbed the news.

Suddenly, I was leery. *Was this another hoax? What if she wasn't dead?* Anxiety overwhelmed me. I stopped pacing. I had to think this through. *Was Hellen the "Sonya" on the answering machine? Was this just another attention getting stunt?*

I had never needed to prove someone dead before. How would I do that? Still pacing, I prayed for help in the moment. I needed clarity.

Soon, my thoughts began to form. Hellen had no friends to call, and us siblings had decided beforehand that there would be no funeral service. *With no viewing or funeral, how could I find out for sure if this was another game?*

The social worker said if I had any questions to call…so I did. "Would it be possible to see my mother?"

"Yes, you have the right to do so," Sonya said. "Come on down and ask for me at the desk."

"Thank you."

I tried paging Greg to ask him go with me, but I was trembling. I didn't know until later, that the page didn't go through.

When Greg didn't call back, I drove to the hospital alone and met the social worker. She guided me towards the elevator and we descended to the basement morgue.

She said, "You're holding up well. Did you drive yourself here?"

"Yes."

I was not up for small talk as I was ushered into a crude viewing room with dusty curtains. There, on a gurney, lay Hellen's body bag.

Sonya whispered, "I can give you about 10 minutes, but you can step out at any time. I'll be right outside the door."

Why was she whispering? Who was going to hear her?

I looked at Hellen's face. A morgue employee had unzipped the body bag about eight inches. Her face had a grey pallor, but I wasn't there to see her coloring. Or the body bag, as weird as that was.

I was there for one thing and one thing alone: I needed to see with my own eyes that Hellen was finally, truly dead.

No phony suicide threats, no police standoffs.

She was actually dead. I would never hear her speak again.

Like a mantra, my thoughts rolled: *Hellen is dead. She is really dead. Oh, thank God, she is finally dead.*

Over and over like a children's rhyme. *Hellen is dead. She is really dead. Oh, thank God, she is finally dead.*

I stared at her face. *Even in death, she looks cold hearted, ugly, and cruel.* Yet I questioned, *shouldn't I feel sad when my mother dies?*

I didn't cry. I just stared. Then, I reached out and touched the zipped-up body bag where I imagined her hands would be. They were inside the zipper. I was kind of grossed out.

I talked to her, and among other things I said, "I'm sorry you chose the path you did. I do not hate you. I'm sorry you've gone to meet God like you have."

The social worker knocked on the door and in a bright singsong voice said, "I'm sorry, but your visitation time is over. Are you okay?"

I assured her I was. We walked out of the morgue and rode the elevator to the main floor of the hospital.

I said, "Thank you. That was important to me."

"Oh, you're welcome. Sorry about your loss! Have a good day!"

She was way too cheery. *Was she trained to talk like that to family members of the deceased?*

~

Seeing Hellen wasn't as difficult as I had expected, I thought.

I was fine. I really thought I was fine.

Until I stepped into the sunshine.

On the sidewalk I stopped, waiting as a police cruiser drove by. The officer's car reminded me of the times the police had tried to help me, but I had been too afraid to tell them the truth. Right there, in front of other hospital visitors and employees, I doubled over, my knees buckled, and I wept.

Viewing Hellen's dead body and seeing the police car, I felt as though I would collapse. Stumbling to my car, I wept, with my head resting on the steering wheel.

It is finally over.

Hellen was dead. I have seen her dead with my own eyes.

Oh, thank God, Hellen is finally dead. The monster is dead.

Her lies, her manipulations, her evil, filthy perversions are all stopped in one breath. I feel guilty for the overwhelming sense of relief. The world is a better place because Hellen has taken her final breath.

Can't the whole world feel it?

I sure can.

~

Later that day, Hugh decided he wanted to schedule a private visitation at the funeral home the next morning.

"I think a private visitation is only proper," he said. "You know, just us four kids and our families."

A private viewing? That was an oxymoron. Hellen had no friends for us to call.

~

The next morning, I drove Tracy to the funeral home an hour before our families arrived.

In the viewing room, Tracy became upset. "There are no flowers for mom. That's not right."

Just then, the poker-faced funeral director stepped in and asked, "How are you ladies doing?"

"This happened so fast, we didn't get flowers ordered for my mom. Do you have any silk flower arrangements you could set in here for the family visitation?" She asked.

"Um, no. We've actually never had that request before, however, it would be a great idea. I'm sorry, the closest store is just a mile down the road."

Tracy drove to the store and purchased flowers. It was that important to her.

~

I stayed at the funeral home. I had a different perspective.

Hellen's straight hair had been cut short by the nursing home staff. I had brought a comb and small barrettes. I didn't want Hellen to be buried with messy hair.

Under close supervision by the funeral director, I gently combed her hair away from her face because I knew it was what she would have wanted, and then I fastened it with the small barrettes.

As I worked, the funeral director remarked, "My, you're so calm. I guess you knew she was near the end of her life, with her health conditions and all."

"Yes, I did," I said, hoping he would leave.

He took the hint.

Stepping back from her cheap particleboard coffin, I considered her new hairstyle.

I had to admit, it looked better than when I started.

While I was still alone and had the chance, I slipped a small note

I had written between Hellen's folded hands. At home, I had chosen a small, floral notepad to write my last sentiments to my mother. I wanted Hellen to be buried, holding my innermost thoughts and feelings towards her. The note was slipped between her nail bitten, aged hands, with no one noticing. I had a strong gut feeling to write the note to Hellen and slip it between her folded hands in the casket. I felt the same way about combing her hair. I have no real reason for either, except my gut feeling is usually right. It's wrong just often enough to keep me humble.

I had done all I needed to do.

Unable to shake the grossness I felt whenever she touched me, or I was forced to touch her, I gathered all the hair styling items and dropped them in the garbage in the restroom. Then, I scrubbed my hands and forearms with hot soapy water. Twice.

I didn't want any of her germs to touch my hair, my purse, or my home. I literally washed my hands of her.

~

I am not responsible for living out the version of me you have created in your head.
~ Courtney J. Burg

~

Hugh and his wife arrived, and visited with the rest of us. After three hours, the funeral director asked Hugh, "How is the family? Have they all said their final goodbyes?"

"Uh, well…it seems as though my brother Danny is running a little late."

"Late? Did he know the visitation time? We are now over the time you'd scheduled here by one hour."

"Yes, I know. He should be here any moment. Sorry."

"Oh. No problem, no problem at all," He said while looking at his watch and wincing.

Ten minutes later, Danny strolled in with a girlfriend we had never met. "Ah, man," he said, "why didn't you tell me this place was out in the toolies? Couldn't you find a cheap place, like man, where we know the streets and neighborhood? I've been driving around for hours!"

I doubted he had, and if so, shame on him. The girlfriend seemed uncomfortable.

We stayed at the funeral home for 20 minutes after Danny arrived.

I noticed that no one cried at Hellen's visitation and whether my siblings admitted it or not, it seemed as though they were all relieved.

I know I was.

~

After the viewing, Greg asked about my experience of arranging her hair. "What made you want to do that? She never cared about how you looked."

"No, she didn't."

"Then why would you want to comb her hair?"

"I wanted to send her off looking her best. It was important to me to treat her better than she treated me. I've never been like her and today was no exception."

Hugging me with tears in his eyes he said, "You're right. You've never been like her and today was no exception."

I do not regret combing Hellen's hair or sending her off holding my note. It felt right at the time. It still does.

~

The next few days, I experienced a sadness that I couldn't understand or identify. Eventually, I realized that hope had died.

Hope for what? I wondered. I had still been hoping that someday, my mother would love me, or find me good enough to love.

Over time, and with help, I realized hope hadn't died.

It had never existed.

~

Hellen's death brought a lot of relief to my life. I was surprised, however, when I realized that even after the abuser is dead, her indoctrinations still controlled me on many levels. Clearly, I had more to sort through.

Hellen didn't possess the heart of a mother, and my hope that Hellen would someday love me, approve of me, or be proud of me, had been no more real than Casper the Friendly Ghost. It was never going to happen, no matter how long she lived. Like Casper, it wasn't real.

But, I was a normal girl with the heart of daughter. I genuinely desired a mother to love, nurture, teach, guide, advise and correct me. I had normal needs. I could not have ever pleased her because she wasn't normal. She didn't have the heart of a mother but instead was an evil, violent child molester. I couldn't relate to her on any level.

∼

Eighteen months after Hellen died, a doctor from New York called me to say, "Your father is dying right now. I mean…uh, right this minute."

"I'm on my way."

I arrived at midnight. Angelo was still alive, and we held hands and talked. He was thankful I was there. I stood by him and held his hand as he died. Watching as he exhaled his last breath, I wished I could have known him better. He was 81.

Hugh flew to New York for the funeral.

Danny asked, "How much did he leave me? Can you cut me a check?"

Tracy was on a long camping trip and we couldn't contact her for days.

My parents' deaths did not devastate me. I never really knew my father or my mother. Their chosen paths had steered them in directions that did not include parenting their children.

1986 to 1995

~ Counseling Notes ~

Ryan was only three hours old when I hung up the phone on Hellen. I was proud of myself at the time, but second-guessed the decision when I spoke about it later.

The counselors said, "It was significant that you stood up to your mother the day Ryan was born. That took grit and resilience at a time when you were physically recovering from childbirth. The fact that you called Hellen to inform her of the birth and have her treat you cruelly is unacceptable. Again, your resilience shines when you refused to be a victim to her bullying and control. When you took control of the short phone conversation and told her to call him Ryan or don't call you and hung up. That took a lot of courage. You had not been away from her control for long."

~

My healing process occurred in large part because I could safely confide in my husband, Greg.

"Greg is a safe person for you to confide in. That kind of safety is worth a million bucks. Then you had one of the best pastors in the world. You had help and counseling extraordinaire. You were able to ask the God questions. You were able to confide the difficult stuff. You felt safe. As tough as it was to do, you had great people helping you. God has been good to you."

~

Meeting my dad was a dream come true. I was also very scared.

The counselors said, "It was a key part of your healing. It's something that you wanted to do since you were a little girl. You wondered about him for over 20 years and when you finally met him, you were not disappointed. Angelo was hurt by Hellen and he sounds like a timid man. But your experience from visiting and travelling to his home was that he was not a mean man. Your gut feelings from childhood proved true."

~

I cried when talking about confronting Hellen and her subsequent death.

"The confrontation at the hospital met your exact guidelines. It was respectful and appropriate. You were kind and firm and you had a right to deal with the violence and torture Hellen perpetrated on you. You will bear the scars for the rest your life and you had the right to confront her. Your Christian character shines through the way you handled the confrontation and the way you conducted yourself at the viewing. It would have been difficult to comb her hair and make her look her best after all she had done to you. It's interesting that you needed to keep silent about it until it was complete and you had 'washed your hands of her' before you talked about it. Sometimes our resolve is best when we are quiet. And we're not surprised that Greg was the first person you told."

1996 to 2015

*It's okay to care about what people think.
Just know there's a difference between valuing
someone's opinion and needing their approval.*
~ Lori Deschene

The Times

Between 1996-2015, the U.S. population increased by over five million people, cellphones became a necessity, and a relative stepped forward and disclosed the long-held family secret.

Time flew by as Greg and I watched our sons mature through their teen years. We had another new home built and from there, our children left for college and went on to be married.

Life as empty nesters made our home much quieter, but we enjoyed our time together and the success of our children and their spouses.

A short time after Angelo died, I was diagnosed with a hereditary bleeding disorder.

One or both parents can be a carrier, but then it passes on to one's children. It was a peculiar ailment since no one in my family had heard of it or been diagnosed with it.

I researched cousins I'd never met, made contact and found there was no trace of the disease in the family. None of the children or grandchildren had any symptoms or diagnosis.

Then, one of the family members I interviewed contacted me. They said they had some information about a family secret that might be helpful, and if I wanted to know, they would disclose the information in six weeks.

I thought, *the wait time is odd, but what choice do I have?*

I waited.

When the time came, the individual divulged the decades-long, family secret.

It was: Hellen had always said that she 'never wanted that pregnancy,' regarding the time she was pregnant with me. I had heard that since I was a young child. It was common knowledge that Hellen became pregnant during the time she spent most of each week with her father, while her custom home was built. As the family member spoke, I wondered, *why are they telling me this common information?*

Then, they finally got to the family secret.

The family secret was that, for many reasons, the family, neighbors and small community believed that Hellen's father, the man I knew as Grandpa Bullard, was my biological father.

I was stunned and speechless.

It took me some time to absorb the information. Yet, it was possible.

Hellen had lived with her father for years after her mother died. Hellen was her daddy's favorite. It seemed odd that Hellen 'had' to have Angelo build her a home near her father, yet, 15 months after we moved in, she fled 2,500 miles away from her father and family.

There are no pictures of Hellen or Angelo holding me as a newborn. The only newborn picture is the one taken by the hospital. There are no pictures of Hellen holding me as an infant until after my first birthday, yet her father was a photographer. When he came to stay with us, I was always grandpa's "special girl." Hellen moved us often to keep us away from our aunts, uncles, and cousins.

The long-held, family secret offered some insight to explain

Hellen's obsession with me and why she hated me—from my earliest memories until the day she died—and her often repeated lament, "What did I ever do to God to deserve a sorry excuse for a daughter like you?" It also explained the bleeding disorder and why I stayed bruised for so long when she beat me. I had purple bruises the whole 17 months I lived alone in her house after Tracy married. When we told the team of hematologists the family secret, they explained that in incestuous conceptions, unusual gene mutations can occur, resulting in unexplained 'hereditary' diseases, which no one else in the family would have.

It also explained Hellen's unusual sexual response when her father died. Information that only I was privy to.

I wondered what other secrets had haunted Hellen throughout her life. Perhaps graveyards bury more secrets than people.

~

A few months later, Greg and I had a short visit with Hellen's retired pastor from Casa Grande. We listened as he reminisced about Hellen. Finally, I worked up the courage to ask the question I'd wondered about for years.

"Do you know what inspired my mother to move to Casa Grande?"

"Why yes, I do. One summer night in 1980, at a family Bible camp, Hellen cried and prayed for a long time at the altar. My wife, good woman that she was, bless her memory, stayed with Hellen until she finished praying. Later that night, my wife said that Hellen turned to her and asked, "Do you think God will ever forgive me for all the bad things I've done?" My wife assured her that God would forgive her and invited her to come to our church in Casa Grande to get a fresh start. My wife told me she had to reassure Hellen several times over that God would forgive her for anything she had done."

I remembered that night at Bible camp. I had been afraid to leave the tabernacle, as we called it, for fear that Hellen would be angry with me. I finally left because there was no one there but the pastor's wife from Casa Grande and Hellen. I didn't get into trouble.

After that visit, I told Greg, "Hellen must have truly believed she had a chance at forgiveness and a new start, for her to sell the house and move to Casa Grande. If she was going to get forgiveness and make a fresh start, there was no way she could have kept me living with her. She had to get me out of her life in hopes of redeeming her own. That's got to be why she let me go about two weeks after family Bible camp. It also explains why she signed for me to get married."

Once again, God answered my prayers.

~

Pastor Sawyer and his wife continued to support me through their ministry and counsel. They also encouraged me to consult with Dr. Laine, an experienced counselor with over 40 years' experience in child trauma. Dr. Laine listened to some of my darkest memories and knew the right questions to ask at the right moments. He provided insight and direction and worked as a team with Pastor Sawyer.

Dr. Laine was patient and listened as the abuse slowly unfolded. He understood it would take time until I found the courage to speak what I'd always believed to be, the unspeakable. I told Dr. Laine details that I'd never told anyone before. It was a great relief to unload the terror and torture of my early years. Dr. Laine helped me to see how some of the troubled memories still affected and controlled my life.

When we first met, I intended to tell Dr. Laine everything. I wanted to unload all the old garbage of my memories in a safe place. But when the opportunity came, I couldn't give a voice to some of the evil Hellen had done to me.

Later, I concluded that perhaps her evil didn't deserve a voice. She knew, I knew, and more importantly, God knew. That was enough.

Dr. Laine said, "We have what we call 'normal abuse' but your mother crossed the line on every level. You were spiritually tortured, emotionally tortured, physically tortured, and sexually tortured. Until you can face that and accept it as the truth that it is, you are still minimizing.

"Spiritual torture uses scriptures to manipulate, not allowing you to pray or go to church. At church, she often controlled the services.

"Emotional torture, in your case, was having no bed, forcing you to abandon Herbie, the dehumanizing, the stripping of your identity, cruel emotional attacks, often including cruel physical torture and pain.

"Physical torture is when you are deliberately deprived of your basic physical needs. It is done to achieve and maintain control. It is deliberately intended to dehumanize, demean, and to strip the victim of their identity. In your case, it was the enemas, the beatings, the sexual abuse, the starvation, lack of hygiene, etc. It is active, intentional torment and torture.

"Sexual torture is different from the other abuse because it is very personally and psychologically invasive. Hellen tortured you through use of enemas, burnings, strip searches, and of course, her sexual perversions and abuse.

"When they are combined–spiritual, emotional, physical torture and sexual abuse–it is called 'Systematic Ritual Abuse' on many levels. It is intended to strip the victim of their identity for life, completely dehumanizing them. This type of abuser deserves the death penalty."

~

It was a slow process, sorting through the messed-up beliefs in my head.

Pastor Sawyer calls them 'false doctrines' because they are stronger than a 'belief' and they are what people use to govern their lives.

I asked him how I would know what was true or false, since I had believed them all my life.

He suggested I write down the things I believed were true–my false doctrines–and then try to prove those things with scripture. My list had 65 false doctrines.

Here are a few of the things I wrote that I believed to be true:

I am stupid.

There is no help or hope for me.

I am permanently physically, emotionally, and spiritually ruined by the things Hellen did to me.

It was hard to believe that I had lived my life with a distorted perception of reality and twisted beliefs. I spent hours studying my Bible, comparing scripture to my list of facts, constantly referring to a concordance. I looked up scriptures about failure, fear, life, being worthy of love, and God's plans about the future. I didn't find any scripture to support my doctrines, but many that contradicted them.

My list of 65 false doctrines were over time, each proved wrong by multiple scriptures.

I began to question where the doctrines originated and with prayer and counseling, I recognized that they came from Hellen and/or as a result of the abuse.

Honestly acknowledging how the doctrines directed a lifetime of choices was difficult for me. It was painful to see that I had made permanent, life-long decisions based on faulty beliefs; essentially Hellen was still controlling my life. I began to work harder to sort through the doctrines in my mind.

Pastor Sawyer encouraged me to continue the Bible study.

It was eye-opening to see there was no truth to the messages I had received; that, in fact they were biblically wrong. However, it was a whole different journey to take those false doctrines out of my mind and insert biblically sound thinking. Transcending the limits Hellen placed on me as a child was hard work.

The process took perseverance, but I was able to see the darkness of Hellen's lies, exposed in the light of Bible truth. As the cataracts of Hellen's lies were removed from my mind, I was able to view life, love, and relationships in the bright light of day. I had fewer dark days. My sense of humor sparked, and I laughed often. The more I experienced healing, the more determined I was to find complete healing.

In my journal I wrote,

> *Removing Hellen's lies (false doctrines) that poisoned my mind and twisted my direction is a lot of work. Yet, each time another old painful piece is removed, I feel a little better and a little stronger. I am getting better.*

Pastor Sawyer and his wife are dedicated to helping people. In addition to pastoring our local congregation for over 42 years, they offer classes for those who have suffered trauma. The classes have been life changing for many people, including me.

After completing the classes, I wrote this poem for the Sawyers.

The Masks

Walking down the road of Life,
I watch each person pass.
Anxious as I alternate through
My endless disguise of masks.

Masks that I am too afraid
To remove and reveal,
That I am dirty, ruined and crying inside
Too afraid to be real.

My innocence robbed years ago,
I'm convinced I have to hide.
I just cannot let anyone glimpse,
The monster that lives inside.

Please don't believe
What you see at first glance,
I'm dying inside,
So, I try another mask.

1996 to 2015

Each day I hide the scars of my life,
They simply must remain undetected.
Survival is always first.
The Secret carefully protected.

If you'll pause and take a second look,
As you pass me by.
Maybe you'll glimpse the awful secret
Some of the masks fail to hide.

The weight of this Secret,
This burden of Shame,
Keeps me wearing my masks,
Keeps me hiding my pain.

I'm hoping you'll take a second look,
That knowing look that can tell,
My fear-filled eyes, I'm a defeated soul,
Standing at the edge of hell.

Your knowing look may well provide,
My only real chance
To be freed from this prison of fear,
And life behind the masks.

As you stop and begin to talk with me,
Fear governs my every word.
I really want to trust in you-
Yet I've never exposed this hurt.

1996 to 2015

I panic at the thought
That I am failing to conceal,
This raging storm of Conflict
So frightening, so real.

Questions rain and flood my thoughts,
Rage thru me and storm my mind.
I am overwhelmed by their fierceness,
Disoriented by the dark clouds of lies.

For, if I could tell, who would I tell?
And just how would I describe?
The fear that controls me, this burden of shame,
The slow-rotting of my insides?

I've spent my whole life
Protecting this Secret.
If I expose it now,
Will I later regret it?

I don't like me with the mask,
And I hate myself without it.
If I trust you with this Secret of mine,
Will you hate me? Will you doubt it?

You see, I'm truly convinced
I'm hopeless...a loser on Life's road.
A dirty pig, a worthless nobody,
If you agree, where will I go?

1996 to 2015

The word Fear doesn't begin to describe,
The terror that I feel-
Revealing this lifelong Secret,
So disgustingly real.

I've never trusted anyone-
This Secret I've kept so close.
I want to trust what you're saying to me,
My very first thoughts of Hope.

I've lived my whole life behind
This endless exchange of masks.
To relinquish them now, I find
Is such a fear-filled task.

The controlling false doctrines,
A lifetime of lies,
Are darkening cataracts
To the vision of my mind.

So, I swing blindly at your help,
Wary of your concern.
Unable to see the road you're leading me down,
Fearful at every turn.

Please don't give up on me.
Take a second look once more.
I don't mean to fight against
The very help I long for.

1996 to 2015

My lifelong doctrines of
Hopelessness, fear, and self-hate,
Have built prison walls around me
That I need your help to escape.

Fear is my prison,
Guilt is my guard.
The Secret my shackles,
Shame forms my scars.

I don't want to live in this prison,
Yet I'm too afraid to leave.
Replacing the lies with truth
Is the only way I can live free.

The time you take to listen,
And explain these life-changing truths.
Helps me to revisit with courage,
The destructive lies and abuse.

Your patience, understanding,
And desire to help,
Provide hope for my future
Beyond my hidden self.

Because of your counsel,
I will not have to grow old,
With this slow-rotting Secret,
A hole in my soul.

Because you stopped, took a second look,
That knowing look one day.
My prison has opened, my vision is clear,
I am no longer afraid.

Thanks for listening, believing and seeing hope
I was too blinded to see.
For leading me down that dark scary road,
Thanks for going the distance with me.

Thank you for not giving up on me,
For stopping to take that second glance.
Thanks for helping me to face,
The hardest thing I've ever faced:

Life – without the masks.

W.M.

~

I kept a journal during counseling. I held nothing back when writing in it. I raged, wept, despaired, questioned, doubted God, everyone I knew and myself. As I wrote, I sorted through doctrines and faced the landfill of lies Hellen swore were truths.

When I had the first thoughts of writing *The Masks,* I went through my journals. The idea of hiding behind a disguise was expressed repeatedly throughout my writing. The inspiration for the lines in *The Masks* came directly from my journals.

I wrote *The Masks* many years ago. I had no knowledge at the time that the word 'masks' is used extensively in writings about trauma, abuse, and healing. The concept of hiding is pervasive throughout the life of victims. It is only through healing and laying aside our masks that we can live and love openly without the fear of being truly seen.

~

While working with Dr. Laine, I was introduced to Maria Iannone, a highly skilled Eye Movement Desensitization and Reprocessing (EMDR) therapist at the Arizona Hemophilia and Thrombosis Center. Maria was exceptional to work with and I found worthwhile results with EMDR therapy. I cannot explain how EMDR works, but it helped with my troubling memories of the abuse. I was blessed to have a skilled therapist. Maria is a professional extraordinaire, and I am honored to have had the opportunity to work with her.

I believe that God let my path cross with the Sawyers, Dr. Laine, and Maria Iannone. I needed help to heal past the trauma of my youth and I couldn't imagine better or more capable group of professionals than them.

I was also introduced to the work of Vincent Felitti, M.D., Chief of Preventive Medicine at Kaiser Permanente in San Diego. He and Robert Anda, M.D., a medical epidemiologist at the Centers for Disease Control, conducted a major study on Adverse Childhood Experiences (ACEs) and their effect on adult health. Adverse Childhood Experiences harm children's developing brains so profoundly that the effects show up decades later; they cause much of chronic disease, most mental illness, and are at the root of most violence.

There are 10 types of childhood trauma measured in the original ACE Study. The studies researchers developed the ACE score to explain a person's risk for chronic disease. There is one point for each type of trauma. The higher your ACE score, the higher your risk of health and social problems. With an ACE score of four or more, things start getting serious. The likelihood of chronic pulmonary lung disease increases 390 percent; hepatitis, 240 percent; depression 460 percent; suicide, 1,220 percent.

I had an ACE score of nine.

As I sorted through the lies, I believed as truths, I gained more confidence to try new adventures.

One day after counseling, Pastor Sawyer asked, "When are you going to quit believing you're stupid?"

I cried on the way home. In spite of all the help I'd had, at times I still felt that I was so stupid I ruined everything I touched.

Growth is no longer blaming others for your lack of limits.
They continue to take, because you continue to offer
~ Courtney J. Burg

A few days later, I saw an ad for GED classes.

Afraid I would fail again; I registered, but told no one.

I took a pretest in reading, English, and math to determine what levels I needed to work on. I tested post-college level for English and reading, and third grade for math.

The waiting list to begin classes was four months long. I waited without telling anyone. I was sure I wouldn't be able to learn the math, history, or the science.

In January, a week before I was to start classes. I said to Greg, "I have an announcement."

"You're pregnant?"

"No. Thank God. I'm too old for another baby. The kids are out of the house."

"Then what could it be?"

"I'm graduating in May."

"Graduating? From what?"

"High school."

"Really? That's wonderful!" Once he knew my plan, Greg was

excited and couldn't understand why I wouldn't want to tell everyone. When I explained, he understood and expressed confidence in my ability to learn.

I'd attended classes for 11 days when the instructor told me I was ready to take the five tests. I went to the testing facility and completed all the tests in one afternoon. The clerk monitoring the testing was impressed because no one had ever been able to finish all of the five timed tests in one afternoon.

Later that evening, the clerk called me. She said, "Wilma, you passed all the tests!"

When the diploma arrived, Greg and I showed the Sawyers first, and then we showed our kids.

A few weeks later I was asked to give the commencement speech at the Orpheum Theatre in downtown Phoenix.

Just prior to walking onto the stage, an usher told the chancellor of the community college and I that they were filled almost to capacity. "We have just about 25 seats left." He said.

I asked, "How many seats does the auditorium hold?"

"Right about 1,360, maybe 1,365 seats."

I was scared, but everything went well.

After the graduation at Orpheum Theatre, I gained more confidence to try new things.

I began to swim and play the piano, things I'd desired to do since I was a young child. Things Hellen said I was too stupid to ever learn to do.

There have been a lot of discoveries and a lot of joy as I've been able to lay aside Hellen's destruction and lies. The healing has let me see life in a whole new way.

I had the courage and curiosity to travel more, hike the Grand Canyon several times and I've done some public speaking regarding abuse, trauma and survival.

1996 to 2015

~ Counseling Notes ~

I asked about the family secret which stunned me, yet shed light on so much.

The counselors said, "Well, it explains a lot of things you have questioned since you were little. Why Grandpa Bullard was into photography, yet there are no pictures of Hellen holding you as an infant. Why she cried, threw fits, and threatened suicide to live by her father, and then when she did, she moved 2,500 miles away. This information is a result of your tenacious research, travel, and interviews in an effort to know all you could discover about Hellen and her early life. Your time, effort, and expense paid off when the interviews yielded more than you thought they would. The family secret was disclosed. Hellen's lesbian relationship(s) was disclosed. So many things came to light you would've never known because she was always moving/working under Tracy's social security number. Perhaps now you know why. Sometimes what you find can be shocking. It's interesting that, according to your family member, besides relatives, members of the community even believed that."

~

In counseling, I was amazed at how I had minimized the significance of Hellen's cruelty and perversions.

The counselors said, "When there is emotional trauma the brain responds with minimizing. That makes it feasible to continue on. When the trauma is greater than what the brain can minimize, then the brain 'blacks' out the memory. Even though the memory is blacked out, it continues to fester in the body like a sore. Physical after effects come from this unresolved, blacked out part of your brain: Headaches, dizzy spells, stomachaches, fibromyalgia and other problems."

∼

I hated that I could only relay the abuse slowly, instead of in one or two counseling sessions.

The counselors encouraged me. "The closer the relationship where the abuse occurs, the deeper the pain. If its family, it's very damaging and very significant. It is the process in the brain that lets a little bit out, and because it is so painful, it waits…then lets another little bit out until finally the traumatic events are told. Trust and safety are very important, but I don't know anyone to sit down and expose the abuse in its entirety at one time. Not with abuse like you had."

∼

It was an honor to give the commencement speech at my G.E.D. graduation in May of 2009 at the Orpheum Theatre.

The counselors said, "That was a huge achievement Hellen had convinced you that you could never attain. You were too stupid, undeserving, unworthy, etc. You pushed past it all and graduated after 11 days of school. You overcame a lot to be there that night, and especially to be the speaker. You deserved it, too."

1996 to 2015

*Phoenix, Arizona
May 14, 2009*

*Graduates filing into the Orpheum Theatre
It was filled to capacity – 1,364 people*

The first line of my speech:

*"Mark Twain said,
'There's two types of speakers:
those that are nervous, and those that are liars.'"*

I was the first type – nervous.

1996 to 2015

Phoenix, Arizona
May 14, 2009

*"...to my fellow graduates, tonight is not just about you and I passing five tests to get a diploma. And we did, and it was important. But this evening is about something much bigger. It's about how we were on our road to graduation and we ran into some obstacles. And the obstacles were able to stall us, and they were able to slow us down, but we're here tonight, because in spite of the obstacles, they were **not**...able...to...**stop**...us."*

After the speech, the Chancellor said, "In my 20 years here at Rio Salado, I have never seen a standing ovation for a student speaker. Congratulations, Wilma!"

1996 to 2015

D'Amor Photography

*Phoenix, Arizona
25th Anniversary
Top of the Rock
Wearing my wedding dress*

Epilogue

*When we write well the story of our pain and wrestle with
the God who allowed it to happen, we face head on the
deception that we were going through it all alone. We fully face
the fact that God will see us through anything.
The end of the pain and wrestling
can only direct the reader
to God's amazing grace.*
~ Dan B. Allender, Ph.D.

I've had the opportunity to speak at events and talk with survivors of abuse, sexual assault, and child trauma. One common fear regarding disclosure, is not being believed or being treated different after the abuse is disclosed. I had similar fears as well, especially when speaking publicly and publishing this book. Pastor Sawyer said, "Real safety, real security, comes from being transparent and finding out that people still love us."

~

I am grateful for all the support I've received, though like others, I've encountered a few skeptics along the way. I've been asked, "Why can't you just let the past stay in the past? Are you always going to live on the dark side of life?"

Acknowledging and overcoming the abuse was a challenge of epic proportions that I didn't believe I had the courage or strength to face. Yet, I found the more I delved into the dark rooms of my memory with the bright light of honesty and Bible truths, the less power the darkness held. It was so liberating, that the more light I saw, the more I *wanted* to examine and shine the light on my dark memories. As discouraging as it could be at times, I didn't *want* to stop.

When dealing with the skeptics, I am stunned by their flagrant display of arrogance to question or deny another individual's experience. I have asked, "Were you there?"

The counselors said, "Some people cannot accept that such evil exists in the world. Your abuse has been well documented. Don't let anyone silence you. You were silenced too long. Just keep going and when you can, help others."

I am thankful for their wise, encouraging words and I live by them.

In this case, silence isn't golden. Freedom to speak is.

~

Since I've shared my abuse experience publicly, I've had victims confide awful horrors perpetrated on them by family members, yet they were sworn to secrecy to 'protect the family name'. Others were bound to a lifetime of silent suffering because 'the Bible tells us to honor our father and mother.' The Bible does say that, and it also instructs us to be honest. In my case, I was told to keep silent by those who did not want Hellen's secret to be exposed. Other victims were not told, it was just 'understood.'

With a lot of help I learned that 'family' doesn't mean suffering the rest of my life–or forgoing the help I need–to protect Hellen's dirty secret.

To fully face Hellen's lies and heal, I had to tell the truth about what happened, even when relatives thought it shameful to discuss.

I couldn't let their pressure hold me back. I was the one burdened with her secret, after all.

So, through public speaking and this writing, I've honored my father and mother the best way any of us can: I've told the truth.

They say the truth hurts, but here's how it worked in my life: I hurt more people, including myself, 'trying to protect the secret,' pretending Hellen 'did her best,' living my own life of pain, denial, repression and pretending, than I ever did just speaking the truth of what actually happened. Though painful in the beginning, it was so worth it.

Though I wouldn't want to–if I could–I'd do it over again and years sooner. I will never go back to a life of hiding again. Truth is not only liberating; it is the only way to live.

~

In addition to the skeptic question's, the "Why?" questions puzzle me and I find them difficult to answer.

"Why didn't you just run, scream, or tell someone? I would have."

My first thought is, *no, you wouldn't have. You're just normal, like me. You would've been scared to death of Hellen.*

But I don't say that.

Instead, a flash of regret crosses my mind that I didn't run, scream or tell anyone. Yet, I did tell someone. I told a whole bunch of 'someones.' I had the normal reactions of a child experiencing trauma. Unfortunately, either the professionals I was around were not trained to recognize those signals, or Hellen was just that good at manipulating those professionals. Perhaps it was a mixture of both. Our world is much more aware of child abuse and its symptoms today than it was 50 years ago.

Also, it was impossible for me to tell at the time I was being abused, not only because awareness and access to help was not like it is today, but because Hellen systematically changed the methods of abuse to find new ways to torture my mind and body until I was unable to reason. I had no chance to step back and gain perspective until after my rescue. Since I left Hellen's house, I have spoken to other adults who were abused and molested as children by Hellen. They weren't able to tell anyone at the time, either. I know of only one who has been

Epilogue

able to accept counseling help. The fear, manipulation, and control was overwhelming.

The fear I experienced living in Hellen's house, went beyond the monster-under-the-bed fear. Experiencing terror–at times for hours on end–wreaked havoc on me physically, mentally and emotionally. There are no words to describe the intensity of that terror now, nor were there at the time. My best attempt is, I felt I was in a whirlwind. It was happening so fast, my head was spinning. I did what I was told, terrified to break yet another new rule. Afraid. Always so afraid, I just couldn't speak. I remember thinking, *if obeying and keeping silent is this painful, what would she do to me, if I told? How much worse could it get? And, just who would believe me?* Unrelenting fear.

For me, until I felt safe–I mean, really safe–I couldn't say one word. And, I didn't.

~

I understand that no amount of healing can change my childhood. Mother-daughter sexual abuse did not make me a lifelong victim, nor does it define me. Hellen's name is on my birth certificate, yet, I do not acknowledge her as my mother. Real mothers are not sexual predators that burn, torture, torment and exploit their children. I did survive Hellen's abuse and torture, and it did profoundly affect my life. But, the abuse no longer controls me. I did not get to choose my parents or my childhood, but I do get to choose my perspective. I do have choices regarding my future, my reputation, and legacy.

~

The first time Pastor Sawyer mentioned forgiving my mother, I put my hand up like a stop sign. "I don't even want to hear it." He was patient. Over time he helped me to understand that forgiving Hellen freed me from the prison of fear and shame she had constructed around me. I had always thought that forgiveness meant having loving thoughts and receiving the person fully back into my life. I was so wrong.

Epilogue

He explained the concept of healthy boundaries. Though it took a period of time, I genuinely believe I have forgiven Hellen. That is different from the question, "If you could get revenge, what would you do?"

Nothing. God will decide.

I've had all kinds of Walter Mitty-like thoughts on revenge, but that is all they are. At the end of the day, my thoughts are best summed up by these two favorite quotes:

~

While seeking revenge, dig two graves – one for yourself.
~ Douglas Horton

The best revenge is to be unlike him who performed the injury.
~ Marcus Aurelius

~

In spite of Hellen's brutal torture, I have the life I truly hoped for. A dedicated pastor, a loving husband, and children who cannot wrap their minds around a childhood like mine. Our children were loved, cared for, disciplined, counseled, praised, fed, clothed, spoiled, and loved some more.

I have the marriage, family, grandchildren, friends, and the life I was sure Hellen had stolen from me. God has been good to me.

Through the grace of God, I have not perpetuated a cycle of abuse. Yet, I have struggled and failed to find the words for how grateful I am that God–and God alone–provided everything I needed to break the cycle of abuse, and to heal.

~

I think of Hellen daily. Now and then I shed a few tears, as I wonder what it would have been like to have a mother who loved me. I wonder about having a real mom and dad. Most of all, I wonder who I would have become without 16 years of violent abuse. Yet, that

Epilogue

lasts only a moment...and then I move on.

~

Counseling helped me lay aside the inner pain and move past the trauma of my childhood years. I didn't know at the time that Hellen's beatings and sexual abuse were leaving permanent physical damage. Doctors, surgeons, and radiologists who've interpreted my MRIs and CAT scans unequivocally confirm the physical damage resulting from the abuse. I've had surgeries to repair the injuries, and I have scars from head to toe, both inside and out. I deal with chronic physical pain daily, as a result of Hellen's brutality.

~

I have not arrived. Instead, healing is an ongoing process. I'm still discovering, learning, and healing. I can't define healing for others, but for me, healing provides freedom from the mind control Hellen worked for years to instill.

I am grateful for the healing I've experienced and the chance to enjoy a completely different, loving, and healthy life.

~

I harbor no feelings of guilt, blame, shame, or fault of any kind towards my siblings. They were older, but they were still developing children, trying to survive in an unpredictable and abusive environment. Hellen was a manipulative liar who fooled clergy, educators, doctors, police, and professionals on every level. It's an understatement to say that my siblings were manipulated as well.

The counselors said, "As children, our bodies, minds, maturity, and emotions are in a continual state of development. It is improbable that a child could accurately assess the things that happen to a sibling when a parent is abusive."

~

Hellen died a slow, miserable death at the age of 62 with her mind clear and aware. She had three lifelong fears: being ill and dependent

Epilogue

on others, dying alone, and dying in our local county hospital. She experienced all three.

My father passed away two years later at the age of 81 in New York. I was with him and holding his hand when he died.

Hugh Proietti married his college sweetheart. They raised a family and are proud grandparents.

Danny Proietti is divorced and his children are grown.

Tracy and Duane raised a family and are proud grandparents.

Greg and I have been married for over 40 years. Our sons and their wives are busy raising their families. We are proud grandparents to several grandchildren.

~

Healing has brought joy for the daily, peaceful things of life. A sound mind, a loving husband, a beautiful family, and lifelong friends. Morning coffee on our back porch, silly rabbits playing in our yard, our grandchildren's laughter, an anniversary trip. A long walk with an old friend. These are the joys in my life. I have a beautiful life surrounded by people that love me.

Without the masks.

Statistics

I have learned a lot in the past twenty-five years. Mostly, I have learned from my clients. I have also gleaned an immense amount of understanding from fellow professional and lay therapists who continue to lean into darkness that most fear to name, let alone enter. While I am encouraged by the advances that have been made in bringing the reality of sexual abuse into the light, I have seen the culture flip from massive denial to indifferent minimization.
~ Dan B. Allender, Ph.D.

Years ago, when I began researching mother-daughter incest, I couldn't find statistics online or in books anywhere. I finally consulted a librarian at a college and she directed my research path.

I have since found several articles, books and websites, and I have listed them in the Reference section at the back of this book.

It is generally accepted that mothers have the daily caretaking responsibilities of their children. In the research I studied, it consistently showed that mothers hide the abuse under the guise of caretaking. That was my experience as well with the enema nights, inappropriate baths, food games, etc.

Researchers Finkelhor and Browne (1985) proposed that the following four factors are most related to traumatization in the child victim:

1. Traumatic sexualization: A process in which a child's sexuality is shaped in a developmentally inappropriate and interpersonally dysfunctional fashion as a result of the sexual abuse.

2. Betrayal: The dynamic by which children discover that someone on whom they were dependent caused them harm.
3. Powerlessness: The process in which the child's will, desire and sense of efficacy are continually contravened.
4. Stigmatization: The negative connotations (badness, shame, and guilt) which are communicated to the child regarding the experience and which then become incorporated into the child's self-image.

The definition presented a clear and relevant guideline. It provided a professional definition of child traumatization and negated the many disturbing comments I had encountered such as, "Well, maybe your mom was just very affectionate and you're not. Maybe you just misunderstood her expressions of love. We have some of that in our family, too."

The librarian could only find textbooks for professional therapists and law enforcement. I had hoped for a book from a daughter/survivor perspective, but I took what she was able to find, and started reading.

The information I read in the first 15 minutes lifted a load of guilt and shame that I had carried for many years. The research clearly showed that Hellen had followed a distinct pattern of mothers that sexually abuse their daughters. Hellen committed specific acts of abuse characteristic of other maternal abusers that researchers tracked all over the United States, British Columbia and Canada.

Hellen would have been horrified by that knowledge. She believed she was original, a trailblazer, and superior to the laws of the land, and God. Through the years, Hellen had blamed me for making her have to hurt me, yet with the textbooks open in front of me the statistics proved her a liar, once and for all. I didn't have the power to make her follow the pattern of all the other maternal sexual abusers.

It was a life-changing moment. I still had a long way to go in the healing process, but when I closed the textbooks, I was on my way.

An overview of the information I discovered is:

Sexually abusive mothers:
- Mothers who sexually abuse their daughters commonly use enemas in a sexually controlling manner. Often, they require nudity, special responses or silence, while performing the enemas for hours. The enemas included penetration vaginally and rectally.
- Forcing their daughters to abandon a beloved pet was another common theme for mothers who sexually abuse their daughters. Poor Herbie.
- Mothers commonly hid, or tried to hide, the abuse under the guise of caretaking.
- Voyeurism was overwhelmingly common in all the statistics: watching their daughters bathe/shower, go to the restroom, dress, undress, as well as requiring their daughters to watch them bathe/shower, go to the restroom, dress, and undress, and view them naked.
- Hellen followed the more violent end of the arc of research involving beatings, burnings, alcohol and drugs. The common theme in some areas of research is the sexual usage of pencils, hairbrushes, hairbrush handles, dildos, vibrators, and burning their daughters with lit cigarettes. Hellen fit right in.

Daughters sexually abused by their mothers:
- I followed a textbook pattern of a sexually abused child. I was afraid of the dark; I ran away, bit my nails, got into fights, and had angry outbursts at school. I was full of fear and had health issues, weight loss/gain, and suffered with depression.
- I desperately tried to please Hellen amping up my efforts as the

abuse escalated. I believed the abuse was my fault, and I hated who I was for causing myself unnecessary pain. I made up excuses for the knots on my head, missing hair, and her public scenes.
- I lied when asked if I was okay and safe. I was suicidal.
- The majority of daughters were sexually victimized by others, after being sexually abused by their mother. Some were pimped out by their mothers.
- Most daughters did not tell anyone until they were around age 45 years old, or after.

Clearly, I was a normal child responding to trauma. Hellen was abstract, breaking all norms.

References & Resources

*I have learned that success is to be measured
not so much by the position that one has reached in life
as by the obstacles which he has had to overcome
while trying to succeed.*
~ Booker T. Washington

Books

The Holy Bible, King James Version.

Brand, Julie A. *A Mother's Touch Surviving Mother-Daughter Sexual Abuse.* Trafford Publishing, 2007.

Burke-Harris M.D., Nadine. *The Deepest Well.* Houghton Mifflin Harcourt, 2018.

Finkelhor, D & Associates. *Sourcebook on Child Sexual Abuse.* Sage, 1986.

Kasl, C. D., *Female perpetrators of sexual abuse: A feminist view.* In M. Hunter (Ed), 1990.
The sexually abused male: Application of 376 treatment strategies (vol.1). New York: Lexington

Karr-Morse, Robin, Wiley, Meredith. *Scared Sick: The Role of Childhood Trauma in Adult Disease.* Basic Books, 2012.

Maté M.D., Gabor. *When the Body Says NO.* John Wiley & Sons, 2011.

Miletski Ph.D., MSW, Hani, *Mother-son incest: The unthinkable broken taboo.* Brandon, VT: The Safer Society Press, 1995.

Mitchell Ph.D., J. & Morse, J., *From victims to survivors: Reclaimed voices of women sexually abused in childhood by females.* Washington, D.C.: Accelerated Development, 1998.

Nakazawa, Donna Jackson. *Childhood Disrupted: How Your Biography Becomes Your Biology and How You Can Heal.* Atria Books, 2015

Ogilvie, Beverly. *Mother-Daughter Incest A Guide for Helping Professionals.* The Haworth Maltreatment and Trauma Press, 2004.

Rosencrans MSW, Bobbie. *The Last Secret: Daughters sexually abused by mothers.* Brandon, VT: The Safer Society Press, 1997.

Shapiro Ph.D., Francine. *Getting Past Your Past.* Rodale Books, 2013.

Terr M.D., L. *Unchained memoires: True stories of traumatic memories, lost and found.* New York: Basic Books 1995.

Turner, M. & Turner, T. *Female adolescent sexual abusers: An exploratory study of mother-daughter dynamics with implications for treatment.* Brandon, VT. The Safer Society Press, 1994.

Turner, V.J. *Secret Scars.* New York. Hazelden Publishing, 2002.

Van Der Kolk M.D., Bessel. *The Body Keeps The Score.* Penguin Publishing Group, 2015.

Websites

Anda M.D., Robert, ACE Study https://robertandamd.com/

Burke-Harris M.D., Nadine. *How childhood trauma affects health across a lifetime* (16-minute TED Talk by Dr. Nadine Burke Harris) www.youtube.com/watch?v=95ovIJ3dsNk

CDC ACE Study website: www.cdc.gov/violenceprevention/acestudy/index.html

Felitti M.D., Vincent. ACE Study https://drvincentfelitti.com/

PACEs Connection. https://www.pacesconnection.com/

The 10 ACE Questions and Resilience Score: www.acesconnection.com/blog/got-your-ace-resilience-scores

Endorsement & Quote Credits

Allender Ph.D., Dan B.
  Redeeming Heartache, Dan B. Allender, Ph.D. with Cathy Loerzel M.D.
  To Be Told, Dan B. Allender, Ph.D.
  The Healing Path, Dan B. Allender, Ph.D.
  The Intimate Mystery, Dr. Dan B. Allender & Dr. Tremper Longman III.
  Intimate Allies, Dr. Dan B. Allender & Dr. Tremper Longman III.
  God Loves Sex, Dr. Dan B. Allender & Dr. Tremper Longman III.
  Bold Love, Dr. Dan B. Allender & Dr. Tremper Longman III.
  The Wounded Heart, Dr. Dan B. Allender.
  The Wounded Heart Workbook, Dr. Dan B. Allender.
  Healing the Wounded Heart, Dan B. Allender.
  Healing the Wounded Heart Workbook, Dan B. Allender with Traci Mullins.
  Leading with A Limp, Dan B. Allender, Ph.D.
  Leading with A Limp Workbook, Dan B. Allender, Ph.D.
  Sabbath, Dan B. Allender.
  The Cry of The Soul, Dr. Dan B. Allender & Dr. Tremper Longman III.
  https://theallendercenter.org/about/team/dan-allender/
Aurelius, Marcus https://www.goodreads.com/author/quotes/17212.Marcus_Aurelius
Burg, Courtney J. https://www.mombojombo.org/ https://www.mombojombo.org/blog
Burke, Edmund https://en.wikipedia.org/wiki/Edmund_Burke
  https://www.brainyquote.com/authors/edmund-burke-quotes

Crane, Frank https://www.brainyquote.com/authors/frank-crane-quotes

Deschene, Lori https://tinybuddha.com/

Drucker, Peter, quote used with permission from interview conducted in 1988, https://billmoyers.com/content/peter-drucker/

Edison, Thomas https://www.brainyquote.com/authors/thomas-a-edison-quotes

Encinas, James https://www.jamesencinas.com/home

Evans, Richard Paul, *The Christmas Box, The Gift,* https://www.richardpaulevans.com/

Frankl, Viktor, *Man's Search for Meaning,* Estate of Viktor Frankl, https://www.viktorfranklinstitute.org/ https://www.viktorfrankl.org/

Gilmore, Leigh, *The Limits of Autobiography: Trauma, Testimony, Theory.*

Halley, LMSW, Dorthy Stucky and Steven M.S. Halley, LSCSW. The Family Peace Initiative (FPI), *The Family Peace Initiative's Course Workbook, The River of Cruelty- How cruelty is passed from person to person and generation to generation, Halley's Alley: Commentaries on Individuals, Families and Society.* https://www.familypeaceinitiative.com/about/history

Hislop, Julie (2001) *Female sex offenders: What Therapists, Law Enforcement and Child Protective Services Need to Know.* Issues Press

Horton, Douglas https://www.thegoldenquotes.net/

Jay, Meg, *Supernormal,* https://megjay.com/

Kirkpatrick, Heather https://aldergse.edu/

Laine Ph.D., James A. https://prabook.com/web/james_alan.laine/279555

Lincoln, Abraham https://www.brainyquote.com/authors/abraham-lincoln-quotes

McDougall, Heather https://www.linkedin.com/in/heather-mcdougall-a600a513

Meili, Trisha, *I am the Central Park Jogger: A Story of Hope and Possibility,* http://centralparkjogger.com/book/index.cfm

Roosevelt, Theodore https://www.goodreads.com/author/quotes/44567.Theodore_Roosevelt https://www.brainyquote.com/authors/theodore-roosevelt-quotes

Sporleder, Jim, *The Trauma Informed School,* https://jimsporlederconsulting.com/

Stone Ph.D., Ryan, Author, *Best Road Yet.*

Tournier, Paul http://www.paultournier.org/en/http://www.paultournier.org/en/mdlp.html

Tubman, Harriet https://www.goalcast.com/2018/01/09/harriet-tubman-quotes-2/ http://www.harriet-tubman.org/quotes/

Twain, Mark https://www.thegoldenquotes.net/

Washington, Booker T. https://www.biography.com/activist/booker-t-washington https://www.brainyquote.com/authors/booker-t-washington-quotes

Surnames

English: https://surnames.behindthename.com/names/usage/english

BULLARD: Derived from Middle English: *bole* "fraud, deceit."

Italian: https://surnames.behindthename.com/names/usage/italian

PROIETTI: Derived from Latin: "abandoned, given to the children of unknown parents."

Acknowledgments

Many people have supported me through the years and in their own way, each had a part in making this book possible.

I will forever be grateful that God kept me through the darkest of times and delivered me from Hellen, and from my own anger and false doctrines.

Words fail to express my love and respect for Pastor Sawyer and his wife. Their patience, wisdom, and hope for my future cast light on dark days. Thanks for seeing hope, when I was blinded by shame. Thank you for never giving up on me. What a difference you have made in my life.

I am grateful I had the opportunity to counsel with James A. Laine, Ph.D. Your willingness to work with Pastor Sawyer greatly supported my healing process. I appreciate your patience and your valuable guidance along the way.

I had the wonderful opportunity to work with Maria Iannone, LPC and EMDR therapist. Thank you for caring and investing so much of your time into my healing. I am truly grateful.

A special thanks to editor, Mary L. Holden. Mary worked with me and this emotionally charged manuscript and helped see it through to publication.

I had the honor to have ten endorsers in addition to my family for my first published book. It has been extraordinary because each individual read the full manuscript before writing their endorsement. A special thanks to each and every one for your time and commitment to this manuscript. It is an important message that we hope will reach many.

A special thanks to my childhood friend, Penny. I am grateful for the heartfelt talks, your wisdom, and the confidences we've shared

Acknowledgments

that have anchored me through life's storms. I am also thankful for all the fun times, coffee, and giggles along the way.

Much love to our children and grandchildren–and the bonus kids who joined our family through the years. Thank you for the love and joy you've brought to my life. I am proud and honored to be your Mom and Grammy.

And finally…I have heart full of love and respect for Greg, my ally and companion since I was 13 years old. Thanks for the coffee, the long drives, and for listening as I sorted through the carnage of my childhood and the overwhelming landfill of memories. Thank you for never faltering in your support and belief that I could heal through it all. I couldn't have done it without you. Really, I couldn't have. You are an amazing gift and it is an honor to walk through life with you. Thanks for being my husband and my friend. I love you.

Art Photography by Adriane Ryann Thompson

Phoenix, Arizona
2021
Greg & Wilma
40th Anniversary

About the Author

Wilma MacLiver was born in Pennsylvania in 1964 and raised in Phoenix, Arizona. She began writing at the age of 10 to relieve the pain of her mother's unrelenting abuse.

When she began to receive help for the abuse, she searched for a book on mother-daughter sexual abuse (MDSA), from a daughter's perspective. There were none available. She decided then, that if she could ever find the courage, she would write her personal memoir, for other daughters searching.

She knew she wasn't alone.

This is her true account of the unspeakable abuse she suffered. When she was 10, Wilma saw a diary with a lock and key. She had no money to purchase it, but she was intrigued by the idea that she could write, and no one be able to read her private thoughts. In her environment, she always had to find a way, and this was no exception; so, she began writing on notebook paper–Hellen would never know–and she flushed the papers down the toilet so Hellen wouldn't find them. Her system worked and provided some relief.

Through the years, she wrote and hid her journals. Eventually, she was able to confide in her husband Greg, and finally her counselors. She kept journals throughout her counseling and healing process.

Wilma continues to journal and to write nonfiction, poetry, fiction, and humor.

She is a public speaker and lives in Arizona with her husband Greg, of forty years.

Wilma enjoys coffee, reading, long walks and spending time with her family and friends.

This is her first book.

Contact@WritingWellInk.com

www.ingramcontent.com/pod-product-compliance
Lightning Source LLC
Chambersburg PA
CBHW020900080526
44589CB00011B/367